DISHING UP® NEW MEXICO

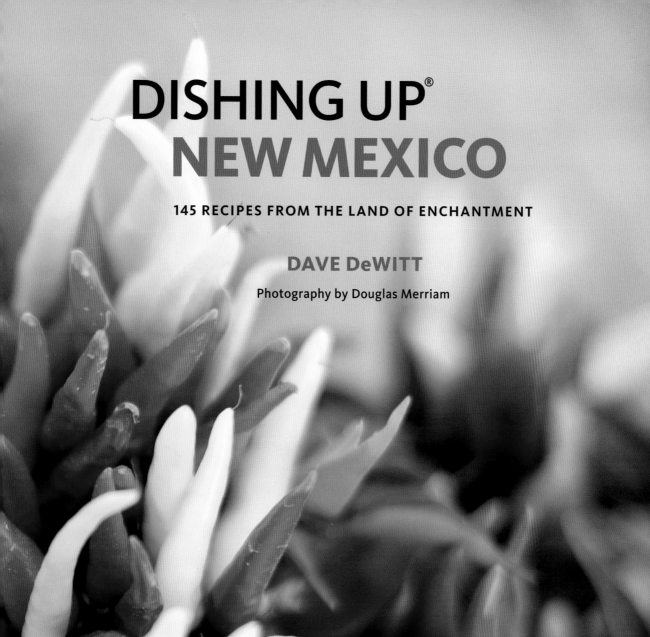

DISHING UP® NEW MEXICO

145 RECIPES FROM THE LAND OF ENCHANTMENT

DAVE DeWITT

Photography by Douglas Merriam

The mission of Storey Publishing is to serve our customers by publishing practical information that encourages personal independence in harmony with the environment.

Edited by Margaret Sutherland and Lisa Hiley
Art direction and book design by Mary Winkelman Velgos,
    based on a design by Tom Morgan of Blue Design
Text production by Liseann Karandisecky
Indexed by Nancy D. Wood

Photography by © Douglas Merriam
Map illustration by © Dawn Cooper

Storey Publishing
210 MASS MoCA Way
North Adams, MA 01247
www.storey.com

Printed in the United States by Versa Press
10 9 8 7 6 5 4 3 2 1

Library of Congress Cataloging-in-Publication Data

DeWitt, Dave.
  Dishing up New Mexico / by Dave DeWitt ; photography by Douglas Merriam.
    pages cm
  Includes index.
  ISBN 978-1-61212-250-2 (pbk. : alk. paper)
  ISBN 978-1-61212-251-9 (ebook) 1. Cooking, American—Southwestern style. 2. Cooking—New Mexico. I. Title.
TX715.2.S69D489 2014
641.59789—dc23
                          2014018154

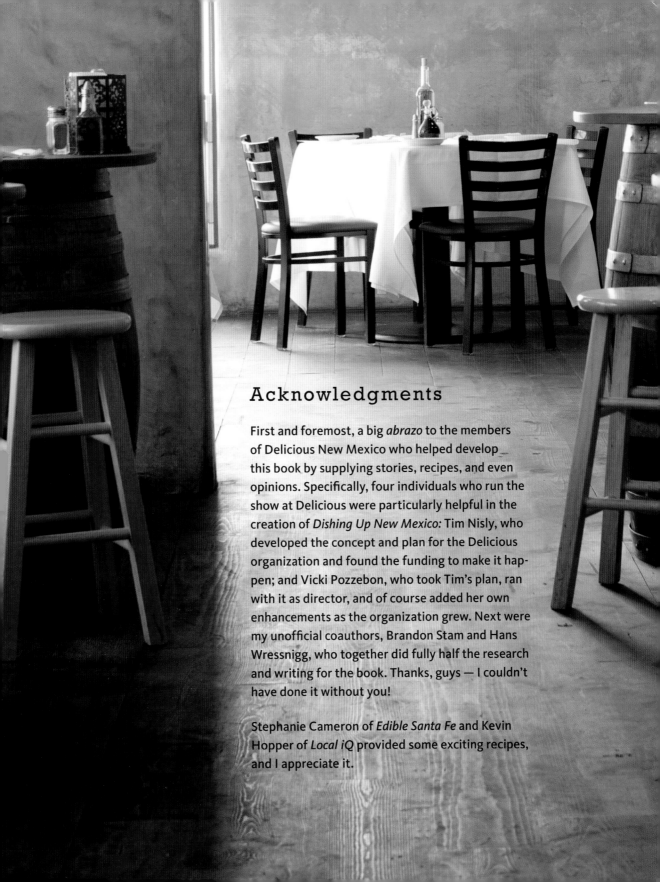

Acknowledgments

First and foremost, a big *abrazo* to the members of Delicious New Mexico who helped develop this book by supplying stories, recipes, and even opinions. Specifically, four individuals who run the show at Delicious were particularly helpful in the creation of *Dishing Up New Mexico:* Tim Nisly, who developed the concept and plan for the Delicious organization and found the funding to make it happen; and Vicki Pozzebon, who took Tim's plan, ran with it as director, and of course added her own enhancements as the organization grew. Next were my unofficial coauthors, Brandon Stam and Hans Wressnigg, who together did fully half the research and writing for the book. Thanks, guys — I couldn't have done it without you!

Stephanie Cameron of *Edible Santa Fe* and Kevin Hopper of *Local iQ* provided some exciting recipes, and I appreciate it.

Contents

FOREWORD

by Vicki Pozzebon, director of Delicious New Mexico

I AM NOT A NATIVE NEW MEXICAN. I am a transplant from Canada, via Vermont with a few stops in between. But I think it's safe to say that New Mexico has adopted me and I, it. It is home. It is the place that most resembles my own upbringing of family gatherings around enormous bowls of freshly picked salad greens, locally raised and butchered meats, dairy, and melt-in-your-mouth vegetables laced with rich flavors that transport you directly back to the soil from whence they grew.

I come from a long line of Italian immigrant farmers, ranchers, dairy producers, and entrepreneurs. It's no wonder I feel so at home in New Mexico, where the entrepreneurial culture is steeped in agricultural tradition mixed with creative new business ideas. And it's no wonder that my local economic development work has led me to create sustainable food systems and to support local food businesses. I am a foodie, a localist, and a proud adopted New Mexican.

What has always struck me about New Mexico's food culture is its inherent creativity. I once asked a chef why he thought Santa Fe had so many chef-owned restaurants (more than 200 at last count!) and the answer was simply, "Because like an artist, a chef must create." Passion, creativity, and a penchant for risk-taking drive New Mexico's food culture. It is not a rare occurrence to meet a New Mexican with a family-tested, mother-approved recipe for a new food idea that they absolutely must get to market, put on a menu, pour into a jar. This is the spirit of New Mexicans at their finest. We are still the Wild West Frontier, where the adventurous gather, the risk-takers succeed, and the land calls our name.

Dishing Up New Mexico brings together those pushing the New Mexico food frontier — food entrepreneurs, farmers, chefs — with a focus on creativity, local food, and great stories. That's the New Mexican way. The culture of food in New Mexico is so strong that just about everything we do involves food: meetings, community gatherings, family time, all revolve around food. It's how we get things done.

And at Delicious New Mexico we get things done by helping our local food businesses grow their products into larger markets and engage consumers in the story of those local food products so that we all make it work together. We dream of New Mexico's rich cultural heritage being experienced through the amazing food products our members grow and create.

We can create greater community wealth for New Mexico farmers and the entrepreneurs who are using their products. We can elevate those food businesses to be the best of the locally owned businesses because their passion for food, culture, and community will shine through in their products. We can create a New Mexico that gets back to our food roots, employs hundreds of people in small, locally owned businesses that contribute to happier, healthier employees, and thereby create happier, healthier communities. All of this coming from the food movement? You bet.

INTRODUCTION

JUST WHEN WE THOUGHT that the fast foodies had won the food wars with their mantras of convenience and eating on the run, a grassroots rebellion began among small farmers, owners of specialty markets, restaurateurs, and concerned consumers who rejected fast food and instead embraced the concept of "slow food." That is, buying locally grown food as much as possible and cooking it at home.

"Food is in season for a reason," chef Kimberley Calvo told me when I interviewed her. Kimberley is a member of Delicious New Mexico, my support group for this book. Members pledge the following: that they are locally owned New Mexico businesses, that they source from in-state farmers and food producers to the greatest extent possible, that they practice waste reduction by

reusing and recycling, and that they use green products whenever possible.

Delicious New Mexico is a nonprofit organization that's part of the South Valley Economic Development Center in Albuquerque, which provides a commercial community kitchen for its members to use to pack specialty products. It is appropriately named "The Mixing Bowl."

Another example of the importance of the locally grown movement is the way we protect our signature crop, the legendary chile pepper. In Spain, Pimentón de la Vera was the first chile pepper product to be granted a Denominación de Origen, or controlled name status. In France, *piment d'Espelette*, was granted a French Appellation d'Origine Contrôlée (AOC). This designation means that other varieties of

pimientos cannot be called *pimentón*, and other French chile peppers cannot be called Espelette. Unfortunately, the United States does not give "controlled name status" to agricultural products such as chile peppers.

The problem in New Mexico was that the state's shrinking chile pepper acreage could not meet consumer demand, and chile peppers not grown in the state were being labeled as "New Mexican." Most of these imports came from Texas, Arizona, Mexico, and China. The legislature attacked the problem by passing a labeling law that forbade the use of the words "New Mexican" if the chiles were grown out of state, even if the growers had bought or acquired seed of the 'NuMex' varieties developed by New Mexico State University.

The law includes brand names and trademarks in existence before the Chile Advertising Act's inception and foreign chiles must be labeled as "Not Grown in New Mexico." The law does allow state restaurants that use imported chile to use the term "New Mexico–style Chile" in their advertisements and menus. Well, it's a start.

In other words, this state as a whole is on top of the farm-to-table concept even to the point that both McDonald's and Blake's Lotta Burger buy locally grown New Mexican green chiles for their burgers. That's because their locally grown customers demand it. Another small victory.

Since many traditional New Mexican recipes are instantly available on your computer from my SuperSite, Fiery-Foods.com, it made sense for this book to emphasize the most innovative recipes that screamed, "I'm a little different, but I'm great!" The recipes come from a wide variety of local sources with one common theme: the evolution of New Mexican cuisine using both traditional and new ingredients. Restaurant chefs, culinary experts, food writers, and home cooks all contributed. Some of the recipes were created by writers in various magazines I edited, especially Nancy Gerlach, a good friend and brilliant recipe developer, now retired, who co-wrote ten cookbooks with me. Our media supporters, *Edible Santa Fe* and *Local iQ*, provided quite a few recipes that were exactly on target.

This was a fun book to work on because it's so positive, and so enthusiastic about the changing food scene in New Mexico, one where we return to our roots. It illustrates how well integrated entire farm-to-table food operations are now, especially since the launch of Delicious New Mexico. And those talented and enthusiastic food lovers of Delicious were wonderful collaborators on this project and helped me create the best book I could about the growing farm-to-table movement in the Land of Enchantment.

New Mexico

SAN JUAN RIVER

HERON LAKE

CIMARRON RIVER

EL VADO LAKE

Rocky Mountains

TAOS

ABIQUIU LAKE

Sangre de Cristo Mountains

CANADIAN RIVER

RIO GRANDE

SANTA FE

CONCHITI LAKE

GALLINAS RIVER

CONCHAS LAKE

RIO RANCHO

BLUE WATER LAKE

ALBUQUERQUE

Manzano Mountains

CLOVIS

Mogollon Mountains

RIO GRANDE

ROSWELL

ELEPHANT BUTTE RESERVOIR

Sierra Blanca Mountains

GILA RIVER

CABALLO RESERVOIR

ALAMOGORDO

Sacramento Mountains

PECOS

Organ Mountains

DEMING

LAS CRUCES

Florida Mountains

N

W   E

S

1 Chile Peppers: The Heart and Soul of the State

THE CHILE PEPPER IS New Mexico's most iconic crop and cooking ingredient. When I moved to New Mexico in 1974, I started my writing career by specializing in the lore and cooking of chiles. In addition to producing many articles and books, I edited two magazines devoted to chiles, developed a trade show for the chile and fiery foods industry, and started a spicy product contest. This is probably why the media often refers to me as "The Pope of Peppers."

Though strongly identified with the American Southwest, chile peppers aren't native to the area, having arrived with the first Spanish explorers and settlers coming up from what is now Mexico. Most historians believe that Capitán General Juan de Oñate, who founded Santa Fe in 1598, introduced chile peppers into what is now the United States. Or it might have been the Antonio Espejo expedition of 1582–83, which brought chiles to the Pueblo Indians of New Mexico.

According to one of the members of the expedition, Baltasar Obregón, "They have no chile, but the natives were given some seed to plant." Chiles were among the crops raised by Indians, according to colonist Francisco de Valverde in 1601; he also complained that mice were a pest that ate chile pods off the plants in the field.

The cultivation of chile peppers exploded all over the region as the Spanish settled. It is likely that many different varieties were cultivated, including early forms of jalapeños, serranos, anchos, and pasillas. But one variety that adapted particularly well to New Mexico was a long green chile that turned red in the fall. Widely called 'Anaheim' because of its transfer to California around 1900, this variety was cultivated in New Mexico with such dedication that several land races developed.

These land races, called 'Chimayó' and 'Española', are varieties that adapted to particular environments and are still planted today in the same fields they were grown in centuries ago; they constitute a small but distinct part of the hundreds of tons of chile pods produced each year in New Mexico.

In 1846, William Emory, chief engineer of the Army's Topographic Unit, was surveying the New Mexico landscape and its customs. He described a meal eaten by people in Bernalillo, just north of Albuquerque: "Roast chicken, stuffed with onions; then mutton, boiled with onions; then followed various other dishes, all dressed with the everlasting onion; and the whole terminated by chile, the glory of New Mexico."

Emory went on to relate his experience with chiles: "Chile the Mexicans consider the chef-d'oeuvre of the cuisine, and seem really to revel in it; but the first mouthful brought the tears trickling down my cheeks, very much to the amusement of the spectators with their leather-lined throats."

Dave's Fresh Red Chile Sauce

This method of making chile sauce differs from others using fresh New Mexican chiles because these chiles aren't roasted and peeled first. Because of the high sugar content of fresh red chiles, this sauce is sweeter than most. When I first made this sauce, I harvested some chiles from my garden one late summer day, made a batch, and ate every drop of it as a soup! It makes a tasty enchilada sauce, too. The sauce will keep in the refrigerator for up to five days, or you can freeze it.

¼ cup vegetable oil

8 New Mexican red chiles, seeds and stems removed, chopped (or more, to taste)

1 large yellow onion, chopped

3 garlic cloves

4 cups water

1 tablespoon minced fresh cilantro

½ teaspoon dried oregano, preferably Mexican

¼ teaspoon ground cumin

Salt

Heat Scale: Mild to medium   ABOUT 3 CUPS

1. Heat the vegetable oil in a large saucepan over medium heat and sauté the chiles, onion, and garlic, stirring occasionally, until the onion is soft, 5 to 10 minutes.

2. Add the water, cilantro, oregano, and cumin, and bring to a boil. Reduce the heat to low and simmer for 1 hour, uncovered.

3. Purée the sauce in a blender or food processor in batches and return it to the saucepan. Cook until the sauce thickens to the desired consistency, usually just a few minutes. Salt to taste.

A BRIEF HISTORY OF CULTIVATED CHILES

The earliest cultivated chiles in New Mexico were smaller than those of today; indeed, they were (and still are, in some cases) considered a spice. But as the land races developed and the size of the pods increased, the food value of chiles became evident. There was just one problem — the bewildering sizes and shapes of the chile peppers made it very difficult for farmers to determine which variety they were growing from year to year. And there was no way to tell how large the pods might be, or how hot. But modern horticultural techniques finally produced fairly standardized chiles. Here's how.

In 1907, Fabian Garcia, a horticulturist at the Agricultural Experiment Station at the College of Agriculture and Mechanical Arts, began experimenting with breeding more standardized chile varieties; in 1908, he published "Chile Culture," the first chile bulletin from the Station. When Garcia became director of the Station in 1913, he expanded his breeding program. After 10 years of experiments with various strains of pasilla chiles, Garcia released 'New Mexico No. 9', the first attempt to

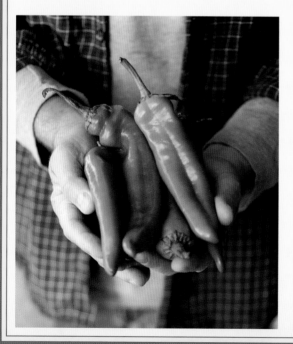

grow chiles with a dependable pod size and heat level. The 'No. 9' variety became the chile standard in New Mexico until 1950, when Roy Harper, another horticulturist, released 'New Mexico No. 6', a variety that matured earlier, produced higher yields, was wilt resistant, and was less pungent than 'New Mexico No. 9'.

The 'New Mexico No. 6' variety was by far the biggest breakthrough in the chile breeding program. According to the late Dr. Roy Nakayama, who succeeded Harper as director, "The 'No. 6' changed the image of chile from a ball of fire that sent consumers rushing to the water jug to that of a multi-purpose vegetable with a pleasing flavor. Commercial production and marketing, especially of green chiles and sauces, have been growing steadily since people around the world have discovered the delicious taste of chile without the overpowering pungency."

In 1957, researchers developed 'New Mexico No. 6-4', a less pungent version of 'New Mexico No. 6'. The new variety became the new chile industry standard in New Mexico and, more than 50 years later, was still the most popular commercially grown chile in the state. Other varieties, such as 'NuMex Big Jim' and 'NuMex R-Naky' became popular mostly with home gardeners.

Today, Dr. Paul Bosland, who took over the chile breeding program from Dr. Nakayama, is developing new varieties that are resistant to chile wilt, a fungal disease that can devastate fields. He has also created varieties to produce brown, orange, and yellow *ristras* (strings of dried chiles) for the home decoration market. The breeding and development of new chile varieties is an ongoing, major project at New Mexico State University, in addition to research into wild species, post harvest packaging, and genetics.

Sichler Chile Blend

John Sichler came up with this chile blend by experimentation and the proportions change each time he makes it, so this recipe is an approximation. He carries a bag of the blend with him when he and his wife, Eleanor, visit their favorite restaurants. The owners welcome them and encourage him to add the blend to the meals they order because they know he will leave them what's left of the blend as a bonus tip — and a real treat. (See How to Roast Fresh New Mexican Chiles, page 29.) Store the blend in the refrigerator for up to five days; it freezes well.

3 yellow chiles

2 New Mexican green chiles

2 New Mexican red chiles

2 green or red jalapeños

3 garlic cloves, unpeeled

Heat Scale: Varies, but usually hot

1½ TO 2 CUPS, DEPENDING ON THE SIZE OF THE CHILES

1. Heat a grill or stove burner to medium hot. Place the chiles and garlic in a grill basket and roast, shaking often to prevent burning, until all the chiles are blistered and slightly blackened, 5 to 10 minutes.

2. Remove the basket from the heat and spread the chiles and garlic on a cutting board to cool.

3. When cool enough to handle, peel the chiles and remove the seeds and stems. Peel the garlic cloves. Coarsely chop the chiles and garlic together and use as you would any fresh green chile.

Sichler Farms

ELEANOR SICHLER SIMPLY did not want to run a retail chile stand, even though she had to admit that her husband, John, had planned it well. But in 1986, she had two small children, and she dreaded the thought of yet another project to worry about and spend precious time on. So she disappointed her husband and said no to his chile stand dream. Repeatedly.

During this time she heard an interview with a group of ladies over the age of 90, during which the reporter asked them what they regretted most about their long lives. The answer was unanimous: not taking risks to achieve their true goals. Eleanor thought about it and realized that she was preventing John from achieving the family goal of financial independence. What if the stand was close to their house? And it was open only during the chile harvest season of August through October? Maybe it could work.

It did. Here's how the Sichlers made it happen. John's father, Jack, was a chile farmer, so they already had a ready supply of the hot pods during the harvest season. John discovered a rundown former used car building and lot within a few blocks of their house and convinced the owners to let him fix the place up as payment for the first

year's rent. Eleanor agreed to manage the retail stand while John visited local farms to secure more chile crop for the stand. They opened the Sichler Farms stand in August of 1987, well supplied with green and red chiles, jalapeños, yellow hots, red *ristras*, and frozen green chiles, along with squashes, pumpkins, cucumbers, melons, apples, and peaches.

The retail stand's clientele grew slowly but steadily because of their high visibility near San Mateo and Lomas — one of the busier intersections in Albuquerque. The couple taught their son, Tim, to roast the chile pods in the large, propane-fired cylindrical roasters. At the age of eight, he drew media attention as the "Youngest Professional Chile Roaster in the World."

The stand is still going strong, and longtime customers — myself included — return every year to order precisely the chiles they want. Eleanor always saves a half bushel of fresh red pods for me. Jack retired from chile farming in 2008, but his nephews Craig and Scott Sichler now supply the Sichler Farms stand as well as food manufacturers and restaurants. During their three-month harvest season, they sell six to seven thousand 40-pound sacks of fresh chile pods, plus dried and frozen chiles and the rest of their produce. No regrets there!

John, Tim, and Eleanor Sichler

THE CHEMIST WHO BECAME A CHILE FARMER

ONE WOULD NOT EXPECT a 72-year-old analytical chemist to be out in a chile field in the hot September sun picking pods for hours, but then my friend and business partner, Marlin Bensinger, is not your typical scientist. Besides, the pods are worth a dollar each, retail, and he can pick a thousand of them in a few hours. Such is the weird world of superhot chiles, and Bensinger is a major player in that world.

His first accomplishments were designing and building oleoresin extraction plants in 18 countries including India, Tanzania, Kurdistan, and the United States. Oleoresins are the essential extracts of plants like nutmeg, celery, black pepper, rosemary, and chile peppers. The oils are extracted for their pungency, their flavors, their aromas, and their colors, and used in food, fragrance, and pharmaceutical manufacturing.

Most of these factories were for extracting oleoresins from chile peppers — either paprika for its intense color or capsicum for its intense pungency. As a chemical engineer, Bensinger had the smarts to build the facilities, but he also is an analytical chemist who can test the oleoresins to determine their color intensity or their pungency. And that's how he became the foremost expert on capsaicin, the compound that makes chiles hot.

When news stories regarding an Indian chile pepper called 'Bhut Jolokia' that measured about four times the heat level of any other pepper known surfaced about a decade ago, Bensinger was in a perfect position to capitalize on what would soon become a craze to find or develop even hotter chile peppers. Fascinated by the superhots, he tested every one he could find, keeping careful records, and eventually started growing some varieties in pots.

Eight plants became 2,000 when he leased part of a farmer's field, and then the project got out of hand at 20,000 plants. That field, in his first year, yielded a net profit of $16,000 — an unheard of crop value for an acre of peppers of any kind. So now Bensinger is a gentleman farmer and part-time chemist — and, by the way, he can't eat anything he grows because it's way, way too hot for him. He views superhot chiles not as a food, but as an industrial ingredient. Ultimate chileheads would disagree.

Marlin Bensinger

Fried Chile Salsa

In northern Mexico, the chiles, tomatoes, and onions are grilled before making *salsa cruda*, so why not fry them instead? Frying the ingredients separately and flavoring them with cilantro keeps this from being a pasta sauce. Serve the salsa with chips or as a topping for grilled meat, poultry, or fish. The salsa will keep in the refrigerator for five days, but do not freeze it.

½ cup olive oil or more as needed

5 mild or 2 hot jalapeños, stems removed

1 large red onion, coarsely chopped

2 garlic cloves, minced

6 medium tomatoes, chopped and drained

3 tablespoons minced fresh cilantro

½ teaspoon dried oregano, preferably Mexican

2 tablespoons red wine vinegar or more to taste

Heat Scale: Medium

6 SERVINGS

1. Heat the olive oil in a large skillet over medium heat until hot, and fry the jalapeños until their skins start to blister and brown, about 5 minutes. Remove them from the skillet and drain on paper towels.

2. While the jalapeños are cooling, add the onion and garlic to the oil and fry for 1 minute. Remove, drain on paper towels, and place in a bowl.

3. Add the tomatoes to the oil and fry for 2 to 3 minutes, stirring often. Remove, drain on paper towels, and add to the onions.

4. Peel the jalapeños, cut in half lengthwise, and remove the seeds. Chop the jalapeños and add them to the onions and tomatoes. Stir in the cilantro, oregano, and red wine vinegar. Serve at room temperature.

Rio Grande Rainbow Salsa

Not only does this salsa display a riot of colors, it also provides an explosion of flavors. When finely minced, as they are in this recipe, fresh New Mexican green chiles do not need to be roasted and peeled. This salsa is delicious served over slices of smoked turkey breast or grilled fish. It also makes a great dip for corn chips. Store any leftover salsa in the refrigerator for up to five days, but don't freeze it.

2 red jalapeño chiles, seeds and stems removed, finely chopped

2 New Mexican green chiles, seeds and stems removed, minced

2 yellow wax hot chiles, seeds and stems removed, finely chopped

1 red onion, diced

2 medium tomatoes, diced

1 mango, peeled and pitted

2 tablespoons vegetable oil

1 tablespoon wine vinegar

Fresh cilantro leaves, for garnish

Heat Scale: Medium

3 TO 4 CUPS

1. Combine the chiles, onion, and tomatoes in a bowl.

2. Purée the mango with the oil and vinegar in a blender, then add it to the bowl. Mix well. Garnish with the cilantro before serving.

Chilaquiles en Salsa Chipotle
(Tortillas with Chipotle Sauce)

Chilaquiles (chee-lah-key-lays) is a term meaning "broken-up sombrero." This simple dish "recycles" day-old corn tortillas by breaking the sombrero (tortilla) in pieces and smothering them in a chile sauce. Simple, yes, but there are a vast number of variations. The sauce can be a basic red sauce, mole, *pipián*, green tomatillo, or, as presented here, a simple chipotle sauce. The toppings can vary also. This recipe calls for cheese, but you can add shredded chicken, cooked chorizo, or beans. *Chilaquiles* is a great breakfast dish, but is also good for brunch or a light supper. This dish does not refrigerate or freeze well because of the tortillas.

2 dried New Mexican red chiles

1 dried ancho chile

1 cup chopped white onion

2 garlic cloves, minced

2 tablespoons vegetable oil, plus more for frying

3 chipotle chiles in adobo sauce

3 medium tomatoes, roasted, peeled, and seeds removed, chopped

1 teaspoon dried oregano, preferably Mexican

Salt

1 dozen stale corn tortillas, each cut into 6 triangles

1 cup crumbled *queso fresco* or grated Monterey Jack cheese

Sour cream and chopped fresh cilantro leaves, for garnish

Heat Scale: Mild   4 SERVINGS

1. Place the dried chiles in a bowl and cover with very hot water. Steep for 15 minutes to soften. Drain the chiles and discard the water. Remove the stems and seeds.

2. Heat a heavy skillet over medium-high heat. Add 1 tablespoon of the oil and, when hot, add ½ cup of the onions and the garlic and sauté until soft, 5 to 10 minutes.

3. Place the chiles, onion-garlic mixture, chipotle chiles, tomatoes, and oregano in a blender or food processor and purée until smooth. Strain the sauce to remove any small pieces of chiles.

4. Add the remaining tablespoon of oil to the skillet and, when hot, carefully add the sauce. Reduce the heat and simmer until the sauce thickens, about 15 minutes. Salt to taste.

5. Pour oil to a depth of 1 inch in a heavy skillet and heat to 350°F over medium-high heat. Fry the tortillas in batches until they are golden, about 1 minute. Remove and drain on paper towels.

6. Place the remaining ½ cup onion in a strainer and run under cold water for 1 minute to remove any bitterness.

7. Add the tortillas to the sauce and quickly stir to coat; you do not want them to soften. Immediately spoon them with some sauce onto individual plates, and top with onions and cheese. Garnish with a dollop of sour cream and cilantro and serve.

FARM-TO-TABLE MEDIA SUPPORT: *Edible Santa Fe*

THE GOAL OF THIS FREE quarterly magazine is to reconnect people to local food supplies so that farm to table becomes a lifestyle. Subtitled "The Story of Local Food from Albuquerque to Taos," the publication is part of Edible Communities, a franchiselike organization that produces 70 titles across North America and is currently adding new magazines at a rate of 10 per year.

The content for each publication is region-specific, focusing on the farmers, fishermen, chefs, and food artisans from that area. *Edible Santa Fe* is big on agritourism, covering state vineyards, museums, and fascinating farm operations like Los Poblanos. Located in Albuquerque's North Valley, Los Poblanos features organic produce gardens, large lavender fields, an inn, a gift shop, and a farm-to-table fine dining establishment, La Merienda (ironically meaning "The Snack").

With material like that, the 20,000 issues printed monthly "disappear as fast as we can supply them," according to copublisher Stephanie Cameron.

As part of her job, Cameron has developed a unique method of managing writers. Edible Communities has an annual Edible Institute, at which publishers and editors swap ideas, attend seminars, and generally brainstorm about how to improve their publications. In the same way that Edible Communities has a national community, *Edible Santa Fe* has a local community of dedicated writers who specialize in covering local food. Cameron has initiated a version of the Edible Institute called the Writers' Forum, quarterly potluck dinners where about 60 writers come to pitch story ideas to the magazine.

I asked her what her biggest surprise as a publisher has been, and she replied that besides the business aspects — magazine publishing is a risky business — she has been amazed by the community interest that started off fairly strong and is now enormous. "I think we're starting to achieve our goal," she said proudly.

Recipe from AMY WHITE, *EDIBLE SANTA FE*

Pepino y Chile Popsicles
(Cucumber and Chile Pepper Popsicles)

Amy, a recipe developer for *Edible Santa Fe*, writes, "There's nothing quite like the real-fruit *paleta*s that Mexican popsicle vendors sell from little pushcarts and from South Valley *paleterias*, and a supreme flavor is *pepino y chile*. Add a little extra lime and sugar to give these a bit more zing. The best thing about making your own popsicles is that you can adjust the flavor to your liking, or come up with your own flavor combinations. You can buy popsicle molds online or at specialty kitchen stores."

3 cups chopped peeled cucumbers

½ cup sugar

Juice of 1 lime

1–2 teaspoons red chile powder

Heat Scale: Medium   8 (2-OUNCE) POPSICLES

Purée the cucumbers, sugar, lime juice, and chile powder in a blender or food processor. Pour the mixture into eight popsicle molds and freeze for at least 4 hours. For aesthetic flare, put one or two thin slices of cucumber on the sides of the mold before you pour in the blended ingredients.

HOW TO ROAST FRESH NEW MEXICAN CHILES

Certain large fresh chiles, such as New Mexican green chiles and poblano chiles, have a tough outer skin that must be removed before you can eat them. The only practical way to do this is to apply strong heat until the skin blisters and pulls away from the meat of the chile, making it easy to peel off. There are several effective methods of blistering chiles; choosing one depends on what kind of equipment you have available, as well as the number of chiles involved.

Oven broilers work well, but require sitting on the floor for extended periods of time if you're working with any quantity. Hold the pods as close to the flame as possible or you'll be there for hours roasting just 10 pounds. Stove-top burners (gas and electric) also do a good job if you cover them with heavy wire mesh. Stove-top grills for indoor use are fine, but can only fit a few chiles at a time.

A charcoal or gas grill makes it easy to regulate the heat, and you can blister a large number of chiles at the same time. Using a chile roaster, available by mail order, is the fastest and easiest method of all. These machines feature a mesh drum for the chiles with one or more burners fueled by propane. Larger models are motor driven. With a roaster, I recommend blistering the chiles slowly to allow the chiles' natural sugar to caramelize and improve their flavor.

Before roasting, wash the pods and let them dry. Wear latex gloves at all times when handling the chiles, to protect your hands from the capsaicin (and keep your hands away from your face!). Cut a small slit in the side of each chile. If you forget, the pods may explode with a loud pop, shooting their seeds five or six feet. Not every chile will do this, but it is a good idea to simply stab every chile as you throw it on the fire.

As you roast the chiles, keep flipping them over to make sure they are not burning. You will actually be able to see the skin blistering, or even blackening somewhat, and pulling away from the meat of

the chile. Whether or not you see that, it is important to brown virtually the entire chile in order to easily remove the skin. Don't be timid — chiles can take a lot of heat before burning — but don't lose sight of the fact that you are merely blistering the skin, not incinerating the pods.

After the chiles are well blistered, place them in a large bowl covered with a damp towel or put them in a heavy plastic bag for at least an hour. This steaming action makes peeling the chiles infinitely easier. (To yield crisper chiles, plunge them into ice water after roasting to stop any further cooking.)

If you've done a good job of roasting your chiles, peeling them is fast and easy, though you should still be wearing gloves. Simply start at either end and pull off the skin. I generally pull from the bottom tip back toward the stem, but the method depends on the roasting job. Occasionally, you will run into problems with the deep indentations; it is hard to blister those "valleys" without burning the surrounding areas. You may have to use a sharp knife to scrape off any remaining skin.

At this point, most people like to cut off the stem and remove the seeds. The easiest method is to cut off the very top of the chile along with the stem, and then scrape the seeds out of the open end. Removing the seeds will cause a slight loss of pungency because they are attached to the veins (the placental tissue) that run the length of the pod. If you really want to reduce the firepower, you can also remove those veins. You've now completed the whole process and have a chile that is ready to eat, cook with, store in the refrigerator for up to four days, or freeze.

Spicy Stuffed Ancho Chiles with Two Sauces

Ancho chiles are dried red poblanos with a wonderful raisiny flavor. They are available in supermarkets in many parts of the country or by mail order. Don't let the many steps in this recipe intimidate you; it is relatively easy to prepare and can all be prepped in advance, then quickly assembled to serve. These do not freeze well, but you can keep them in the refrigerator for up to five days.

TOMATO-CARROT SAUCE

- 6 medium tomatoes, peeled, seeded, and diced
- 4 carrots, peeled and diced
- 2 tablespoons oil
- 4 cups vegetable stock
- 1 tablespoon lime juice
- Salt and freshly ground black pepper

CHIPOTLE SAUCE

- ¾ cup sour cream
- 1 chipotle chile in adobo sauce, minced
- 1 tablespoon vegetable stock
- Salt

STUFFED CHILES

- 6 large dried ancho chiles
- 1 cup cooked black beans or pinto beans
- ½ cup grated Manchego cheese
- ½ cup minced sun-dried tomatoes
- ¼ cup chopped scallions
- ¼ cup minced roasted and peeled New Mexican green chiles
- 3 garlic cloves, minced
- 2 tablespoons New Mexican red chile powder
- ½ teaspoon freshly ground white pepper
- 2 tablespoons lime juice

Heat Scale: Medium   6 SERVINGS

1. Make the tomato-carrot sauce: Sauté the tomatoes and carrots in the oil in a large saucepan over medium-high heat until the carrots are soft, about 10 minutes. Add the stock and lime juice, bring to a boil, and boil rapidly for 1 minute. Lower the heat to low and cook, uncovered, until the mixture is slightly thickened, about 5 minutes, stirring occasionally. Remove the saucepan from the heat and let the mixture cool. Salt and pepper to taste.

2. Make the chipotle sauce: Mix the sour cream with the chipotle chile and the stock in a bowl. Salt to taste.

3. Make the stuffed chiles: Preheat the oven to 200°F. Soak the ancho chiles in warm water for 20 minutes. Drain them, pat them dry with paper towels, and make a lengthwise slit into each chile. Remove the seeds and the membrane.

4. Combine the beans, cheese, tomatoes, scallions, green chiles, garlic, chile powder, pepper, and lime juice in a bowl. Divide the mixture and stuff it into the ancho chiles. Warm them in the oven for 15 minutes.

5. To assemble the dish, pour a portion of the tomato-carrot sauce onto a small plate, top with a stuffed ancho chile, and drizzle the chipotle sauce over the top. Repeat with the remaining chiles. Serve warm or at room temperature.

THE CHILE PEPPER INSTITUTE AT NEW MEXICO STATE UNIVERSITY

The Chile Pepper Institute is the only international, nonprofit organization devoted to education and research related to chile peppers. Established in 1992, the Institute builds on the research of chile peppers since the famous horticulturist Fabian Garcia (the father of the American chile pepper industry) began standardizing chile pepper varieties in 1888 (see A Brief History of Cultivated Chiles, page 16). Visitors to the Institute can peruse research posters, books, and art pertaining to chiles and discover hundreds of high-demand and hard-to-find seed varieties.

Research is conducted at the Fabian Garcia Horticultural Center on the corner of University Avenue and Main Street, which maintains a public teaching and touring garden showcasing dozens of chile pepper varieties from around the world. Prominently featured in the demonstration garden are about 40 'NuMex' varieties, which were developed at NMSU. In addition to the famous '6-4', 'Big Jim', and 'Sandia', there are ornamental chiles with colorful names like 'NuMex Garnet', 'Piñata', 'Sunrise', 'Sunburst', 'Suave Red', and 'Suave Orange'. Many of the ornamentals are tied to holidays, such as 'NuMex Christmas', 'Valentine's Day', 'Easter', and 'St. Patrick's Day'.

"The purpose of the garden is educational," says Danise Coon, assistant director of the Institute. "We want to teach everyone about the incredible diversity of chile peppers." During the summer, school groups, 4-H groups, and Future Farmers of America groups tour the garden along with NMSU students, Elderhostel groups, and dozens of chilehead tourists.

Work-study students maintain the garden under the direction of Coon and Dr. Paul Bosland, who serves as the director of the Institute. The garden adjoins the greenhouse where Dr. Bosland conducts his breeding program and experiments. Most varieties do very well, except for the *Capsicum pubescens* species (*rocotos*). Coon also mentioned that "it's a little too hot and dry for many of the bell varieties."

Every year the garden has a central theme, and past themes have included "World's Hottest," "Hungarian Peppers Everywhere," "A Passion for Purple" (featuring chile plants with purple pods), and "Chile Flavors Around the World." Admission to the demonstration garden is free.

Grilled Green Chile Polenta with Roasted Salsa Verde

Here's a grill concept that needs no meat itself but is a great accompaniment to grilled beef, pork, or chicken. We give Italians credit for inventing polenta, but it's really just corn gruel, a dish that goes back to the Maya civilization. Keep leftovers in the refrigerator for up to five days but do not freeze.

GRILLED GREEN CHILE POLENTA

1½ cups milk

¾ cup coarse yellow cornmeal

½ cup grated cheddar or Asiago cheese

¼ cup roasted, peeled, and chopped New Mexican green chiles

2 tablespoons coarsely grated yellow onion

1 garlic clove, minced

Salt

Olive oil

ROASTED SALSA VERDE

1 pound fresh tomatillos, husks left on

1 small yellow onion, quartered

2 New Mexican green chiles, pierced once with a knife tip

1 teaspoon sugar

2 tablespoons lime juice

Salt

¼ cup chopped fresh cilantro

Heat Scale: Medium   4 TO 6 SERVINGS

1. Make the polenta: Bring the milk and 1½ cups water to a boil in a large saucepan. Slowly sprinkle the cornmeal into the liquid, stirring constantly. Reduce the heat to medium, and continue to stir until the mixture is thick and starts to pull away from the sides of the pan. This can take up to 10 minutes. Quickly add the cheese, chiles, onion, and garlic. Stir well, salt to taste, and remove from the heat.

2. Lightly coat a 10-inch cake or pie pan with oil and pour the polenta into it. Place in the refrigerator for 3 hours to firm.

3. Make the salsa: Combine the tomatillos, onion, and chiles in a basket on the grill over medium flames and roast until the vegetables are slightly blackened, shaking the basket often. Remove the tomatillos, onion, and chiles from the basket and peel, but don't worry about removing all the peels from the chiles. Do remove the stems and seeds.

4. Combine the vegetables, sugar, and lime juice in a blender or food processor and purée until smooth. Season with salt and stir in the cilantro.

5. Clean the grill and brush it with more oil. Slice the polenta into wedges or squares, brush with the oil, and grill over a medium fire until they begin to brown, 8 to 12 minutes.

6. Place the polenta on a serving platter, top with the salsa, and serve.

Recipe from GWYNETH DOLAND, ALBUQUERQUE

Grilled Green Chile Cheese Tamales
with Avocado Cream

This recipe from former chef and current food writer Gwyneth Doland is one of the most unusual tamale recipes you will ever find. Your first thought might be: Oh, no, not a grilled tamale! But it works, if you can prevent the corn husks from burning — so arm yourself with a spray bottle filled with water. You can tie the tamales together with string or with a thin strip of corn husk. Serve these tamales as an entrée or as a side dish with Mexican rice, squash with tomatoes and green chile, and flan for dessert. Leftovers can be refrigerated for up to five days, or you can freeze them.

TAMALES

- 15 dried corn husks
- ½ cup cornmeal
- 1 tablespoon instant masa mix
- 1 tablespoon sugar
- 1 teaspoon salt
- ⅓ cup milk
- 2 tablespoons butter
- ½ cup cooked corn kernels

GREEN CHILE CHEESE FILLING

- 6–8 roasted, peeled New Mexican green chiles, stems and seeds removed, cut into thin strips
- ⅓ cup finely chopped yellow onion
- ⅓ cup finely chopped black olives
- 6 ounces asadero or Monterey Jack cheese, coarsely grated

AVOCADO CREAM

- 2 medium avocados, peeled, pitted, and chopped
- 2 jalapeños, stems and seeds removed, chopped
- 2 tablespoons chopped yellow onion
- 2 teaspoons chopped fresh cilantro
- ¼ teaspoon garlic salt
- 1 tablespoon lemon juice
- Sour cream and chopped fresh cilantro leaves, for garnish

Heat Scale: Medium

6 TAMALES

1. Make the tamales: Place the corn husks in water in a large bowl, weigh down with a plate, and soak until soft, about 30 minutes.

2. Combine the cornmeal, masa mix, sugar, salt, milk, and butter in a saucepan and simmer for a couple of minutes to thicken slightly. Cool to room temperature, and stir in the corn kernels.

3. Drain the husks, pat dry with paper towels, and lay on a flat surface. Place two husks together, overlapping slightly. Spread some of the cornmeal mixture on a husk, cover with chile strips, then the onion, olives, and cheese. Place another layer of the cornmeal on top, pull the husks over the top, and tie at both ends. Repeat until you have 6 packets.

4. Preheat the grill to high. If using charcoal, move all the coals to the edges of the grill, and keep the tamales in the center. If using gas, arrange the tamales around the edges of the grill. Cook, turning occasionally, until the filling sets, 45 to 60 minutes, spraying with water to keep the husks from burning. Check for doneness by opening up one of the tamales.

5. Make the avocado cream: Combine the avocados, jalapeños, onion, cilantro, garlic salt, and lemon juice in a blender or food processor and purée until smooth.

6. Slice open the tamales, spoon in the avocado cream, top with a dollop of sour cream, sprinkle with cilantro, and serve.

Pipián Rojo
(Red *Pipián* Sauce)

Squash has been a staple of the Mexican diet for millennia, and *pipián* sauce is a traditional southern Mexican condiment based on *pepitas* (squash or pumpkin seeds). The addition of chiles and tomatoes makes this even more of a New World dish. This thick sauce, excellent on tamales, is bright red from the achiote (annatto seed); there is also a green *pipián* sauce made with only tomatillos and no tomatoes. Cooked ground chicken or turkey is typically added, but in this recipe, just chicken stock is used. The sauce will keep in the refrigerator for up to five days and it freezes well.

1½ cups chopped tomatoes

½ cup chopped tomatillos

1 pasilla chile, seeds and stem removed

1 guajillo chile, seeds and stem removed, or 1 dried New Mexican red chile

¼ cup lime juice

¾ cup water

½ cup white sesame seeds

1 tablespoon dried squash or pumpkin seeds (*pepitas*)

1 cinnamon stick, 1 inch long, broken up

2 teaspoons crushed hot New Mexican red chile

½ cup cubed French bread

1 tablespoon all-purpose flour

¼ teaspoon achiote

2 cups chicken stock

Heat Scale: Medium   ABOUT 2 CUPS

1. Combine the tomatoes, tomatillos, pasilla chile, guajillo chile, lime juice, and water in a saucepan and cook over medium heat for 10 minutes.

2. Toast the sesame seeds, squash seeds, cinnamon stick, and crushed chile in a dry skillet over low heat for about 10 minutes, stirring occasionally.

3. Transfer the toasted ingredients to a blender or food processor, add the tomato mixture, and blend to a smooth paste. Add the bread, flour, achiote, and stock, and blend until smooth. Return the sauce to the stove and heat through.

Southwest Shredded Chicken Tamales
with Chile Verde Sauce

Preparing tamales for the Christmas holidays is a tradition in the Southwest. Shredded pork and red chiles are the most common stuffing, but since you can fill tamales with almost anything, including poultry, seafood, fruits, and vegetables, I always include a batch of chicken tamales for variety. Tamales are surprisingly easy to make and they freeze well, so make a big batch and enjoy them all year long. Reheat by steaming or in the microwave oven until the tamales are hot to the touch. Do not defrost first or they will become soggy.

The name "tamalli" comes from the Nahuatl Indian word *tamalli*, and it is one of the oldest Mexican foods. These wrapped dishes migrated north and are as popular in New Mexico as they are in Old Mexico. Traditionally, lard is used as the fat in making them, but vegetable shortening can be substituted. Leftovers can be kept in the refrigerator for five days.

CHICKEN FILLING

2–3 cups shredded cooked chicken

½ cup grated asadero or Monterey Jack cheese

½ cup roasted, peeled, and chopped New Mexican chiles

½ cup minced yellow onion

2 tablespoons chopped fresh cilantro

1 teaspoon minced garlic

1 teaspoon chopped fresh marjoram (½ teaspoon dried)

½–¾ cup sour cream

1½–2 cups commercial tomatillo sauce

Salt and freshly ground black pepper

CHILE VERDE SAUCE

2 cups roasted, peeled, and chopped New Mexican green chile

1 cup chicken stock

½ teaspoon dried oregano, Mexican preferred

TAMALES

24 dried corn husks

4 cups dried masa harina

¼ teaspoon baking powder

1 teaspoon salt

2½ cups vegetable stock or water

⅔ cup vegetable shortening

¾ cup Mexican *crema* (or substitute sour cream thinned with a little milk)

1. Make the filling: Combine the chicken, cheese, chiles, onion, cilantro, garlic, marjoram, and sour cream in a large bowl and toss to combine. Add just enough of the tomatillo sauce to hold the mixture together, lightly mix, and salt and pepper to taste.

2. Make the sauce: Combine the green chiles, chicken stock, and oregano in a small saucepan over low heat and simmer for about 10 minutes, until slightly thickened.

3. Make the tamales: Arrange the corn husks in a shallow pan, cover with water, weight them with a plate, and soak to soften for about 30 minutes.

4. Combine the masa, baking powder, and salt in a bowl and stir. Slowly add the stock or water until the mixture holds together.

5. Whip or beat the shortening in a separate bowl until fluffy. Add the masa mixture to the shortening and continue to beat until fluffy. Drop a teaspoonful of the dough into a glass of cold water; if it floats, it is ready. If it sinks, continue to beat and test until it floats.

6. Drain the husks and pat dry. Place a couple of tablespoons of the masa in the center of a large husk, or 2 smaller overlapped husks, and spread thinly. Place a couple of tablespoons of the filling down the center of the masa and top with a dollop of *crema*. Fold the husks and use two strips of leftover husks, or two pieces of string, to tie the tamales together at both ends. Repeat with the remaining husks, masa, and filling.

7. Place a rack in the bottom of a steamer or large pot and add water to cover the bottom. Arrange the tamales either standing up or in layers, but do not pack them tightly as they will expand. Cover the tamales with a damp towel or additional corn husks. Steam until the masa has cooked, 30 to 40 minutes. To test for doneness, open the end of one tamale. If the masa pulls away from the wrapper, it is done.

8. Allow the tamales to cool slightly, pile them on a platter, and serve with a bowl of Chile Verde Sauce on the side.

Black-Bean Corned-Beef Chile Stew

Corned beef in a stew? Why not experiment? Cooks can either prepare their own corned beef or purchase it from a butcher. You'll find this easy-to-make dish a delightful mix of flavors; just be sure to skim off any fat that comes to the surface after the beef cooks. Serve it with an Irish soda bread because of the corned beef, accompanied by a Marble Oatmeal Stout. Leftover stew can be refrigerated for up to five days or frozen.

2½ pounds corned beef

2 cups black beans

8 New Mexican chiles, roasted, peeled, and chopped

2 carrots, peeled and chopped

1 large onion, chopped

½ bunch of fresh Italian parsley, chopped (about ¼ cup)

1 tablespoon freshly ground black pepper

1 tablespoon freshly ground white pepper

½ teaspoon salt

Heat Scale: Mild

8 TO 10 SERVINGS

1. Combine the corned beef, black beans, chiles, carrots, onion, parsley, black pepper, white pepper, salt, and 3 quarts water in a large stockpot and bring to a boil. Reduce the heat to low and cook, uncovered, for 2 hours.

2. Strain the stew and transfer all the solids to a bowl, returning the liquid to the stockpot. Skim the fat off the stew liquid. Trim the fat off the corned beef and discard it; cut the meat into 1½-inch lengths. Return the beef and the rest of the solids to the stock in the stockpot.

3. Add enough water to the pot to make the stew about 1 gallon. Bring to a boil, stir well, and serve.

Creamy Green Chile–Chicken Soup

Here's a southwestern classic featuring New Mexican green chiles. It was one of the favorites at the late, lamented W. C.'s Mountain Road Cafe. If W. C. neglected to post it for a while on his specials board, his regulars complained. Serve the soup as a starter before Mexican or southwestern entrées or grilled meats. Leftover soup can be stored in the refrigerator for five days or frozen.

2 tablespoons vegetable oil

1 small onion, finely chopped

1 garlic clove, minced

1 tablespoon all-purpose flour

4 New Mexican green chiles, roasted, peeled, and chopped

3½ cups chicken stock

1 (3½-pound) chicken, poached, skin and bones discarded, and meat chopped (3–4 cups)

½ teaspoon salt

½ teaspoon finely ground white pepper

¼ teaspoon dried oregano, preferably Mexican

1 cup heavy cream

Chopped fresh Italian parsley, for garnish

Heat Scale: Medium

6 SERVINGS

1. Heat the oil in a saucepan over medium heat. Add the onion and garlic, and sauté, stirring occasionally, until the onion is soft, 5 to 10 minutes. Add the flour and stir well. Add the chiles and chicken stock, and simmer, uncovered, for 20 minutes.

2. Add the chicken, salt, white pepper, oregano, and heavy cream to the saucepan, stir well, and simmer, uncovered, for 10 minutes.

3. Ladle the soup into bowls and garnish with parsley.

SALSA: MORE THAN JUST A CONDIMENT

Are you still using salsa merely as a dip for chips? That's so yesterday. Thousands of brands of salsa offer a myriad of combinations and flavors, providing many more uses for America's best-selling condiment. It's a great marinade and baste for just about anything you can put on the grill. Think of it as a topping for grilled meats, baked potatoes, and even pizzas. Imagine adding it to your meatloaf, scrambled eggs, or chile con queso. Try it in fillings for wontons, empanadas, or egg rolls. Here are some more ideas for adding salsas to your meals.

Beverages. Salsa in a Bloody Mary or Virgin Mary? Simply use your blender. Or, instead of buying a chile pepper vodka, add salsa to your favorite vodka, let it steep for a few days, strain it through cheesecloth, and, voila, salsa-infused vodka to astonish your friends.

Breakfast. Picture your favorite breakfast burrito transformed by your favorite salsa. Or huevos rancheros (ranch-style eggs). Even menudo, a tripe soup that is the real breakfast of champions, needs salsa in it. And yes, you can make breakfast sausage with salsa in it. My wife regularly makes our Sunday breakfast omelets with salsa and a flavorful cheese like feta or gorgonzola.

Appetizers. Add salsas to commercial dips for an instant flavor improvement. Shrimp cocktails served with salsa replacing the standard cocktail sauce? Works for me. Want to shock your guests? Spice up a standard pâté by adding salsa to it or update an old-school appetizer like toast points with a cheddar-salsa spread.

Seafood. Marinate a whole, cleaned fish in your favorite salsa before baking it on indirect heat in a closed grill. Add salsa to shrimp creole, tuna salad, fish chowder, ceviche, raw oysters, and clams. Top sashimi with it like we were served at a restaurant in Todos Santos, Baja California Sur.

Meat. Slice open the thickest pork chop you can find and stuff it with salsa before grilling. Add salsa to meat gravies. Mix some salsa with your barbecue sauce before basting. Add it to your chili con carne, mix it in with your ground beef for hamburgers, or combine with chorizo. Making carnitas? Toss in some salsa during the last minute of frying.

Poultry. For Thanksgiving, surprise the family with cornbread-salsa stuffing in the turkey. Chicken pot pie with chipotle salsa in it? Fantastic. Take a hint from cooks in Barbados: lift the chicken skin from the meat and insert salsa (they use a spicy herb blend) before frying, roasting, or grilling. Chicken soup for the salsa lover's soul? I love it. Can you imagine chopped liver with salsa? I can, on dark rye.

Side dishes. Baked beans will never be the same after you've cooked them with salsa. When preparing rice pilaf, substitute ¼ cup of salsa for ¼ cup of the stock, and wow! *Calabacitas* with salsa is a Southwest treat, as are salsa-filled, fried squash blossoms. Instead of garlic mashed potatoes, substitute salsa for the garlic, which also gives them some color. Salsa-scalloped potatoes are a real treat. If you live in the South, think about salsa and grits. And of course, salsa makes a great tomato-based salad dressing.

Desserts. It's sweet heat time, with fruit salsa over vanilla ice cream. Mix some mango salsa into your fruit pie filling. Instead of bananas Foster, why not bananas sweet salsa? And with some red chile salsa, you can easily make a warm chocolate pie or custard much spicier.

Warning: After you've tried all these ideas, you may become a salsaholic. Lucky you.

Anasazi "Refried" Beans

The Anasazi bean (also called the Aztec bean, Cave bean, or New Mexico Appaloosa bean) is a red and white heirloom bean native to the North American Southwest; it was grown by the Anasazis, the ancestors of the Pueblo tribes. The term "refried" is a misnomer because the beans are only fried once. In Mexican Spanish, the prefix "re-" is an informal form of emphasis meaning "very" or "well," so these "refritos" are really well-fried beans, not refried beans. Serve these beans with enchiladas or tamales.

NOTE: This recipe requires advance preparation.

1 pound dried Anasazi beans

¼ cup finely chopped yellow onion

5 slices bacon, coarsely chopped

1 garlic clove, crushed

1 jalapeño chile, seeds and stem removed, finely chopped

¼ teaspoon ground cumin

Salt and freshly ground black pepper

Heat Scale: Medium   8 SERVINGS

1. Soak the beans in water overnight, then drain.

2. Cook the beans in 6 cups of water at a gentle boil until tender, about 1½ hours. Drain the beans, reserving the liquid.

3. Sauté the onion, bacon, garlic, and jalapeño in a large skillet over medium heat, stirring occasionally, until the bacon is crisp. Add the beans and cumin and mash everything together, adding the reserved cooking liquid a little at a time until the mixture is smooth. Salt and pepper to taste.

Chiles Stuffed with Port-Salut and Crispy Churro Lamb

Chiles rellenos, or stuffed green chiles, is a classic New Mexican dish that usually calls for stuffing roasted and peeled whole chile pods with Monterey Jack cheese and deep-frying them. But of course, restaurant chefs could not tolerate such a simple dish. After dining on restaurant versions of this dish from Mexico City to Phoenix to Santa Fe, I came up with this variation. I suggest using 'Big Jim' peppers if you can find them, but any variety will do. Stuffed chiles will keep for about five days in the refrigerator but, because of the breading, do not freeze well.

TOMATILLO-CILANTRO SAUCE

- 6 tomatillos, quartered
- 2 garlic cloves, chopped
- ¼ cup chopped fresh cilantro
- 2 cups water

STUFFED CHILES

- 2 tablespoons olive oil, plus more for frying
- ½ pound Churro lamb leg meat, cut into thin strips
- 2 garlic cloves
- ½ cup milk
- 1 egg
- ½ cup flour
- 12 ounces Port-Salut cheese, cut into thin strips
- 4 New Mexican green chiles, roasted, peeled, and seeded (remove the seeds through a small slit in the top of each pod)
- 8 sprigs fresh mint, for garnish
- Freshly cooked tortilla chips, for garnish

Heat Scale: Mild   4 SERVINGS

1. Make the sauce: Combine the tomatillos, garlic, and cilantro in a saucepan with the water. Simmer over medium heat until the tomatillos are very soft, about 15 minutes. Reduce the heat to low, and continue cooking while preparing the chiles.

2. Make the stuffed chiles: Heat the oil to medium-hot in a skillet, add the lamb and garlic, and sauté, stirring occasionally, until the lamb is cooked to medium, about 10 minutes. While the lamb cooks, mix the eggs and milk in a shallow bowl and put the flour in another shallow bowl. Remove the lamb from the skillet, reserving the oil. Toss the lamb with the cheese and fill the chiles with equal portions.

3. Dip each stuffed chile in the flour, then the egg-milk mixture, and sauté in the skillet over medium heat, adding more oil if necessary, turning once, until golden brown, about 5 minutes per side.

4. While the chiles are cooking, drain the water off the tomatillo mixture, transfer the solids to a blender, and purée.

5. Spoon some sauce onto each plate and put a chile on top of the sauce. Garnish with mint and tortilla chips, and serve.

TIO FRANK'S

TIO FRANK'S HAS MADE SOME remarkable progress for a specialty food company with only two products: red chile sauce and green chile sauce. Well, four products if you include the mild and hot versions of each sauce. Frank "Paco" and Emma Dean Najar started the company in 2008; it is now managed by their son, also named Frank, who credits the company's success to the Mixing Bowl, the community kitchen at the South Valley Economic Development Center in Albuquerque.

"Without that kitchen," he says, "we never would have been successful." So successful, in fact, that their production outgrew the Mixing Bowl and now Comfort Foods, a regional contract packer, packages their products.

Emma Dean Najar

Two additional factors in the company's growth have been the demand for their traditional products and the way they are marketed and distributed. First, they don't make salsa, a product that Frank Jr. says has oversaturated the Southwest. "We make cooking sauces," he insists, "not for dipping chips but for creating entire meals."

The chiles that form the basis for those sauces come chopped and frozen from Quality Produce in the southern part of the state. The company's marketing is based upon demonstrating products at growers' markets, festivals, shows, and even flea markets. "Once a customer tastes it," says Frank, "we get repeat orders from regulars who buy it by the case."

The small business currently produces about three thousand jars a month, which are sold by about 115 retail locations in New Mexico and Colorado, including Whole Foods, Sprouts, and Smith's supermarkets. Frank has big plans for the future. "We want our own manufacturing facility, and eventually to produce a line of frozen entrees." And of course they will be New Mexican dishes. "People around here want their chile, and we're here to give them the best we can make."

Cheesy Shrimp Flautas with Hot Orange Sauce

Flautas, or "flutes," have been basic appetizers for centuries. They usually consist of ground beef, red or green chile sauce, and a little cheese placed in a tortilla, rolled tightly into a tube resembling a flute, then fried crisp. When Santa Fe chefs took on flautas in the early '90s, they came up with modern interpretations like this recipe. It demonstrates how innovative chefs have taken "peasant food" (as any ethnic cuisine has been labeled for years) and elevated it to new heights using classic techniques.

Serve the flautas with Spanish rice and guacamole. The flautas don't freeze well, but they can be stored in the refrigerator for up to five days.

NOTE: This recipe requires advance preparation.

BASIL MARINADE

- 2 cups fresh basil, mostly leaves
- ⅓ cup piñon nuts, toasted
- ½ cup sun-dried tomatoes
- 1 tablespoon minced garlic
- ½ cup olive oil
- Salt and freshly ground black pepper

HOT ORANGE SAUCE

- 4 scallions, white part only, minced
- 1 tablespoon hot New Mexican red chile powder
- ½ teaspoon tomato paste
- 1 pint heavy cream
- 2 tablespoons white table wine
- Juice of 1 orange
- Salt
- 1 teaspoon honey (optional)

FLAUTAS

- 10 medium shrimp, peeled, deveined, and tails removed
- 4 small flour tortillas
- 3 scallions, julienned
- ½ red bell pepper, seeded and julienned
- ½ green bell pepper, seeded and julienned
- ½ yellow bell pepper, seeded and julienned
- 8 ounces smoked cheddar cheese, grated (2 cups)
- Vegetable oil, for frying

Heat Scale: Varies with amount of sauce   4 SERVINGS

1. Make the marinade: Blend the basil, piñon nuts, sun-dried tomatoes, and garlic in a food processor while drizzling in the olive oil until finely chopped. Transfer the marinade to a bowl and salt and pepper to taste.

2. Add the shrimp to the bowl with the marinade, toss to combine, and marinate for 4 hours.

3. Make the sauce: Combine the scallions, chile powder, tomato paste, cream, wine, orange juice, and salt to taste in a small pot over low heat. Simmer until the cream thickens, about 3 minutes. Drizzle the honey into the sauce, if desired.

4. Make the flautas: Sauté the shrimp and marinade in a small pan over medium heat for 3 minutes, stirring occasionally, then remove from the heat, and cut each shrimp into 3 or 4 pieces.

5. Divide the shrimp into 4 portions and spread each portion on the edge of a tortilla. Add the scallions, bell peppers, and cheese to each tortilla in equal proportions. Roll the tortillas into tubes and secure the edges with toothpicks.

6. Heat the oil in a large frying pan to hot. Fry the flautas, turning occasionally, until golden brown, 3 to 5 minutes. Remove from the oil and drain on paper towels. Place each flauta on a plate, cut it in half, and top with the orange sauce. Serve immediately.

Red Chile Linguine with Mussels and Saffron Crème

At Il Piatto in Santa Fe, chef Matt Yohalem serves this nontraditional recipe for mussels. He notes, "We serve the linguine with fresh mussels and a saffron crème sauce. The crème is a nice counter to the spice, and the yellow sauce and black mussels [are] a nice visual contrast to the red pasta." It also tastes heavenly.

RED CHILE SAUCE

- 1 tablespoon olive oil
- 1 cup crushed dried New Mexican red chiles, seeds removed
- 1 tablespoon minced garlic
- 1 cup finely chopped yellow onion
- 1 teaspoon minced fresh basil
- 1 teaspoon minced fresh oregano
- 1 teaspoon minced fresh Italian parsley
- 1 bay leaf
  Zest and juice of 1 lemon
- 1 large tomato, roughly chopped
- 1 cup white table wine
  Salt and freshly ground black pepper

MUSSELS

- 2 pounds black mussels, cleaned
- 1 tablespoon butter
- 1 tablespoon minced garlic
- 1 tablespoon minced fresh Italian parsley
- 1 tablespoon finely chopped shallots
- ½ teaspoon saffron threads
- 1 cup white table wine
- 1 cup heavy cream
- 10 ounces linguine
  Lemon wedges, for garnish

Heat Scale: Medium   4 TO 6 SERVINGS

1. Make the sauce: Heat the oil in a saucepan over medium heat. Add the chiles and sauté for about 1 minute. Add the garlic and sauté for 30 seconds longer. Add the onion and sauté for 1 minute longer. Add the basil, oregano, parsley, bay leaf, lemon zest, and lemon juice. Cook for 3 minutes. Add the tomato, wine, and 1 cup of water, and bring to a boil. Reduce the heat and simmer for 20 minutes. Let the sauce cool slightly before puréeing it in a blender. Strain, salt and pepper to taste, and set aside.

2. Make the mussels: Heat a skillet over medium heat, add the mussels, and cook, covered, for 2 minutes. Add the butter. Add the garlic, parsley, shallots, saffron, and white wine, and cook for 1 to 2 minutes. Add the cream, reduce to a simmer, and cook, covered, for 10 minutes.

3. Make the linguine: While the mussels cook, cook the linguine in a pot of boiling water for 10 minutes, then drain.

4. Transfer the mussels to a serving platter. Add the linguine to the sauce and simmer, stirring, for 1 to 2 minutes, or until the pasta is well coated.

5. Pile the pasta in the center of a serving platter, surrounded by the mussels. Garnish with lemon wedges and serve with a side bowl for the shells.

Blue Corn–Chile Cornbread

Blue corn is making a comeback in products such as chips and cornmeal. Blue corn has 20 percent more protein than yellow corn, and, in my opinion, offers a depth of flavor not found in its more common cousin. Its preparation and usage are identical to yellow corn. Adding green chiles to cornbread is an ancient Pueblo tradition. Serve this delectable version with butter and/or local honey.

1½ cups blue cornmeal

2 tablespoons sugar

2 teaspoons baking powder

½ cup chopped El Pinto Roasted Green Chile, or 3 New Mexican green chiles, roasted, peeled, and chopped

¾ cup milk

1 egg

2 tablespoons bacon fat or vegetable oil

Heat Scale: Mild   6 TO 8 SERVINGS

1. Preheat the oven to 350°F. Grease an 8-inch square baking dish.

2. Combine the cornmeal, sugar, and baking powder in a large bowl and mix well. Combine the chile, milk, egg, and bacon fat in a separate bowl and mix well. Add the wet ingredients to the dry ingredients and mix well.

3. Pour the batter into the prepared baking dish and bake for 30 minutes, or until lightly brown and set.

Jalapeño-Cheddar Cornbread

Once you taste this version, you'll never eat plain old cornbread again. Serve it with chili con carne and your guests will grovel at your feet. Adjust the heat upward by doubling the jalapeños. You can also make this recipe with blue cornmeal.

1½ cups buttermilk

¼ cup finely chopped jalapeño chiles, stems removed

2 eggs, beaten

1 cup coarse cornmeal

1 cup all-purpose flour

2 teaspoons sugar

1 teaspoon baking soda

1 teaspoon baking powder

1 teaspoon salt

¼ teaspoon garlic powder

1 cup grated cheddar cheese

Heat Scale: Medium   6 TO 8 SERVINGS

1. Preheat the oven to 350°F. Grease a 9-inch square baking dish.

2. Heat the milk with the jalapeños in a small pan over medium heat for 3 minutes. Remove from the heat and set aside to cool.

3. Combine the cornmeal, flour, sugar, baking soda, baking powder, salt, and garlic powder in a medium bowl. Whisk the eggs and cheese together in a separate bowl. Add the milk mixture and the egg mixture to the dry ingredients and blend with a fork until smooth.

4. Pour the batter into the prepared pan and bake for 40 to 50 minutes, or until the cornbread is lightly brown on top.

Southwestern Chile Lasagna

If you like making your own pasta, try substituting blue corn flour for the wheat flour when making your lasagna noodles. The color and flavor are definitely not Italian! In the larger cities in the state, there are still butcher shops that make their own sausage and many small-scale pork producers make a fine product — it's worth searching out the best available. You can refrigerate or freeze any leftovers.

¾ pound spicy sausage

1 large yellow onion, chopped

3 garlic cloves, minced

3 large tomatoes, peeled and chopped

¼ cup tomato paste

2 tablespoons medium-hot New Mexican chile powder

1 tablespoon chopped fresh cilantro

½ teaspoon sugar

¼ teaspoon dried oregano, preferably Mexican

12–14 strips lasagna noodles

2 cups ricotta cheese

1 egg, lightly beaten

6 New Mexican green chiles, roasted, peeled, and stems and seeds removed, cut in strips

8 ounces provolone cheese, thinly sliced

¼ cup grated Parmesan cheese

Salt and freshly ground black pepper

Heat Scale: Medium

6 TO 8 SERVINGS

1. Crumble the sausage into a medium-hot skillet and cook, stirring occasionally, until browned, about 10 minutes. Pour off any excess fat, add the onion and garlic, and sauté until the onion is soft, 5 to 10 minutes.

2. Add the tomatoes, tomato paste, chile powder, cilantro, sugar, and oregano, and bring the sauce to a boil. Reduce the heat to low and simmer for 20 to 30 minutes, or until thickened.

3. Preheat the oven to 350°F. Cook the lasagna according to the package directions until al dente, then rinse and drain.

4. Combine the ricotta with the egg in a bowl.

5. Place a layer of noodles in the bottom of a greased 9- by 13-inch baking dish. Top with a layer of the cheese mixture, then a layer of the sauce, a layer of green chiles, and a layer of provolone cheese. Cover with a layer of noodles and repeat the procedure, ending with the provolone on top. Top with the Parmesan.

6. Bake for 30 minutes, or until the lasagna is thoroughly heated and the cheese has melted. Let stand for 10 minutes before cutting and serving.

Recipe from J. P. HAYES, SGT. PEPPER'S HOT SAUCE

Chipotle–Pumpkin Seed Pesto

My friend J. P. Hayes of Sgt. Pepper's Hot Sauce makes this excellent pesto, which you can serve over homemade bread or pasta or use as a pizza topping. Mix it with mayonnaise or ranch dressing to create a tasty dip. I'll always remember J. P.'s dramatic performance as he demonstrated how to make this pesto during a power outage at one of my Fiery Foods and Barbecue Shows. The pesto will keep in the refrigerator for about five days and can be frozen.

1 can chipotle chiles in adobo sauce, or ½ cup dried chipotles rehydrated in red or white wine vinegar

¼ cup tomato paste

8 garlic cloves

2 tablespoons cider vinegar or lime juice

1 cup grated Parmesan cheese or Romano cheese

1 cup pumpkin seeds (*pepitas*) or piñon nuts, toasted

1 cup canola oil

Heat Scale: Medium hot   1½ CUPS

1. Combine the chipotles and sauce with the tomato paste, garlic, and vinegar in a food processor and purée.

2. Add the cheese and pumpkin seeds. With the motor running, drizzle in the oil until you reach the desired consistency. (You may not need all the oil.)

Black Bean Chili

This unusual recipe stars black beans, probably the most flavorful of all the beans. Yet black beans rarely appear in chili recipes, which are dominated by pinto beans. Serve this chili with any type of cornbread and a fresh garden salad.

NOTE: This recipe requires advance preparation.

1 pound dried black beans

1 tablespoon red chile powder

1 tablespoon dried oregano, preferably Mexican

2 teaspoons paprika

1 teaspoon ground cumin

½ teaspoon cayenne pepper

1 bay leaf

1 tablespoon olive oil

1½ pounds beef tenderloin tips, cut into small cubes

1 yellow onion, chopped

4 garlic cloves, minced

1 green bell pepper, seeded and chopped

1 (14.5-ounce) can chopped tomatoes, with liquid

1 ham hock

2 jalapeño chiles, stems and seeds removed, chopped

1 dried New Mexican red chile, stem and seeds removed, crushed

1 tablespoon chopped fresh cilantro

1½ teaspoons freshly ground black pepper

1 teaspoon salt

½ cup red Burgundy wine

Fresh cilantro sprigs, for garnish

Heat Scale: Hot

8 TO 10 SERVINGS

1. Soak the beans overnight in water.

2. Drain and refill the pot until the water just covers the beans and bring to a boil. Reduce the heat and simmer, uncovered, for 1 hour. Drain and reserve the beans.

3. Combine the chile powder, oregano, paprika, cumin, cayenne pepper, and bay leaf in a small skillet and toast over medium heat, stirring occasionally, until the spices are brittle, but not burnt, about 1 minute.

4. Heat the olive oil in a separate skillet and brown the cubed tenderloin over medium heat, stirring occasionally. Add the onion, garlic, and bell pepper, and sauté until soft, 5 to 10 minutes. Add the toasted spices and tomatoes and cook for 15 minutes over medium heat.

5. Transfer the mixture to a 6-quart slow cooker. Add the beans, the ham hock, the chiles, cilantro, black pepper, salt, and wine, cover, and cook on the high setting for 6 to 7 hours. Remove the lid during the last hour of cooking. Before serving, adjust the water if the chili seems to be too dry. Remove the ham hock and bay leaf and serve in bowls garnished with cilantro sprigs.

Eggs Benedict Arnold with Hot Hollandaise Sauce

You may have noticed that in New Mexico, we constantly reinvent classic dishes by spicing them up. This popular breakfast dish is made pungent by the addition of both green chiles and the spicy sauce. If you're not already keeping your own chickens, it's increasingly easy to find eggs from a local producer, where they are likely to be fresher and tastier than ones from the supermarket. I have a standing trade with amateur chicken-raiser Gwyneth Doland — her eggs for my fresh culinary herbs.

Hot Hollandaise Sauce
- ½ teaspoon cayenne pepper
- 3 egg yolks, lightly beaten
- 1 tablespoon lemon juice
- ⅔ cup butter, softened
- Salt and freshly ground black pepper

Eggs Benedict Arnold
- 4 eggs
- 2 English muffins, halved
- 4 thin slices ham or Canadian bacon, at room temperature
- ½ cup green chile strips
- 4 ounces cheddar cheese, finely grated (½ cup)

Heat Scale: Medium   2 SERVINGS

1. Make the sauce: Place the cayenne pepper in a double boiler over a pan of simmering water over medium heat. Add the egg yolks and lemon juice to the pan and whisk briskly until light and creamy, about 1 minute. Whisk in half the butter, a little at a time, until a thick emulsion forms, and the whisk leaves a trail in the sauce. Reduce the heat to low and gradually whisk in the remaining butter. Whisk well until the sauce is glossy. Salt and pepper to taste. Keeping the heat on low, cover the pan to hold the sauce while you cook the eggs.

2. Make the eggs: Crack the eggs into a small bowl, making sure the yolks are intact. Bring a quart of water and ½ teaspoon salt to a boil. Carefully add the eggs to the boiling water, reduce the heat to low, and simmer for 5 minutes.

3. While the eggs poach, toast the muffins. Place one slice of ham on each muffin half and place the chile strips on top of the ham. Remove the eggs from the pan with a slotted spoon, and put on each muffin half. Top with the sauce and the cheese before serving.

2 Farm-to-Table Seasonal Delights

I RADICALLY EXPANDED my garden into a micro farm as part of a writing assignment in 2013. A micro farm is nothing more than a large garden with the goal of making a profit, so I was experimenting to see if I could do that by growing the crops I was really good at, namely tomatoes, culinary herbs, and the superhot chile peppers that are a lot more valuable than New Mexico chiles.

I had a total harvest of 310 pounds of tomatoes and lots of herbs, which I sold to local restaurants. I made a small profit, especially on the superhot chiles, which I sold for 50 cents per pod. And the best part of my micro farm was that instead of paying outrageous prices for tomatoes, I could use my surplus at home and sell the rest.

Micro farms are just part of the thriving produce scene in New Mexico. The term "farmers' market" can be confusing because many small retail markets include it in their name. But I'm referring to markets in parks, fields, and parking lots where growers assemble to sell directly to their customers.

The New Mexico Farmers' Marketing Association administers the 63 true farmers' markets in New Mexico and lists as its three major goals sustaining the farmers and producers who grow and sell food at farmers' markets and other local and direct marketing venues; educating the public about the importance of eating healthy, locally grown and produced food; and encouraging the purchase of healthy, locally grown food by all New Mexicans, including low-income and/or food insecure members of our communities.

The association has three main special assistance programs. Supplemental Nutrition Assistance Program (SNAP), formerly known as food stamps, is available at about half of the farmers' markets in New Mexico. SNAP can be used for fruits, vegetables, meats, cheeses, breads, jams, and other foods. The WIC Farmers' Market Nutrition Program for women, infants, and children offers funds to purchase fresh fruits and vegetables at participating farmers' markets. Finally, the Senior Farmers' Market Nutrition Program (SFMNP) provides income-eligible seniors age 60 and over with checks that can be used to purchase fresh fruits and vegetables as well as honey at participating farmers' markets.

For small growers and food producers, neighborhood farmers' markets are an ideal retail way to support their wholesale distribution. The best way for growers and producers to find an appropriate market is to visit markets and meet the market managers. Managers can provide farmers with information about government regulations, licensing, nutrition programs that the market participates in, market rules and fees, and the application process. While nearly all markets accept new farmer vendors at any time, some markets restrict the number of other types of vendors such as food processors and artists/craftspeople.

Recipe from AMY WHITE, *EDIBLE SANTA FE*

Fresh Grape Salsa

Amy White, a recipe developer for *Edible Santa Fe*, notes: "Grapevines grow wild and domestically all over New Mexico, and we celebrate a long viticulture tradition. While they're often left for the birds in residential landscapes, many farmers' market growers offer different varieties in late summer. I like small, sweet, seedless green varieties for this recipe. Along with grapes, you can find jalapeños and sweet onions at many farmers' markets in late July. Try this simple variation on a traditional Mexican salsa with your favorite grilled meat tacos, or as a snack with tortilla chips."

1 bunch seedless grapes (about 2 cups), halved

1 jalapeño chile, finely chopped

2 tablespoons finely chopped red onion

1 tablespoon olive oil

Salt and freshly ground black pepper

Heat Scale: Medium　　　　ABOUT 1 PINT

Toss the grapes, jalapeño, onion, and olive oil together in a pretty bowl. Salt and pepper to taste. Serve immediately or store in the refrigerator for up to five days.

Calabacitas Caliente
(Spiced-Up Squash)

This recipe combines three Native American crops: squash, corn, and chiles. It is one of the most popular dishes in New Mexico and makes a colorful accompaniment for meat, chicken, and fish entrées.

4 tablespoons butter

3 yellow summer squash, peeled and cubed (about 2 cups)

½ cup chopped yellow onion

2 cups fresh corn kernels

½ cup roasted, peeled, and chopped New Mexican green chiles

1 cup milk

2 ounces Monterey Jack cheese, coarsely grated (½ cup)

Heat Scale: Medium   4 TO 6 SERVINGS

1. Melt the butter in a skillet over medium heat and sauté the squash and onion, stirring occasionally, until the squash is tender, 5 to 10 minutes.

2. Add the corn, chiles, and milk. Simmer the mixture on low heat for 15 to 20 minutes to blend the flavors, stirring occasionally. Add the cheese and heat until the cheese melts.

HARTFORD SQUARE

WHEN I VISITED SARAH HARTFORD at her nicely designed café, Hartford Square, my first question was how long she had been open. "One week," she answered, "and you'll probably want to know why I opened it the week my daughter was getting married." I looked at her inquisitively.

"You tell me," she said, attempting to answer her own question. "I don't know. But it worked."

Her first weekly menu reflected that, with Best Man's Breakfast Strata with Greens and Roasted Potatoes, Bridal Toasted Rice Salad with Oranges, Olives, and Almonds, Groom's Steak and Potato Salad, and Apricot and Almond Wedding Cake with Almond Buttercream.

"Leftovers from the reception?" I joked.

Hartford smiled. "Everything's special," she said.

"I'm sure it is. . . ."

"No, I mean everything on the menu is designed to be a special because I don't have a regular menu. It changes every week according to what's available, the season, or my mood. So everything's a special and everything is designed first for takeout."

"But people can sit down and eat."

"Sure, we're flexible, but these are my rules. Everything on the menu is available all day long. Everything is designed for takeout, but you can eat it here. And all the ingredients for the dishes — or as many as humanly possible — are sourced locally."

Hartford credits Delicious New Mexico with helping her source the ingredients, and many of her suppliers have their own stories in this book; she looks to Tio Frank's for chile sauce (see page 45), and Old Windmill Dairy for goat cheese (see page 101).

And she operates Hartford Square with customer convenience in mind. "Say you don't feel like cooking dinner. You go to our website, read the menu, find something you like, and call or e-mail us with your selections and tell us when you'll be by to pick it up. We'll have it ready for you."

"And you're just 13 minutes from our house," I said. "I'd better take one of your menus and show it to my wife."

"We'll have a new one starting on the fourth of July," Hartford said. "With a cookout theme."

Sarah Hartford

Recipe from AMY WHITE, *EDIBLE SANTA FE*

Honey-roasted Radishes

Amy White, a recipe developer for *Edible Santa Fe*, created this recipe and sent it to me with this comment: "Radishes come into season in early spring and continue to be available all summer. Plant them around Presidents' Day, along with peas, and replant every couple of weeks to harvest radishes for months to come. This is a lovely little dish for those who don't like the sharp bite of raw radishes. The combination of honey and black pepper lends the radishes a beautiful sweet-spicy complement. Add fresh mint just before serving, or, for a more savory dish, add a few chopped green onions."

½ pound radishes

1 tablespoon Taos Valley Honey or other local honey

1 teaspoon butter

½ teaspoon ground cinnamon

¼ teaspoon freshly ground black pepper

Salt

1 teaspoon red wine vinegar

4 SERVINGS

1. Preheat the oven to 400°F. Trim, scrub, and halve each radish (or leave them whole, just for fun). Steam the radishes until tender, about 5 minutes. Meanwhile, combine the honey, butter, cinnamon, pepper, and a pinch of salt in a small shallow baking dish and melt in the oven.

2. Toss the radishes in the honey-butter glaze, and spread them out in the baking dish. Bake for 10 to 20 minutes, or until the glaze is bubbling and the radishes are slightly shriveled.

3. Toss the radishes with the vinegar while they are still hot, and serve immediately.

VALLEY GURLZ GOODZ: A PICKLED BUSINESS

IT ALL BEGAN WITH an experiment. Maria Gamboa wanted to learn how to preserve the vegetables she was growing in her garden. She had an overabundance of green beans so she began to play around with pickling them, adjusting the pickling spices with each batch and giving them to her friends and relatives for feedback. Her cousin, Angie Rodriguez, enthusiastically suggested that Maria could have two versions of the beans, one spicy and one not, by adding a little chile powder to her recipe. "In the back of my mind," Angie says, "I started seeing Maria's pickled beans not as a hobby but as a product."

Maria agreed and they began the planning. They found a licensed, professional kitchen to produce their beans at the Mixing Bowl, the food processing kitchen at the South Valley Economic Development Center. And since Maria's small garden couldn't

Angie Rodriguez and Maria Gamboa

provide enough beans, they needed a grower. As if by magic, a friend, Ken Armijo, offered to grow all the beans they would need.

But the biggest challenge facing the business they called Valley Gurlz Goodz was introducing pickled green beans to an entirely new market. After all, pickled beans are more a southern food than a southwestern specialty. After the La Montañita Co-op accepted their product, Maria and Angie went on a tasting mission to give samples of the beans to the co-op's customers. One of the first questions the people tasting the beans always asked was, "Other than being a snack, what do I do with the beans?"

"Salads," the Gurlz replied. "Use them in spinach salads, pasta salads, potato salads, and even tuna salads." And one of the more creative uses for the pickled beans was — surprisingly — in Bloody Marys. The pickling solution flavors the drink and the beans are the garnish! (See recipe on page 213.)

I asked the Gurlz if they thought a single product was enough to support their business, and they admitted that they need to develop a variety of pickled products to sustain it. But they were in a pickle about what to pickle next. Asparagus? Okra? Peppers?

It will be interesting to see what the Valley Gurlz do next. They want to quit their day jobs and have a company with employees, no matter what they have to pickle to accomplish that goal.

Green Bean Pasta Salad

Maria Gamboa and Angie Rodriguez of Valley Gurlz Goodz are always coming up with inventive ways to use their pickled green beans, and this is one heck of a delicious use for them that's also quick and easy to make! See their profile on facing page.

8 ounces tricolor fusilli or dried pasta of choice

1 cup halved grape or cherry tomatoes

4 ounces feta cheese, crumbled

10–12 Valley Gurlz Goodz Dill or Spicy Pickled Green Beans, quartered

½ cup oil-based Caesar dressing

Salt and freshly ground black pepper

Heat Scale: Mild   4 SERVINGS

Cook the pasta according to the package directions. Drain, then combine the pasta, tomatoes, cheese, green beans, and dressing in a large bowl. Stir well. Salt and pepper to taste. Chill for at least 1 hour before serving.

Grilled Corn and Chipotle Soup

This is actually a very simple soup; its most prominent components are corn, chipotles, and cream. The chipotles can be either canned chipotles in adobo sauce or dried chipotles; just reconstitute the dried ones in hot water before using them. These little devils are smoked red jalapeños, so use them sparingly. The corn relish as a topping adds more texture to the soup.

GRILLED CORN AND CHIPOTLE SOUP

- 6 medium ears of corn, shucked
- Vegetable oil, for grilling the corn and frying
- Salt
- 2–3 chipotle chiles in adobo sauce
- ¼ cup diced red onion
- ¼ teaspoon ground cumin
- ¼ teaspoon freshly ground white pepper
- 2 cups heavy cream
- 2 corn tortillas, cut into wedges

CORN RELISH

- 1 cup reserved grilled corn
- 1 tablespoon diced green bell pepper
- 1 tablespoon diced red bell pepper
- ¼ teaspoon minced jalapeño chile
- 3 tablespoons white wine vinegar
- 1 teaspoon Taos Valley Honey or other local honey
- Salt

Heat Scale: Medium to hot   **4 TO 6 SERVINGS**

1. Rub the ears of corn with vegetable oil. Sprinkle with salt and grill over an open flame over medium heat. Allow some of the kernels to pop and blacken, which will add flavor and character to the soup. Using a sharp knife, scrape off the kernels, right down to the cob. Set aside one-quarter of the corn (about 1 cup) for the relish.

2. Make the relish: Combine the reserved corn, green bell pepper, red bell pepper, jalapeño, vinegar, and honey in a bowl. Stir to mix. Salt to taste. Allow the relish to sit for at least 1 hour at room temperature to blend the flavors.

3. Make the soup: Combine the remaining corn, the chiles, onion, cumin, white pepper, and about 1 cup of water in a blender or food processor and pulse briefly until a coarse paste forms. Add more water as needed but don't overblend the mixture as you want it to add texture to the soup.

4. Transfer the corn mixture to a large saucepan over high heat, add another cup of water, and bring to a boil. Reduce the heat and simmer until reduced by half, 15 to 20 minutes. Add the cream and stir well over low heat.

5. Meanwhile, heat about ¼ inch of oil in a heavy skillet over high heat. Add the tortilla wedges and fry until crisp. Remove and drain on paper towels.

6. Ladle the soup into individual bowls and garnish with a dollop of the corn relish and a couple of tortilla wedges.

OLD TOWN FARM

SINCE 1977, Linda Thorne and her husband, Lanny Tonning, have owned and operated Old Town Farm near the Rio Grande (which humorist Will Rogers called the only river he had ever seen that needed irrigating). Thorne calls her farm "the green heart of the city" because downtown Albuquerque has grown up around it over the years.

The city's BioPark, museums, and bike paths surround the farm, all within walking or biking distance. The Duranes Lateral, reputedly the oldest registered irrigation ditch in North America, forms the western boundary of Old Town Farm and supplies the water for its crops. Linda and Lanny are striving to keep Old Town Farm's agricultural character while accommodating its increasingly urban location.

On their 12-acre farm, they grow a wide variety of produce including heirloom tomatoes, raspberries, Japanese *shishito* and *Fushimi* peppers, and *misome* — a nutritious Japanese green that is great for pickling. They have expanded their produce garden in order to accommodate their walk-in and bike-in customers as well as their customers at the Downtown Growers' Market in Robinson Park. The farm also sells flowers, eggs, and honey.

This expansion resulted in a downsizing of their horse-breeding operation, which had long been part of Old Town Farm. Thorne reminisces fondly about the hundreds of horses that have passed through the property, which has direct access to the Bosque Trail. While the equine part of their business may not be as big as in years past, she assures everyone that "once a horse farm, forever a horse farm!"

The farm hosts weddings and events and, in October 2012, launched Bike-In Coffee, which welcomes cyclists to enjoy great coffee, fresh pastries, and quiche that uses many of the ingredients from the garden. In addition, the coffee shop has free Wi-Fi, fire pits for chilly days, and U-pick veggies from the garden to take home. Bikers can access the farm from the bike path on the south side of I-40 between Gabaldon and Rio Grande Boulevard or from the Mountain Road Bike Trail via Montoya.

Squash and Fresh Corn Medley

This southwestern take on succotash includes many of the vegetables that farmers harvest in the summer and fall. Serve it as a side dish with roasted or grilled meats, or make it a main dish by adding cooked pinto beans.

2 tablespoons vegetable oil

3 small zucchini or crookneck squash, peeled and cubed

1 medium yellow onion, chopped

1 garlic clove, minced

4 New Mexican green chiles, roasted, peeled, and stems and seeds removed, chopped

1 large tomato, peeled and chopped

2 cups fresh lima beans

¼ pound green beans, cut into 2-inch pieces (about 1 cup)

2 cups fresh corn kernels

Heat Scale: Medium   4 SERVINGS

1. Heat the oil in a small skillet over medium heat. Add the zucchini, onion, and garlic, and sauté, stirring occasionally, until the onion is soft, 5 to 10 minutes. Add the chiles, tomato, lima beans, green beans, and ½ cup water, and simmer, stirring frequently, until the lima beans are done, about 10 minutes.

2. Add the corn and cook, stirring frequently, for 10 minutes longer. Add salt to taste.

THE THREE SISTERS OF NEW WORLD AGRICULTURE

The three main food staples of the Americas — maize (corn), squash, and common climbing beans — were often referred to as "the three sisters." Grown by Native Americans from New England down to Patagonia, these were the crops people depended on for survival.

In some native cultures, people planted the three sisters together in what is now known as companion planting. They planted the corn first, and when the seedlings were about six inches tall, they planted the beans and squash around them. The corn supported the climbing vines while the beans fixed nitrogen into the soil to provide nutrients to the corn and squash. The squash became a kind of living mulch, with its large leaves shading the base of the planting and conserving water.

Cooked together, corn and beans provide good nutrition. Corn lacks the amino acids the body needs to produce proteins and niacin, but the beans provide both of these essential nutrients. And squash adds to the vitamin count with high levels of vitamins A, B, and C. Having provided a nearly complete nutritional package for the early peoples of the Americas, these three sisters still play an important role in New Mexico's food scene.

Corn for Grain and Silage

New Mexico's farmers plant approximately 125,000 acres of corn annually, but only about 35 percent of that is harvested for grain. The bulk is silage corn used to supply food (along with alfalfa, New Mexico's most valuable crop) for the dairy cows that make the milk for New Mexico's huge commercial cheese production (see chapter 3). Silage corn, which grows 12 feet tall, is harvested by being mowed and chopped up — ears, leaves, stalks, and all.

Blue corn, originally known as "Hopi maize," is a variety of flint corn grown in the Southwest and particularly in New Mexico and Arizona. It is a staple of New Mexican cuisine, appearing in tortillas and cornmeal. In addition to its striking blue color, it contains 20 percent more protein than yellow or white corn varieties and has a sweeter and nuttier flavor. There is no dedicated corn festival in New Mexico, but there are plenty of corn festivities across the state, most of them with maize mazes.

Plenty of Beans about It

From the standpoint of acreage, pinto beans are the fifth most important crop in the state. More than three-quarters of that acreage is in or around the Estancia Valley, which lies just east of Albuquerque and covers an area of almost 2,000 square miles.

Every second Saturday in October since 1981, the town of Moriarty (The Pinto Bean Capital of the World) holds its Pinto Bean Festival, and there's even a Pinto Bean Museum in nearby Edgewood. In addition to pinto beans, numerous heirloom beans are cultivated, including the ancient Anasazi bean (see Anasazi "Refried" Beans, page 43).

Squash and Pumpkins

Summer squash is grown all over the state in home gardens and truck farms, while winter squash, in the form of the pumpkin, is a significant crop. Pumpkins were originally cultivated for their seeds, not their flesh, because early pumpkins had a bitter flavor and their seeds were tastier. The seeds are often roasted and salted and are a nutritious snack.

Male pumpkin blossoms can be sautéed in butter or dipped in egg batter and fried. There are more male blossoms than female blossoms, and limited harvest of male blossoms probably will not affect yields of pumpkins or their seeds.

The annual New Mexico Pumpkin Festival in Las Cruces features a day of "pie eating, seed spitting, slides, a carving contest, the pumpkin glow, pumpkin shuffleboard, and a corn maze."

THE SEASONAL PALATE

"FOOD IS IN SEASON FOR A REASON," Chef Kimberley Calvo told me. "That's why every chef knows to use canned tomatoes in the winter, not those vile 'fresh' ones in supermarkets."

You may have already guessed why Calvo named her multifaceted culinary enterprise "The Seasonal Palate." Seasonal food drives her food truck, her catering business, her supper club, and her occasional gigs as a private chef. And she's very, very picky about how she acquires that food. I imagine her chanting before the mirror every morning, "Use local purveyors and small vendors, avoid food service suppliers, and tell your diners where the ingredients come from!"

Since graduating from culinary school, Calvo has wanted to be independent and self-employed, and she's certainly accomplished that goal. Her challenge with the Seasonal Palate Food Truck was not only to be seasonal and farm-to-truck, but also to be different. So she decided to do what no other food truck operator would dare to do: serve fresh seafood in the desert.

Through her Santa Fe seafood supplier, Above Sea Level, she is able to plan her menu according to some seasonal seafood patterns, but also can access a ready supply of fish and shellfish that is flown in from the West and East Coasts daily. Seafood dishes are the biggest sellers on her menu.

I asked her what job she had that she'd like to repeat sometime, and she told me about being a private chef for a wealthy Santa Fe couple who entertained at home several times a week and threw charity parties at other locations. "So many people just dropped by that I had to run the household like a restaurant because everyone had certain food preferences and dietary concerns. So I just handed them a short menu with their options. I had to have desserts that were gluten-free and dairy-free. But my employers never questioned my food and service help costs."

Calvo may have given up the high life for a food truck, but hey, at least she's the boss every season of the year and is producing, in her words, "artful, simple, clean cooking." Her truck is usually parked alongside the road that runs from Bernalillo to Placitas just north of Albuquerque.

Recipe from NANCY GERLACH, ALBUQUERQUE

Curry Pumpkin Soup

My former longtime coauthor, Nancy Gerlach, has experimented with a lot of pumpkin recipes beyond just pumpkin pie, including pumpkin cheesecake, muffins, and this spicy soup with an island taste. If you don't want to use pumpkin, any winter squash — butternut, acorn, or Hubbard squash — will do. Or for preparation ease, use canned pumpkin purée.

1 quart vegetable stock

2 medium winter squash, peeled and diced (about 4 cups), or 1 (15-ounce) can pumpkin purée

2 tablespoons butter or margarine

1 cup chopped yellow onion

1 tablespoon chopped fresh ginger

2 teaspoons curry powder

¼ teaspoon ground coriander

¼ teaspoon habanero chile powder

Ground cloves

White pepper

¼ teaspoon orange zest

3 tablespoons orange juice

2 tablespoons rum (optional)

Finely chopped scallions, for garnish

Heavy cream, for garnish

Heat Scale: Medium hot   4 TO 6 SERVINGS

1. If using fresh squash, bring the stock to a rapid boil in a large saucepan. Add the squash, cover, and boil until soft, about 10 minutes.

2. Reduce the heat, transfer the squash to a blender or food processor, reserving the stock, and process until smooth, adding some of the stock if needed to thin the purée. Add the purée back to the stock. (Or, cook the canned pumpkin purée and the stock over medium-high heat for 5 minutes. Do not bring the mixture to a boil.)

3. While the squash is cooking, melt the butter in a small skillet, add the onion and ginger, and sauté, stirring occasionally, until the onion is soft, 5 to 10 minutes. Add the onion mixture, curry powder, coriander, chile powder, and a pinch each of cloves and white pepper to the pumpkin purée.

4. Simmer the soup for 15 minutes. Strain to remove the ginger and onion, stir in the orange zest, juice, and rum, if desired. Divide the soup among bowls, garnish with scallions, swirl the cream on the top, and serve.

Recipe from W. C. LONGACRE, FORMERLY OF THE MOUNTAIN ROAD CAFE

Acorn Squash and Corn Stew with Chipotle

Chipotle chiles contribute a rich, smoky flavor to this simple stew. This recipe is from retired chef W. C. Longacre, with whom I coauthored two books, *Great Bowls of Fire* and *Great Salsas by the Boss of Sauce.*

---

2 medium acorn squash

4 teaspoons bacon fat or unsalted butter

1 tablespoon peanut oil

1 medium yellow onion, chopped

1 tablespoon minced garlic

2 cups fresh corn kernels

2 tablespoons finely chopped chipotle chiles in adobo sauce, or 3 rehydrated dried chipotle chiles

1 teaspoon salt

4 cups tomato sauce

1 teaspoon ground cinnamon

½ teaspoon crushed bay leaf

3 cups chicken stock

½ cup teriyaki sauce

½ teaspoon vanilla extract

1 tablespoon sugar

1 cup orange juice

1 tablespoon raw Taos Valley Honey or other local honey

1½ tablespoons lime juice

Garlic croutons, for garnish

Heat Scale: Mild   8 SERVINGS

1. Preheat the oven to 350°F. Cut the squash in half, remove the seeds, and add 1 teaspoon bacon fat to each half. Bake skin side down for 1¼ hours, or until soft. Let cool, then scrape the flesh from the skins and mash slightly. You should have about 3 cups.

2. Heat the oil in a large pot over medium heat and add the onion and garlic. Sauté, stirring occasionally, until the onion is soft, 5 to 10 minutes. Add the corn, chipotle chiles, salt, and tomato sauce, and cook, uncovered, over medium heat for 15 minutes.

3. Add the squash, cinnamon, bay leaf, chicken stock, teriyaki sauce, vanilla, and 3 cups water, and stir well. Cook, uncovered, for 20 minutes.

4. Combine the sugar, orange juice, honey, and lime juice in a small bowl and stir it into the stew. Cook, uncovered, for 5 minutes.

5. Divide the stew among 8 bowls and serve garnished with garlic croutons.

Recipe from AMY WHITE, *EDIBLE SANTA FE*

Hopi Squash with Green Chile and Piñon Stuffing

Amy White, a frequent contributor to *Edible Santa Fe*, comments about this recipe. "New Mexico is host to diverse, beautiful, and delicious winter squash varieties. Hopi squash is a lovely round, pinkish-orange pumpkin. They have a cute little turban at the blossom end, and weigh 2 to 7 pounds. Winter squash should be cured anywhere from 7 to 10 days in preparation for long-term storage — up to three months. Ask your farmer if the squash you're buying has been cured and buy several at the end of summer in preparation for holiday meals. Stuffed squash is great because you can easily make it so many different ways, you might not even get tired of it before spring! This stuffing, with green chiles, piñon nuts, and apples, is tasty with either cornbread or regular bread. It's a perfect vegetarian main dish, but you could add meat, such as browned sausage or shredded chicken as well."

2 small winter squash (about 2 pounds each)

3 tablespoons olive oil, plus more for baking the squash

4 cups small stale bread or cornbread cubes

¼ cup piñon nuts

1 large yellow onion, diced

1 carrot, diced

1 celery stalk, peeled and diced

1 large baking apple, peeled, cored, and coarsely chopped

6 New Mexican green chiles, roasted, peeled, and chopped

Vegetable or chicken stock to moisten bread

Salt and freshly ground black pepper

Heat Scale: Medium

4 SERVINGS AS AN ENTRÉE OR 8 AS A SIDE DISH

1. Preheat the oven to 375°F. Cut the squash in half through the stem end and scoop out the seeds. Rub the insides with a little olive oil and sprinkle with salt. Place the halves, cut side down, in a deep baking pan. Bake for 45 minutes, or until tender.

2. Meanwhile, combine the bread cubes and piñon nuts in a large bowl. Heat the olive oil in a large skillet. Add the onion, carrot, and celery, and cook, stirring often, until very soft and lightly browned, about 15 minutes. Add the apple and chiles, and cook, stirring often, until the apple is soft, a few minutes longer. Toss this mixture with the bread cubes and piñon nuts. Add the stock, a little at a time, until the bread is moist but not soggy. Salt and pepper to taste.

3. Remove the squash halves, and drain any liquid from the pan. Put the squash back in the pan, skin side down, and fill each half with stuffing. Bake for 15 minutes longer, or until the top of the stuffing is lightly browned.

NEW MEXICO FARM AND RANCH HERITAGE MUSEUM

In addition to being the only museum in the state with live longhorn cattle on display, the New Mexico Farm and Ranch Heritage Museum offers excellent exhibits highlighting the farm-to-table movement in the state. Located on Dripping Springs Road in Las Cruces, the museum is a 47-acre agricultural oasis in the city that brings to life the three-thousand-year-old history of farming and ranching in New Mexico. The enormous main building contains more than 24,000 square feet of exhibit space and interactive displays, plus catering space for meetings and events, a shop, and a theater. Fun and learning go hand in hand as visitors can watch a cow being milked, stroll along corrals filled with livestock, explore several gardens, and watch one of the growing number of demonstrations like blacksmithing and adobe-making. Full disclosure: I'm chair of the board of this museum.

Calabacitas (Summer Squash) with Red Serranos

In New Mexico, this dish is traditionally made with green chiles, but one year I grew a particularly prolific serrano plant that produced so many pods I had to use them up before the green chiles arrived from the southern part of the state. For this recipe, I used the gray or Mexican zucchini, which is a family favorite, but you can use any type available. If you have some fresh corn, you can add ½ cup of the kernels to this mix in step 1.

2 tablespoons olive oil

½ cup finely chopped yellow onion

3 red serrano chiles, seeds removed, minced

2 garlic cloves, minced

4 small zucchini, thinly sliced into rounds

Heat Scale: Medium hot   4 SERVINGS

1. Heat the oil in a skillet to medium, add the onion, chiles, and garlic, and sauté, stirring often, until the onion and chiles are soft, 5 to 10 minutes.

2. Add the zucchini slices and continue to cook until they are soft, about 5 minutes, depending on their thickness. Serve immediately.

Grilled Eggplants with Caprese Dressing

Eggplants come in a variety of shapes and sizes. One year I planted long and slender Japanese eggplants, so I had to slice them in half lengthwise to grill them, but you could also use the larger ones, cut into rounds or several lengthwise slices. Caprese is usually a salad made with tomatoes, basil, and mozzarella cheese, but here I use those same ingredients to make a dressing for the grilled eggplant.

CAPRESE DRESSING

1 large tomato, seeded and minced

5 ounces mozzarella cheese, cut into ¼-inch dice

8 fresh basil leaves, minced

2 tablespoons olive oil

Salt and freshly ground black pepper

2 tablespoons lemon or lime juice

GRILLED EGGPLANTS

2 tablespoons coarse sea salt

4 small Japanese eggplants, peeled (optional) and sliced lengthwise

3 garlic cloves, minced

3 tablespoons minced fresh Italian parsley

3 teaspoons minced fresh oregano

1 teaspoon coarsely ground black pepper

1 teaspoon hot red chile flakes

3 tablespoons olive oil

Heat Scale: Medium   4 SERVINGS

1. Make the dressing: Combine the tomato, mozzarella, basil, and olive oil in a bowl, and season with salt and pepper to taste. Cover and refrigerate until needed.

2. Make the grilled eggplants: Sprinkle the salt over the eggplant slices and let stand on a plate for 30 minutes. Rinse off the slices and pat dry with paper towels.

3. Combine the garlic, parsley, oregano, black pepper, and pepper flakes in a small bowl. Brush the olive oil over both sides of the eggplant slices and sprinkle them with the herb mix.

4. Prepare the grill for direct grilling. Grill the eggplant slices over medium heat until soft, 5 to 8 minutes per side depending on their thickness. Remove the eggplant slices from the grill and transfer to a serving plate. Allow the slices to cool to room temperature.

5. Meanwhile, add the lemon juice to the dressing and gently mix everything together. Top the cooled eggplant slices with the dressing, and serve.

Grilled Summer Squash with Lemon-Garlic Marinade

Here's a delectable way to prepare the tons of squash (especially zucchini) that all your gardening friends bring over. Grill the squash on a vegetable screen, so they don't fall into the coals.

NOTE: This recipe requires advance preparation.

8 garlic cloves

1 teaspoon cayenne pepper, or ½ teaspoon for medium heat

½ cup lemon juice

½ cup white table wine

3 medium yellow squash, peeled and cut into ¼-inch slices

3 medium zucchini, peeled and cut into ¼-inch slices

Heat Scale: Hot

8 SERVINGS

1. Purée the garlic in a food processor, then add the cayenne, lemon juice, and wine, and pulse to blend. Place the squash and zucchini in a deep bowl and pour the garlic mixture over the top, tossing gently to coat. Marinate for 3 hours at room temperature.

2. Prepare the grill for direct grilling and cook the squash over high heat for about 5 minutes per side, until the slices are easily penetrated with a fork. Remove from heat and serve immediately.

THE FIRST RESTAURANT CHAIN IN NEW MEXICO — AND THE UNITED STATES

After the Homestead Act of 1862 and the arrival of the railroad between 1879 and 1882, settlers from the eastern United States flooded the state. The railroad also led to the first chain restaurants in the United States, called Harvey House. New Mexico boasted sixteen of these establishments as well as five hotels that were the grandest of the national Harvey House system: the Montezuma and Castañeda in Las Vegas, the La Fonda in Santa Fe, the Alvarado in Albuquerque, and the El Navajo in Gallup. Only the La Fonda and the El Navajo are still open.

Harvey House came to New Mexico in 1882 when the Santa Fe Railway reached Raton.

Ironically, one of the main reasons the Harvey House restaurants succeeded was the antithesis of the modern "grow locally, eat locally" movement. The restaurants could serve fresh, high-quality meat, seafood, and produce at remote locations across the Southwest because the trains could deliver beef from Kansas City and seafood and produce from Southern California all year long.

Another reason was the fact that Fred Harvey hired young women between the ages of 18 and 30 to be his hostesses. They were quite an attraction on the western frontier, where women were scarce. The humorist Will Rogers once said, "Fred Harvey kept the West in food and wives."

Recipe from NELLE BAUER, RESTAURANT JENNIFER JAMES

Sweet Freezer Pickles

Nelle Bauer is one of the chefs and owners of Restaurant Jennifer James and a fellow columnist at *Local iQ*. She writes, "As there is really no good way to preserve a cucumber, except for pickling, it is only appropriate to pickle the summer surplus of these fruits. It doesn't have to be a lengthy sterile process; cucumbers can be quick-pickled with a short soak in vinegar. If you are feeling unadventurous, this is an easy, no-special-stuff-required recipe for pickles.

NOTE: This recipe requires advance preparation.

2 quarts unwaxed cucumbers, peeled and thinly sliced

1 tablespoon kosher salt

1½ cups sugar

½ cup distilled white vinegar

2 QUARTS

1. Mix the cucumbers and salt in a large bowl and cover with plastic wrap. Set aside for 2 hours at room temperature, then drain off the accumulated liquid and return the cucumbers to the bowl.

2. Combine the sugar and vinegar and stir until the sugar dissolves. Pour the sugar-vinegar mixture over the cucumbers.

3. Transfer the cucumbers and brine to small freezer containers and put them in the freezer. The pickles will be ready to thaw and eat in three or four days. They will keep in the freezer for up to one year.

Blistering Baked Squash with Blueberries

Squash with apples, sure, but combined with blueberries too? Why not? This side dish is best when blueberries are in season, although frozen blueberries will work as a substitute. This is a good accompaniment to grilled meats, especially pork or lamb chops.

4 acorn squash, halved lengthwise and seeds removed

4 tablespoons butter

2 tablespoons canola oil

2 cups fresh blueberries, or 2 cups frozen, thawed and drained

1 cup finely chopped apple

1 habanero chile, seeds and stem removed, finely minced, or 1 teaspoon habanero powder

⅓ cup firmly packed brown sugar

Heat Scale: Medium   8 SERVINGS

1. Place the cut squash in a shallow baking pan (or pans) skin side down and pour ½ cup water into each pan. Cover tightly with aluminum foil and bake at 375°F for 30 minutes.

2. Melt the butter and oil in a small skillet over low heat. Add the blueberries, apple, habanero chile, and brown sugar, and sauté for 1 minute.

3. Remove the squash from the oven and make several slices in the flesh, taking care not to cut through the skin. Divide the sautéed mixture among the squash, pressing it into the slits. Cover tightly with aluminum foil and bake for 15 minutes.

4. Remove the foil and bake, uncovered, for 15 to 20 minutes longer, or until the squash is soft.

Succulent Southwest Potato Salad

I avoid eating potato salad at restaurants because about 90 percent of it is food service–supplied and monotonous. I prefer to buy locally grown potatoes and get innovative with the salad, often spicing it up with chile powder and sauce to elevate the heat level. This salad can be refrigerated for up to five days.

4 medium russet potatoes

2½ teaspoons New Mexican red chile powder

¼ cup olive oil

¼ cup white wine vinegar

1 teaspoon bottled hot sauce

1 (8-ounce) can whole kernel corn, rinsed and drained, or 1 cup fresh corn, lightly cooked

½ cup peeled and coarsely shredded carrot

½ cup sliced green olives

½ cup chopped yellow onion

⅓ cup chopped green bell pepper

Heat Scale: Medium

4 TO 6 SERVINGS

1. Place the potatoes in a large pot and cover with water. Bring the water to a boil, then reduce the heat to medium, and cook at a gentle boil until a knife pierces the potatoes easily, 15 to 20 minutes. Drain, peel, and cube the potatoes and transfer to a large bowl while they are still warm.

2. Combine the chile powder, oil, vinegar, and hot sauce in a small glass jar and shake vigorously. Pour the dressing over the potatoes and toss gently. Add the corn, carrot, olives, onion, and bell pepper, and toss gently.

3. Refrigerate for at least 1 hour before serving.

Beatific Beets

There are so many varieties of beets available in grocery stores and specialty food stores that I would be remiss if I didn't give the beet some credit as a terrific vegetable. Not only are beets flavorful and packed with antioxidants and other healthful nutrients, they also come in a rainbow array of colors, from the traditional deep red to pink, gold, and even striped. And they are easy to grow, so if you can't find the variety you like best in a store, you can put it in your garden! Use the smallest beets you can find; they will be the most tender.

NOTE: This recipe requires advance preparation.

1 pound small beets, roasted or boiled, peeled, and cut into ¼-inch matchsticks

1 cup chopped red onion

¼ teaspoon salt

¼ teaspoon freshly ground black pepper

⅓ cup olive oil

¼ cup raspberry vinegar

1 tablespoon bottled hot sauce

Heat Scale: Medium   4 TO 6 SERVINGS

1. Combine the beets, onion, salt, pepper, oil, vinegar, and hot sauce in a small nonmetallic bowl and lightly toss. Cover and refrigerate for 4 hours or overnight to allow the flavors to meld.

2. Bring the mixture up to room temperature and toss before serving.

Recipe from AMY WHITE, *EDIBLE SANTA FE*

Balsamic Chard Pizza with Fig-infused Chèvre

"Chard is incredibly good for you, and best when dressed with balsamic vinegar and lots of black pepper," says Amy White, who created this recipe for *Edible Santa Fe*. "If you've never liked chard before, it's worth trying this way. A funny thing about chard is that it is naturally a bit salty, so don't add too much salt when cooking it. It's actually the same exact plant species as beets, just bred for tender leaves rather than big roots. Amazingly hardy, chard is one of the best vegetables to grow in New Mexico because it can tolerate the intense heat of our summers as well as the cold nights of early spring and late fall. For these reasons, it is abundant at our farmers' markets three seasons of the year.

"This pizza combines cooked chard with the creamy, tangy sweetness of dried figs mixed with chèvre. It's a perfect spring treat absolutely packed with vitamins and minerals. Try a whole-wheat crust if you want to go extra-healthy."

NOTE: This recipe requires advance preparation.

PIZZA DOUGH
- 2 cups all-purpose flour
- ¾ teaspoon salt
- ½ teaspoon active dry yeast

FIG-INFUSED CHÈVRE
- ½ cup chopped dried figs
- ½ cup chèvre

CHARD
- 1 tablespoon olive oil
- 6 garlic cloves, minced
- 1 large bunch chard, with stems, sliced into ½-inch ribbons
- 2 tablespoon balsamic vinegar
- Salt and freshly ground black pepper
- Olive oil, for serving

4 (8-INCH) PIZZAS

1. Make the dough: At least one day ahead of time, mix the flour, salt, and yeast with 1 cup warm water in a large mixing bowl. (Substitute 1 cup of whole-wheat flour for 1 cup of the white flour for a heartier crust.) Cover the bowl with plastic wrap and let sit at room temperature overnight. In the morning, transfer the dough to a lightly floured work surface and knead for a few minutes until the dough is no longer sticky and you can shape it into a ball. Cut the dough into four equal pieces, wrap the pieces in plastic wrap, and refrigerate until you're ready to make your pizza. The dough will keep up to three days in the fridge.

2. When you're ready to make your pizza, remove the dough from the fridge, unwrap it, and place it on a floured surface to come up to room temperature.

3. Make the chèvre: Soak the figs in a bowl filled with just enough hot water to cover. Set aside until they reach room temperature, then drain off the water, add the chèvre, and mix thoroughly.

4. Make the chard: Heat the olive oil in a large skillet over medium heat and sauté the garlic until fragrant, stirring occasionally. Add the chard and cook until completely wilted and dark green, stirring occasionally, then toss with the balsamic vinegar. Salt and pepper to taste.

5. Preheat the oven to 500°F. Stretch a piece of dough into a circle measuring about 8 inches in diameter and then repeat with the remaining dough to make 4 small pizzas. Place the pizzas on a lightly oiled pizza pan or stone. Top with the chard and dot with the chèvre. Bake for 8 to 12 minutes, or until the crust is golden brown. Drizzle with olive oil, cut, and serve.

Asparagussied Up with Heat

The ancient Egyptians cultivated asparagus and offered it to numerous gods, and the Romans had an expression, *Velocius quam asparagi coquantur*, meaning "faster than you can cook asparagus."

When I lived in Los Chavez, between Belén and Los Lunas, wild asparagus sprouted beneath the cottonwood trees, where I could collect as much of it as I wanted. This was before the Internet, so I was constantly combing through cookbooks to find new recipes for this unusual, leafless plant with the odd name. In coming up with this version, I had some chile peppers in the freezer, so I decided to spice up the asparagus.

One of the most revered spring vegetables, asparagus is a nutritional gem. It has only 22 calories per half cup (approximately six spears) and contains vitamins A and C plus 2 grams of fiber. This dish will keep in the refrigerator for about five days or you can freeze it.

Cooking spray

1 pound asparagus, trimmed, peeled, and cut into 2-inch pieces

2 teaspoons white sesame seeds, toasted

1 teaspoon minced fresh ginger

1 serrano chile, seeds and stem removed, minced

Freshly ground black pepper

2 tablespoons low-sodium soy sauce

Heat Scale: Mild   4 SERVINGS

Coat a large nonstick skillet with cooking spray and heat over medium-low. Add the asparagus, sesame seeds, ginger, serrano, a pinch of black pepper, and the soy sauce. Cook, stirring constantly, for 5 minutes. Serve immediately.

Southwestern Asparagus Strata

Serve this great entrée when asparagus is at its peak flavor — that is, harvested while it is still rather small in height. This recipe has variations all over the place! Basically, a strata is an egg and bread–based dish that you can enhance with vegetables, spices, or herbs. The classic base is 6 eggs to 3½ cups of milk; you can cut down the mix to 4 eggs and 2 egg whites (or egg substitute) and use low-fat milk. Use a full-bodied bread here, though — nothing bland. I suggest day-old French bread from a good bakery.

1 pound day-old French bread, cut into 1½-inch cubes

½ teaspoon freshly ground white pepper

½ teaspoon salt

6 eggs

3½ cups low-fat milk

1 pound asparagus, trimmed and cut into 2-inch pieces

2 tablespoons butter

½ pound button mushrooms, thinly sliced

½ cup finely chopped sweet onion

1 cup chopped green chiles

2 teaspoons finely chopped fresh chives

1 pound Jarlsberg, Gruyère, or Swiss cheese, shredded (2½ cups)

2 tablespoons grated Parmesan cheese

Heat Scale: Mild   6 TO 8 SERVINGS

1. Preheat the oven to 400°F. Arrange the bread cubes in a single layer on a large baking sheet and toast 4 inches under the broiler, stirring occasionally, until the cubes are golden brown, about 5 minutes. Transfer the cubes to a large bowl. Reduce heat to 325°F.

2. Beat the pepper, salt, eggs, and milk together, and pour 1½ cups of the beaten mixture over the bread cubes, tossing to coat them thoroughly. Set aside the cubes and the remaining egg-milk mixture.

3. Steam the asparagus for 3 minutes, rinse in cold water, drain, and set aside.

4. Melt the butter in a skillet over medium heat. Add the mushrooms and onion and sauté until the onion softens and the mushrooms begin to give up their moisture, about 10 minutes. Transfer the mixture to a small bowl with a slotted spoon, allowing any liquid to drain into the skillet. Add the chiles and chives to the mushroom mixture and toss to combine. Set aside.

5. Lightly grease a shallow 3- or 4-quart ovenproof casserole dish or a 9- by 13-inch baking dish. Lay one-third of the bread cubes in the bottom of the pan. Top them with half of the asparagus and half of the mushroom-chile mixture. Combine the Jarlsberg cheese with the Parmesan in a small bowl and sprinkle half of the cheeses over the top. Repeat the next layer with half of the remaining bread cubes, the remaining asparagus, the remaining mushroom-chile mixture, and the remaining cheese mixture. Top with the remaining bread cubes and pour the reserved egg-milk mixture over the top.

6. Bake the strata for 45 minutes, covering the top of the dish with aluminum foil if it starts to brown too quickly. (This dish can also be covered and refrigerated overnight. To serve the next day, allow the casserole to stand at room temperature for 20 minutes while preheating the oven to 325°F.) Bake uncovered for 60 to 70 minutes. Remove from the oven and let stand for 10 minutes before cutting; then, using a spatula, carefully transfer the strata to plates and serve.

THE TWO STATE "VEGETABLES"

In 1965, the New Mexico State Legislature was locked in a bitter struggle, with pinto bean growers on one side and chile pepper producers on the other. Each group was lobbying fiercely for the legislature to name their crop the official state vegetable. New Mexico politics being what they are, there was only one real solution: declare them state co-vegetables.

The only problem, as agronomists and horticulturists love to point out, is that neither beans nor chiles are actually vegetables. Beans are legumes, like the peanut, and chiles are fruits. The politicians didn't care. If it's eaten like a vegetable, a vegetable it must be, they reasoned.

Well, beans are beans, but chiles are a bit more complicated. Botanically, they're berries. Horticulturally, they're fruits. When used fresh in their green form, the produce industry calls them vegetables. When used dried in their red form, they're a spice. No wonder the politicians were confused.

Recipe from SAM ETHERIDGE, FORMERLY OF AMBROZIA

Roasted Tomato Bisque

Chef Sam Etheridge was one of the best chefs Albuquerque has ever seen (see Red Wine and Chile Stew, page 132, and Prickly Pear BBQ Sauce, page 160). His restaurant in Old Town, Ambrozia, was our favorite dinner restaurant for years, and Sam did great cooking demonstrations at the Fiery Foods and Barbecue Show as well. My wife and I never had even an average meal there — they were all great. But when Sam's wife, a doctor, accepted a great position in North Carolina, they moved and the restaurant closed. Sob.

This recipe, which ran in *Local iQ,* is a great way to use up surplus tomatoes from your garden or from the farmers' market. Serve the bisque with cheese quesadillas, sour cream, and avocado. It will keep in the refrigerator for about five days and it freezes well.

1 yellow onion, chopped

2 garlic cloves, minced

1 teaspoon olive oil

2 pounds very ripe tomatoes, quartered and strained

Salt and freshly ground black pepper

1 teaspoon chopped fresh basil

¼ cup dry red wine

¼ cup vegetable or chicken stock

2 tablespoons heavy cream

Heat Scale: Medium   **4 SERVINGS**

1. Preheat the oven to 400°F. Spread out the onion and garlic in a roasting pan, and top with the olive oil. Place the tomatoes on top of the onion and garlic, and salt and pepper to taste. Place in the oven and roast until the tomatoes are slightly charred, about 45 minutes. There is no need to turn or stir the tomatoes.

2. Place the tomato mixture in a blender, add the basil, wine, and stock, and purée. Reduce the blender speed and slowly add the heavy cream. Salt and pepper to taste, if necessary. Add the soup to a saucepan and bring to a boil. Reduce the heat and simmer until the desired consistency is reached.

Variation: The New Mexican Twist

For this version of the bisque, you will need a stove-top or outdoor smoker. Use the original ingredients except replace the basil with cilantro and add two jalapeño or fresh green chiles and two corn tortillas to the list. Combine the tomatoes, chiles, garlic, and onion in the smoker. Smoke on high heat for 15 minutes. Add the red wine and smoke for 15 minutes longer. Fry or bake the corn tortillas until crisp. Combine all the ingredients in a blender, including the cilantro and tortillas, and purée, then slowly add the cream. Cook the purée in a saucepan as above before serving.

Double-Chile Vegetable Stew

This hearty stew uses poblano chiles for their flavor and serranos for their serious bite. It's perfect for a crisp fall day. This is an understated dish that can use vegetables from local gardens and small farms. Serve this stew with cornbread (see recipes on pages 50 and 51). Store in the refrigerator for five days or freeze it.

2 pounds russet potatoes, peeled and diced

2 large carrots, peeled and diced

4 large tomatoes, peeled, seeded, and chopped

1 medium bunch bok choy, chopped medium

1 bunch scallions, chopped medium

1 leek, white part only, cut into ¼-inch rings

1 large head cabbage, chopped medium

1 medium yellow onion, finely chopped

1 red bell pepper, seeded and finely chopped

6 serrano chiles, seeds and stems removed, finely chopped

3 poblano chiles, roasted and peeled and seeds and stems removed, finely chopped

1¾ tablespoons sugar

1 tablespoon salt

1 teaspoon freshly ground black pepper

⅛ teaspoon freshly ground nutmeg

3 cups beef stock, preferably homemade

1 (12-ounce) can crushed tomatoes

¼ cup dry white wine

2 tablespoons red wine vinegar

2 tablespoons teriyaki sauce

Heat Scale: Medium   8 TO 10 SERVINGS

Combine the potatoes, carrots, chopped tomatoes, bok choy, scallions, leek, cabbage, onion, and bell pepper with the chiles, sugar, salt, pepper, nutmeg, stock, crushed tomatoes, wine, vinegar, and teriyaki sauce in a slow cooker. Cover and cook on the high setting for 3 to 4 hours.

IL PIATTO, SANTA FE'S ITALIAN FARMHOUSE KITCHEN

MATT YOHALEM AND HIS WIFE, Honey, left life in the fast lanes of the Manhattan and then New Orleans restaurant scenes to enjoy the slower pace of a farm outside of Santa Fe. Why? Maybe it's the produce, which Yohalem insists is better in New Mexico than his previous homes. So much better, in fact, that when they opened Il Piatto in 1996, Matt began his quest for the finest fruits and vegetables from New Mexico's best small farmers.

"What is available seasonally determines my daily menus," he told me, "and I have exclusive arrangements with some of the growers for specialty items, who bring what they've grown — or made — for me through the front door of the restaurant." Local amateur mycologists grow specific mushrooms for Yohalem, and the South Mountain Dairy has made so much goat-milk pecorino cheese for him that he has a year's supply stashed away.

Since Yohalem based his menus on available produce, meat, and cheeses, how does he select the dishes to serve during the winter? "You'd be surprised at what's available," he said. "Some growers have root cellars so I can get rutabagas and organic carrots; others have products like jams and jellies. And some enterprising growers have hot houses where they grow culinary herbs, microgreens, and other vegetables."

The menus at Il Piatto change constantly. For his summer menu in 2013, Yohalem created some dishes you won't find at The Olive Garden, such as Rabbit Cannelloni with Arugula, Ricotta, Wild Mushrooms, and Pistachio Pesto; and Roast Beef Gnocchi with Caramelized Onions, Walnuts, Apricots, and Goat

Cheese. See his Red Chile Linguine with Mussels and Saffron Crème on page 48.

Yohalem, who has served on the board of the Santa Fe Farmers' Market, haunts the stalls there every week looking for new and interesting menu items. And during the height of the summer produce season, a market comes to him: on Thursdays, so many trucks line up on Marcy Street with deliveries for Il Piatto and neighboring restaurants that they create an impromptu farmers' market where the growers sell directly to passing locals and tourists.

Matt Yohalem

Recipe from MATT YOHALEM, IL PIATTO

House-cured Wild Salmon
with Late Spring Garnish

Although New Mexico residents are a bit seafood challenged because we live in this thing called a desert, several purveyors fly in fresh seafood daily to our larger cities. Then talented chefs like Matt Yohalem of Santa Fe's Il Piatto (see page 95) figure out many creative ways to prepare and serve that seafood. This is Matt's take on gravlax. It will keep for up to five days in the refrigerator; do not freeze.

NOTE: This recipe requires advance preparation.

HOUSE-CURED WILD SALMON

1½ cups finely ground sea salt

1½ cups sugar

¼ cup freshly ground black pepper

2 tablespoons chopped fresh Italian parsley

1 tablespoon ground red chile

2 bay leaves, finely crushed

Zest of 3 lemons

3–4 pounds skin-on wild salmon fillets, bones removed

CREMA

1 cup heavy cream

Juice and zest of 1 lemon

¼ cup olive oil

RECOMMENDED GARNISHES

6 squash blossoms, torn

1 cup thinly sliced spring onion bulbs

¼ cup fresh pea shoots

10 radishes, trimmed and thinly sliced

15 cherry tomatoes, halved

Heat Scale: Mild   6 TO 10 SERVINGS

1. Make the salmon: Combine the salt, sugar, pepper, parsley, chile, bay leaves, and lemon zest in a large bowl. Spread about one-third of the cure on top of a large sheet of plastic wrap. Place the salmon on top in a single layer and cover with the remaining two-thirds cure. Turn the salmon over twice to coat it evenly. Wrap the salmon well and place it on a large baking sheet. Place another baking sheet and 5 pounds of weight on top to weigh it down (3 quarts of liquid or several bricks work well). Refrigerate the salmon, weighted, for 24 hours.

2. Make the *crema*: Combine the cream, lemon zest, and lemon juice in a stainless steel or glass container. Let sit at room temperature for 24 hours while the salmon cures. After a day, the mixture should solidify to the consistency of sour cream. Add the olive oil and mix well.

3. After 24 hours, rinse off the salmon and pat it dry. Slice some salmon against the grain with a very sharp knife and place it on a plate. Top with desired combination of squash blossoms, spring onions, pea shoots, radishes, and tomatoes. Drizzle the *crema* on top and serve as a salad or with toast points, bagels, or crackers.

La Montañita Co-op

THE TERM "FOOD-SHED" describes the flow of food from the area where it is grown and processed to the place where it is consumed. La Montañita Co-op's goal is to shorten the food-shed from international to regional and local distribution, and they are accomplishing that goal in New Mexico.

From its modest beginnings in 1976, the co-op struggled with competition, growth, and a viable business model, but the organization now successfully operates in four locations — two in Albuquerque and one each in Santa Fe and Gallup — with more than 17,000 family memberships. Each family pays a mere $15 a year to join. Their reward is not only the finest organically grown local food they can buy, but the satisfaction of keeping their money in the local economy, providing a stable market for farmers and producers, and participating in the vision of a sustainable agricultural economy.

One of the co-op's chief successes is its distribution center, which it developed in 2006. Two drivers and one truck delivered over $100,000 of meat, eggs, milk, and produce from about 30 regional producers during the first year of operation. La Montañita was assisted by Whole Foods, Raley's, Cid's, Los Poblanos, and other grocers to build the wholesale market for this service. In January of 2007, La Montañita opened its Co-operative Distribution Center

(CDC) in Albuquerque to deliver to small markets and big chain supermarkets.

Farmers and producers throughout New Mexico can either sell their products directly to co-op locations or utilize the services of the CDC's warehouse to expand their markets and save on gas and transport costs. The CDC also offers local producers postharvest and production cooler and freezer space and storage.

Vicki Pozzebon, director of Delicious New Mexico — a project of the South Valley Economic Development Center to raise awareness of local foods — praises the co-op highly. "La Montañita Co-op is an integral part of the food system in New Mexico as they provide retail outlets for producers around the state," she says. "And their distribution center and creation of food-related co-operatives help small farmers and producers be profitable."

Recipe from AMY WHITE, *EDIBLE SANTA FE*

Pasta Salad with Garlic Scape Pesto, Peas, and Arugula

"Turkish Giant garlic, planted in the fall, shoots up its twisty green flower stalks, also known as scapes, in late spring," notes *Edible Santa Fe* contributor Amy White. "Only hardneck garlic varieties do this, and you have to cut them [the scapes] so that the plant can put more energy into growing bigger cloves. They can be found at many growers' markets for just a precious few weeks in mid-June, a riot of crazy corkscrew curls that embody the exuberance of spring. They taste intensely garlicky when raw, without quite the bite of mature garlic cloves, but when cooked, they simply become vegetable-like with a delicate hint of garlic flavor.

"This wonderful, creamy pesto freezes well, so that you can enjoy a taste of this short-lived spring treat later in the year. This recipe calls for pistachios for an interesting twist, but piñon nuts would be just as good. If you find the pesto too intense to eat raw, just toss it with hot pasta. The flavors mellow quickly with even the slightest heat. Try it in cold pasta salads, especially since scape season always coincides with New Mexico's June heat wave! Peas and arugula are in season at the same time as scapes, but later in the summer this recipe would be great with grilled zucchini, raw or grilled sweet peppers, or cherry tomatoes."

GARLIC SCAPE PESTO

- 10 large garlic scapes (about ¼ pound), cut into 1-inch pieces
- ⅓ cup finely grated Parmigiano-Reggiano cheese (leave out if freezing; just add it later when serving)
- ⅓ cup pistachios, toasted
- ⅓ cup extra-virgin olive oil
  Salt and freshly ground black pepper

PASTA SALAD

- 1 cup shelled peas
- 1 pound orecchiette or other small, shapely pasta
- 2 big handfuls arugula, roughly chopped
- ¼ cup pistachios, toasted

8 SIDES OR 4 TO 6 ENTRÉES

1. Make the pesto: Blend the garlic scapes, cheese, pistachios, and oil in a food processor until smooth. Salt and pepper to taste. Set aside. Makes about 1 cup.

2. Make the pasta salad: Bring a small pot of water to a boil, blanch the peas for 30 seconds, remove them to a bowl with a slotted spoon and set aside to cool.

3. Cook the pasta according to the package directions. Rinse the pasta with cold water until completely cool. Toss the pasta with ½ cup of the pesto, the arugula, and the pistachios in a large bowl before serving. (Reserve the remaining ½ cup pesto for another use.) You can make this dish ahead of time and refrigerate it.

3 Enchanting Cheeses

WHILE IT MAY LACK THE MILES of rolling green pastures commonly associated with contented cows, New Mexico is currently ranked seventh in the nation for milk production and eighth for cheese. Dairy facilities range from the small, family-owned Old Windmill Dairy in Estancia to the Leprino Foods Roswell facility, the largest manufacturing plant for mozzarella in the world.

The latter is somewhat farm to table, or at least farm to dairy to plant. The company operates a 450-acre farm that produces silage and alfalfa to feed the dairy cows that make the milk for the mozzarella. Huge machines turn up to 290,000 pounds of milk per hour into cheese.

Elsewhere in the state, the Glanbia cheese plant near Clovis is the largest producer of cheddar in North America, producing in excess of 400 million pounds of high-quality cheese annually. The facility contains 60 miles of stainless steel piping and 742 miles of electrical cable, and requires about $12,500 for electricity and $9,500 for natural gas *every day*. That's an awful lot of energy usage, but it is somewhat offset by the more than 500,000 gallons a day of water that are recovered from milk, then treated and recycled for irrigating fields that produce the crops eaten by the dairy cows.

Contrast these cheese mega-plants with Old Windmill Dairy. It was established in 2002 when partners Ed and Michael Lobaugh purchased land in Estancia and purchased two Nubian goats, then created a building for them. Ed had

fond memories of goats since he had spent his childhood on his grandparents' farm in California, where they raised goats. That childhood experience with goats led to his desire to explore raising goats as more than just a hobby.

Old Windmill Dairy offers a variety of cheesemaking classes from novice to more advanced, and has a cheese club you can join to receive five types of cheese every month. Visitors mostly interested in the goats can feed and pet them or even unofficially adopt one and get a custom-made name tag and collar for their own goat. Ed is also a psychiatric nurse practitioner, and many of his patients have enjoyed the therapeutic effects of visiting Old Windmill Dairy and hanging out with the goats.

Ed and Mike now have around 60 goats on their farm, and they have become one of the most iconic goat cheese producers in New Mexico. They make 13 flavors of chèvre (soft goat cheese), plus blue cheese and feta, which often feature local ingredients. The chèvres include flavors like Wild Dill, Pesto & Pine Nuts, and Figs and Cream.

Despite the size, the farm is far from a factory operation. The kids are bottle-fed and the adult animals dine on premium feed and hay when they aren't roaming about grazing on high-desert plants. There is a lot of TLC at the dairy, both for animals and visitors. And that makes for better cheese!

Pungent Pizzas on the Grill

This recipe lets you re-create wonderful thin-crust wood-fired oven pizza on a grill in your very own backyard. My homemade crust has something that Pizza Doodle Express does not: chile. If you don't want to make your own dough, you can use a 12-inch, prebaked pizza shell. You can also easily make the dough in your bread machine. It is very important to have a clean grill for this recipe as any residue on the grill will give the crust an off flavor.

Here are two of my favorite toppings — each recipe makes enough for one small pizza or half of a large one. Have all the ingredients ready at hand when you put the dough on the grill, as the cooking process goes quickly.

CHILE PIZZA DOUGH

- 1 teaspoon sugar
- 1 teaspoon active dry yeast
- 1½ cups all-purpose flour
- 2 teaspoons red pepper flakes
- ¾ teaspoon salt
- Freshly ground black pepper
- 2 tablespoons olive oil, plus more for grilling

POWERFUL PUTANESCA TOPPING

- 3 cups chopped tomatoes, such as cherry or Roma
- 2 tablespoons chopped capers
- 2 tablespoons chopped niçoise olives
- 1 tablespoon chopped fresh basil
- 2 teaspoons red pepper flakes
- 1 cup grated Parmigiano-Reggiano or Pecorino Romano cheese
- Garlic salt
- Olive oil

SOUTHWEST GREEN CHILE TOPPING

- 8 New Mexican green chiles, roasted, peeled, and cut lengthwise into ½-inch-wide strips
- 1 cup grated mozzarella cheese
- ½ cup grated provolone cheese
- Olive oil

1. **Make the dough:** Combine the sugar and 1 cup warm water (100°F) in a bowl and stir in the yeast. Let stand for 10 minutes, or until foamy. Combine the flour, pepper flakes, salt, and black pepper to taste in a large bowl. Make a well in the flour mixture and pour in the yeast mixture and olive oil. Stir until almost mixed, turn onto a lightly floured work surface, and knead until the dough is smooth and elastic.

2. Place the dough in a large, lightly oiled bowl and cover with plastic wrap. Place in a warm, draft-free location and let rise until doubled, about 90 minutes.

3. Punch down the dough and divide it into 2 balls to make roughly 6-inch pizzas or leave it as one ball if a larger pizza will fit on your grill. (If preparing the dough ahead of time, wrap it and place in the refrigerator until ready to use. Bring the dough back to room temperature before proceeding with the recipe.) Roll out each portion of the dough into a round or oval pizza or do it free-form.

4. Heat a gas grill to hot. If using a charcoal grill, bank the coals to one side, creating a hot side and a warm side.

5. Brush one side of each pizza with olive oil and gently drape them, oil side down, on the hot grill. Within a minute or two, the dough will start to rise and bubbles will appear. Gently lift an end to see that the underside is browned and has grill marks. Immediately invert the crust from the grill onto a metal cooling rack or a baking sheet, and turn the gas grill to low. Brush the cooked side with additional oil.

6. **Add the putanesca topping:** Place the tomatoes on the cooked side of the pizza and sprinkle the capers, olives, basil, pepper flakes, and cheese over the top. Shake a little garlic salt over the pizza and drizzle with olive oil.

7. **Add the green chile topping:** Lay the chile strips over the cooked side of the pizza. Top with the mozzarella and provolone and sprinkle some olive oil over the top. Slide the pizza(s) back onto the grill.

8. Shut the lid and cook, rotating once or twice, until the toppings are heated through, the cheese is melted, and the crust is browned, about 5 minutes on the cooler part of the grill.

AMORE NEAPOLITAN PIZZERIA

THE TYPICAL NEAPOLITAN *pizzaiolo* (pizza chef) doesn't have to make his own mozzarella because it's everywhere in Naples, where the mozzarella is made from the milk of the water buffalo, which is richer in fat and protein than cow's milk. But there aren't too many water buffalos hanging around Amore Pizzeria on Monte Vista Boulevard near the University of New Mexico, so pizza expert Gabriel Amador needs to be a cheesemaker in order to justify his APN certification. That distinction, of course, comes from the Associazione Pizzaiuoli Napoletani, better known in North American pizza circles as the Association of Neapolitan Pizza Makers.

Neapolitan pizza is the mother of all pizza, having spawned nearly an infinite number of variations that made this the world's favorite food. But those variations are not happening at Amore Neapolitan Pizzeria, where they use only classic ingredients from centuries ago to create a thin flatbread topped with tomatoes, herbs, and house-made mozzarella and baked in an 850-degree oven for just 90 seconds before being served up.

Amador opened the only authentic Neapolitan pizza restaurant in the state in 2013. Unable to find the curds he needs to make mozzarella locally, he ships them in from Wisconsin. Amador also imports canned Marzano tomatoes from Naples, and his unbleached, organic flour comes from Italy too. He sources as many products as he can locally, however, buying dairy products from Rasband Dairy in the South Valley, chiles from Armijo Farms, and coffee beans from Villa Myriam (see page 221).

Amador gained his pizza expertise from his mentor Roberto Caporuscio, the owner of the two top-rated pizzerias in New York City, Keste Pizza and Vino and Don Antonio by Starita. The year before they opened Amore, Amador and his wife, Kimberly, went to New York to train with Caporuscio and become certified in the making of authentic Neapolitan pizza.

He may have learned out of state, but Amador has brought all the little tricks he needs to New Mexico to create a near-perfect version of Mozzarella di Bufala Campana for his customers in search of the best Neapolitan pizza outside of Naples.

Farmers' Market Scramble
with Pesto & Pine Nuts Chèvre

A popular flavor of chèvre at the Old Windmill Dairy in Estancia (see page 101) is Pesto & Pine Nuts, which uses locally grown herbs and wild New Mexican pine nuts. It is delicious on its own as a dip, and can be a pizza topping or even a breakfast ingredient. In this dish, it adds a spectacular dimension to ordinary scrambled eggs.

2 tablespoons bacon fat

10 eggs

1 (4-ounce) container Pesto & Pine Nuts Chèvre, or 4 ounces chèvre mixed with 1 tablespoon commercial pesto and 1 tablespoon of pine nuts

4 Roma tomatoes, chopped

1 medium green bell pepper, seeded and finely chopped

Freshly ground black pepper

4 TO 6 SERVINGS

1. Heat the bacon fat in a cast-iron skillet over medium heat.

2. Whisk the eggs in a large bowl. Add the chèvre and whisk the eggs and chèvre until fluffy. Add the tomatoes, bell pepper, and black pepper to taste.

3. Pour the mixture into the skillet and cook over low heat, stirring and scrambling until the desired consistency is reached, about 10 minutes.

ButterBeautiful's Enchanted Eggs

We New Mexicans, of course, regularly eat spicy breakfasts, and rarely have I seen a better use for butter or, in this case, a compound butter from ButterBeautiful (see facing page) than this recipe. I'd never tasted a compound butter made with habanero chiles before, but this habanero Dragon Breath butter nicely tames down the intense heat of that chile pepper.

BUTTER SAUCE

- 3 egg yolks
- 1 tablespoon habanero Dragon Breath butter

EGGS

- 1 (6-ounce tub) habanero Dragon Breath butter (12 tablespoons), or 6 ounces soft butter mixed with ½ teaspoon of bottled habanero sauce
- 3 pounds kale, veins removed and coarsely chopped
- 1 cup chopped roasted and peeled green chiles
- 3 large shallots, diced
- 4 slices Canadian bacon
- 2 tablespoons white wine vinegar
- 8 eggs
- New Mexican red chile powder, for garnish

Heat Scale: Medium   4 SERVINGS

1. Make the sauce: Heat water in the bottom pot of a double boiler to boiling. Combine the yolks and butter in the top pot, place it over the bottom, and cook the mixture, whisking constantly, until it thickens, about 3 minutes; do not over-cook. Keep the sauce warm in the oven while the eggs cook.

2. Make the eggs: Melt the butter in a large skillet over medium heat and sauté the kale, chiles, and shallots, stirring often, until the kale starts to wilt slightly, about 4 minutes. Transfer the kale mixture to an ovenproof bowl and keep warm in the oven. Sauté the bacon in the remaining butter, turning three times, then transfer to an ovenproof plate and keep warm in the oven.

3. Add enough water to the double boiler to equal 1 quart. Add the vinegar and bring to a low boil over medium heat. Break the eggs into the water carefully to make sure the yolks do not break. Poach the eggs until the whites are no longer clear but actually turn white, about 5 minutes.

4. Divide the kale mixture among 4 plates and top with the Canadian bacon, and two poached eggs (remove them from the water with a slotted spoon). Drizzle with the sauce. Lightly dust with red chile powder and serve.

BUTTERBEAUTIFUL

KIRK LUCAS, who describes himself as an inventor, has always had a penchant for creating food-related things. The idea for ButterBeautiful started back in 2005 when Lucas moved to Santa Fe. He fell in love with New Mexican cuisine, especially the great regional variety that existed. While many creative food trends have started up throughout the state, Lucas felt that one area was poorly represented: butter.

In addition to it being part of human culinary tradition for thousands of years, Lucas notes that butter, in reasonable quantities, offers some often overlooked health benefits. Butter is rich in calcium and potassium and helps with thyroid and adrenal health. Lucas also points out that butter is far less processed and more natural than many of the available alternatives.

With that in mind, Lucas took this familiar ingredient and created a line of compound butters filled with the flavors of the Southwest. Using butter from grass-fed cows in the northern New Mexico town of Chimayó, also known for its Chimayó chile, Lucas produces his butters at the Taos Kitchen, where a number of other small regional producers make products. These butters are quite diverse and extremely versatile, giving an exotic and flavorful touch to simple foods such as eggs or meats.

One standout flavor is the Dragon Breath butter, which uses habaneros and has a smoky yet spicy flavor. More refined palates might prefer the Shallot Shiraz or Pinot Grigio Mushroom varieties. Lucas has even created Chile Chocolate Azteca, spicy with a hint of honey. ButterBeautiful products, available online, are a must for the chef in your family or if you're just looking to create some excitement in your everyday culinary adventures.

Chili N Hot Chèvre–Artichoke Dip

Who says goat cheese can't be spicy? Certainly not the creative cooks at the Old Windmill Dairy in Estancia (see page 101). This is one of the more flavorful dips you'll ever make in your kitchen. Serve it with homemade corn tortillas or gourmet crackers. Refrigerate leftovers but do not freeze.

1 (12-ounce) jar marinated artichoke hearts, drained and quartered

1 (4-ounce) container Chili N Hot Chèvre, or 4 ounces chèvre mixed with 2 teaspoons roasted and peeled green chile

⅓ cup mayonnaise

4 ounces cheddar cheese, shredded (1 cup)

Freshly ground black pepper

Heat Scale: Mild

ABOUT 2 CUPS

1. Preheat the oven to 350°F.

2. Place the quartered artichokes in a large bowl and break them up with a spoon as much as you can. Mix in the chèvre and mayonnaise and stir well.

3. Pour the mixture into a 9-inch pie pan and top with the cheddar and black pepper to taste. Bake the dip for 20 minutes, or until hot and bubbling.

Upscale Mean Mac

The variety of cheese in this tasty dish raises it from the realm of the kiddie menu and makes it dangerously delicious! The chiles and the flavored pasta add a subtle punch that contrasts nicely with the New Mexican cheeses and the herbs. You can use any shape of pasta, but I recommend green or red chile linguine for extra bite. Leftovers can be refrigerated or frozen.

1½ teaspoons salt

½ cup olive oil

1 pound flavored pasta

8 ounces mascarpone cheese, softened

1 teaspoon coarsely ground white pepper

½ teaspoon coarsely ground black pepper

4 ounces fontina cheese, cut into ¼-inch cubes

4 ounces blue or feta cheese, crumbled

¾ cup grated Parmesan cheese

1 habanero chile or 3 serrano chiles, seeds and stem removed, minced

¼ cup finely chopped fresh Italian parsley

2 teaspoons finely chopped fresh thyme or 1 teaspoon dried thyme

1 teaspoon dried savory

¾ teaspoon dried oregano, preferably Mexican

4–5 cups mixed greens, such as Boston Bibb lettuce, endive, or escarole

Heat Scale: Medium   8 SERVINGS

1. Bring a large pot of water to a boil, and add 1 teaspoon of the salt and 2 tablespoons of the olive oil. Add the pasta and cook according to the package directions. Drain thoroughly and place the pasta in a large microwave-safe bowl.

2. While the pasta cooks, mix the remaining 6 tablespoons olive oil, the mascarpone, the white pepper, and the black pepper together in a small bowl.

3. Mix the mascarpone mixture with the pasta. Add the fontina, blue cheese, Parmesan, chile, parsley, remaining ½ teaspoon salt, the thyme, savory, and oregano, and toss the mixture lightly.

4. Microwave the mixture on low for 2 minutes to warm it up.

5. Arrange a bed of mixed greens on each plate and mound the pasta on top. Serve immediately.

Chile con Queso de Cabro
(Chèvre Chile Dip)

Of all the chile con queso recipes I've tried, this one — made by my wife, Mary Jane — is, in my admittedly prejudiced opinion, by far the best. It is tastiest when served with homemade corn tortilla chips. It can also be used as a sauce with baked potatoes, refried beans, freshly cooked vegetables, and grilled vegetables. If you like a spicier dip, add a few dashes of your favorite hot sauce to the recipe. This dip doesn't freeze well, but you can refrigerate any leftovers for up to five days. In fact, it tastes even better if it's made a day in advance.

1 tablespoon olive oil

1 medium tomato, finely chopped

2 garlic cloves, minced

2 scallions, finely chopped

2 New Mexican green chiles, roasted, peeled, and chopped

8 ounces sharp cheddar cheese, cut into ½-inch cubes

4 ounces New Mexican chèvre, crumbled

¼ cup light cream or half-and-half

Heat Scale: Medium   ABOUT 3½ CUPS

1. Heat the olive oil in a skillet over medium heat, then add the tomato, garlic, scallions, and chiles. Sauté, stirring often, until the scallions are soft, about 5 minutes. Remove the mixture from the skillet using a slotted spoon and drain on paper towels.

2. Melt the cheddar cheese and chèvre in a heavy saucepan or a double boiler over low heat, stirring occasionally. Add the cream, stirring constantly to incorporate. Add the chile mixture and stir thoroughly. Add more cream if the mixture looks too thick. Continue heating the mixture, stirring constantly, until it is hot, about 5 minutes.

3. Serve immediately or let the mixture cool slightly and refrigerate to serve the next day. In that case, bring the mixture to room temperature, and then heat slowly over low heat, stirring constantly.

Recipe from ROSA RAJKOVIC, FORMERLY OF MONTE VISTA FIRE STATION RESTAURANT AND BAR

Goat-Cheese Poblanos Rellenos with Chipotle Cream

Rosa Rajkovic was the brilliant chef of the Monte Vista Fire Station Restaurant and Bar in Albuquerque for years, and created these cheese-infused stuffed peppers, which I enjoyed many times. She says that because of the varying heat scales of poblanos (they are usually quite mild but occasionally deliver heat), preparing this recipe is "culinary roulette." However, the cheese does cut the heat of any renegade poblanos.

CHIPOTLE CREAM

- ½ cup sour cream
- 4 ounces goat cheese
- 1 small chipotle chile (if dried, soak in warm water to soften)
- Half-and-half or heavy cream
- 1 tablespoon finely chopped fresh cilantro

GOAT-CHEESE POBLANOS RELLENOS

- 6 large poblano chiles
- 8 ounces goat cheese
- 5 ounces low-fat cream cheese
- 4 ounces blue cheese
- 2 eggs, beaten
- 1 cup blue cornmeal
- ½ cup canola or vegetable oil

Heat Scale: Mild to medium   **6 SERVINGS**

1. Make the chipotle cream: Process or blend the sour cream, goat cheese, and chipotle until very smooth in a food processor. Add enough half-and-half to create a pourable consistency, about ¼ cup. Add the cilantro and process for a few seconds longer. Pour the cream into a squeeze bottle or small pitcher and set aside.

2. Make the rellenos: Roast the peppers on a gas grill over high heat or under a broiler until the skins blister and blacken. Remove the peppers from the heat, place them in a bowl, and cover tightly with plastic wrap. Allow the peppers to cool completely in the bowl. Peel the peppers, carefully slit them along one side with a sharp knife, and remove the seeds. Leave the stem intact.

3. Mix the goat cheese, cream cheese, and blue cheese together in a bowl with a fork. Spoon the filling into the cavities of the peppers. Refrigerate the peppers in a covered bowl until ready to assemble the final dish. (Chilling the peppers until they are very cold will help the blue corn coating stay crispy after the peppers are sautéed.)

4. Place the eggs and cornmeal in two separate shallow bowls. Heat the oil in a large skillet over medium-low heat. Dip the rellenos in the egg mixture, then into the cornmeal. Sauté the rellenos until lightly browned, turning each one three times in the hot oil to ensure even crisping. Drain on double layers of paper towels.

5. Place the rellenos in shallow bowls and drizzle the chipotle cream over them to serve.

CAMINO DE PAZ SCHOOL AND FARM

CAMINO DE PAZ is a Montessori School for grades 7 to 9 located in Santa Cruz, just north of Santa Fe. Their philosophy is to provide an environment in which young adolescents can engage their intellectual and spiritual capabilities, as well as their bodies, through physical activities. In addition to teaching the basics such as math and science, Camino de Paz believes in giving students a real, working community in which to operate, so the school operates a farm on the campus that is integrated into the curriculum.

The farm helps the students gain practical experience and build their social skills with their peers and mentors. The animals on the farm include sheep, Angora goats, hens, and Belgian draft horses. All of the animals are holistically integrated into the farm, and students learn the vital roles that each creature brings to the ecosystem.

Camino de Paz also offers a community supported agriculture program (CSA), which offers members a selection of seasonal produce each week throughout the farming season. The students participate in the total farm experience from the planting to selling the produce and other farm products.

In addition to growing produce, the school operates a USDA Certified Grade A goat dairy that makes yogurt, raw and pasteurized goat milk, chèvre, feta, and *cajeta*, a milk syrup flavored with caramel. Students have the opportunity to be involved in the entire process of the dairy operation including milking, pasteurizing, and cheese and yogurt making as well as the bottling, labeling, and marketing of their products in the region. (All products are sold in reusable glass bottles in order to cut down on plastic waste.)

It is increasingly rare for younger generations to receive practical knowledge and experience about subjects like farming, and Camino de Paz students develop a deeper understanding thanks to the in-depth and practical curriculum.

Holy Chipotle! Chèvre, Cucumber, and Avocado Dip

Here's an innovative summer appetizer made with one of the Old Windmill Dairy's chile cheeses. Owners Ed and Michael Lobaugh think lemon cucumbers are the best cucumber variety for this dip, but you can use English cucumbers if they are not available. Your local farmers' market is the best place to find lemon cucumbers. Serve this dip with homemade corn tortilla chips or gourmet crackers for dipping. This dip does not freeze well, but you can refrigerate any leftovers for up to five days.

2 avocados, peeled, pitted, and chopped

1 lemon cucumber, peeled and finely chopped

¼ cup fresh cilantro

¼ cup chopped red onion, finely chopped

1 (4-ounce) container Holy Chipotle! Chèvre, crumbled, or 4 ounces chèvre mixed with 1 finely chopped canned chipotle chile

1–2 jalapeño chiles, finely chopped

Juice of 3 limes

Heat Scale: Mild   ABOUT 2 CUPS

Toss the avocados, cucumber, cilantro, onion, chèvre, and jalapeños to taste in a bowl. Add the lime juice and stir gently to combine. Serve immediately or cover and refrigerate until ready to serve.

Green Chile and Chèvre Muffins

These unusual and spicy muffins are perfect for a picnic when accompanied by fresh fruit or a fruit salad, and, of course, a New Mexican white wine. Wrap leftovers in plastic wrap and keep them in the cupboard for up to three days; they can also be frozen for a couple of months.

2¼ cups all-purpose flour

2 tablespoons yellow cornmeal

3 teaspoons baking powder

Salt

1 cup skim milk

¼ cup olive oil

2 eggs

½ cup coarsely chopped pitted black olives

½ cup chopped roasted and peeled green chiles

¼ cup drained oil-packed sun-dried tomatoes, chopped

6 ounces herbed chèvre, cut into 12 pieces and rolled into balls

12 pecan halves

Heat Scale: Medium   12 MUFFINS

1. Position a rack in the center of the oven and preheat the oven to 375°F.

2. Grease a 12-cup muffin pan with butter. Combine the flour, cornmeal, baking powder, and salt in a large mixing bowl, then set aside. Whisk the milk, olive oil, and eggs in a separate mixing bowl. Pour the egg mixture into the flour mixture and stir with a wooden spoon until just moistened. Gently fold in the olives, chiles, and sun-dried tomatoes. The batter should not look smooth.

3. Fill each muffin cup halfway full with the batter. Press a ball of the cheese on top of the batter in each cup. Spoon the rest of the batter equally into each muffin cup. Finally, place a pecan half on top of each muffin.

4. Bake the muffins for 24 minutes, or until the muffins are brown but not over baked. Remove the muffins from the oven and let them rest in the pan for 5 minutes. Turn them out onto a wire rack and cool to room temperature before serving.

Chicken and Chèvre Enchiladas with Black Bean Sauce

This recipe showcases the versatility of enchiladas, which are served with a sauce made from black beans in addition to the more traditional chiles. For a variation on this recipe, leave the beans whole and add them to the filling, then top the enchiladas with a red chile sauce.

BLACK BEAN SAUCE

- 2 tablespoons vegetable oil
- ½ red onion, chopped
- 2 garlic cloves, minced
- 2 jalapeño chiles, halved and stems and seeds removed
- 1 cup canned black beans, rinsed and drained
- 1 cup chicken stock
- 2 tablespoons dry sherry
- 1 tablespoon lime juice
- 2 teaspoons orange zest

CHICKEN AND CHÈVRE ENCHILADAS

- 1 tablespoon ground New Mexican red chile
- 1 teaspoon garlic powder
- ½ teaspoon ground cumin
- ½ teaspoon dried oregano, preferably Mexican
- 1½ cups shredded cooked chicken
- ½ red onion, chopped
- 4 tablespoons vegetable oil
- 1 medium tomato, chopped
- 8 corn tortillas
- 8 ounces chèvre, crumbled
- ¼ cup chopped fresh cilantro, plus more for garnish
- Sour cream, for garnish

Heat Scale: Medium   4 SERVINGS

1. Make the sauce: Heat the oil in a skillet over medium heat, then sauté the onion, garlic, and jalapeños until the onion is soft, 5 to 10 minutes. Add the beans, stock, sherry, lime juice, and orange zest, and stir to combine. Remove from the heat, transfer the mixture to a food processor, and purée until smooth.

2. Make the enchiladas: Preheat the oven to 350°F. Combine the chile, garlic powder, cumin, and oregano in a medium bowl and toss the chicken in the mixture to coat. Sauté the onion in 2 tablespoons of the oil in a skillet over medium heat until the onion is soft, 5 to 10 minutes. Add the chicken and heat through, stirring occasionally, for 2 minutes. Add the tomato and cook for 2 minutes, stirring occasionally. Remove the skillet from the heat.

3. Heat the remaining oil in a small skillet over medium heat. Using tongs, place a tortilla in the oil for 3 seconds, turn, and cook for 3 seconds. Remove and drain on paper towels. Repeat with the remaining tortillas.

4. Place 2 softened tortillas on an ovenproof plate and top with some of the chicken mixture. Sprinkle the chèvre and cilantro over the chicken and roll the tortillas up. Repeat with the remaining ingredients on 3 ovenproof plates. Pour some of the sauce over each enchilada and heat in the oven for 10 minutes to melt the cheese.

5. Garnish the enchiladas with additional cilantro and a dollop of sour cream and serve.

Grapevine-grilled Quail with Chèvre Rounds

New Mexico's most common quail is the Gambel's quail with its cute little topknot, and there is a hunting season for them in New Mexico. They can be used in this recipe if you are a hunter or know one. If not, domestic quail meat is available in specialty markets and from online sources such as D'Artagnan.com.

Although many Southwest barbecues and grilled meats utilize mesquite, it is not the only aromatic wood available. You can experiment with pecan, apple, peach, or grapevine clippings, as called for here. Be sure to soak the wood in water for 1 hour before grilling.

12 1-pound semiboneless quail (wing tips, backbone, ribs, and thigh bones removed)

2 ancho chiles, seeds and stems removed

1 garlic clove

⅔ cup plus 2 tablespoons olive oil

¼ cup orange juice

2 tablespoons lime juice

6 (2-ounce) chèvre rounds

¼ cup dried cornbread crumbs

6 (6-inch) pieces thick grapevine clippings, soaked in water

Salsa

Heat Scale: Mild · · · · · · · 6 SERVINGS

1. Wash the quail and pat them dry with paper towels.

2. Simmer the chiles in a small pot filled with water for 15 minutes. Drain the chiles. Place the chiles, garlic, ⅔ cup of the olive oil, orange juice, and lime juice in a blender and purée until smooth. Pour the sauce over the quail and marinate for 1 hour.

3. While the quail are marinating, prepare a medium-hot charcoal fire and preheat the oven to 350°F.

4. Brush the chèvre rounds with the remaining 2 tablespoons olive oil, coat with the cornbread crumbs, and bake for 5 minutes. (If you start baking the chèvre when the quail hit the grill, they should be done at the same time.)

5. Add the grape clippings to the coals, arrange the quail skin side down on the rack, and grill for 2 minutes, taking care not to burn them. Turn the quail and grill until slightly brown, about 2 minutes longer. If the skin is not yet brown, turn the quail again and grill for 1 minute longer.

6. Serve 2 quail on each plate with a chèvre round and garnished with salsa.

Frijoles Indios
(Indian Pinto Beans with Chorizo and Cheese)

Beans in some form are served with almost every traditional meal in New Mexico, including breakfast. And when you combine beans with another staple — steamy, hot corn tortillas — you have a healthy, low-fat meal with complete protein. In New Mexico, the beans of choice are pinto beans, an official state vegetable that, of course, is not really a vegetable but a legume (see page 91).

Frijoles are usually cooked in clay pots, called *ollas*, which impart an earthy taste to the dish, but cooking beans in a saucepan, crockpot, or pressure cooker produces a tasty result as well. You must use lard to get an authentic flavor to these beans, but you may replace it with vegetable oil. Remember not to salt them until they are done or they will never become tender.

2 cups dried pinto beans

2 tablespoons lard

¼ pound Mexican chorizo, crumbled

1 small yellow onion, chopped

2 garlic cloves, crushed

1–2 teaspoons crushed chile de árbol or piquín chile

1 teaspoon dried oregano, preferably Mexican

Salt

8 ounces finely/coarsely grated Chihuahua, Monterey Jack, or queso anejo cheese (2 cups)

Heat Scale: Mild   4 TO 6 SERVINGS

1. Combine the beans and 2 quarts water in a large saucepan or stockpot and remove any beans that float to the top. Bring the mixture to a boil over high heat, cover, and reduce the heat to low. Simmer until the beans are tender, about 2 hours, adding more water if necessary. When the beans begin to wrinkle, add the lard. When they are completely done, add salt to taste and simmer for 2 minutes longer. Drain the beans, reserving the liquid.

2. Return the beans to the saucepan and mash, adding the bean liquid to produce a smooth consistency. Add enough liquid to make the beans rather soupy as they will thicken as they sit.

3. Heat a skillet over medium heat, add the chorizo, and cook, stirring occasionally, until done, about 10 minutes. Using a slotted spoon, transfer the chorizo to the beans.

4. Add the onion and garlic to the skillet and sauté, stirring occasionally, until soft, 5 to 10 minutes. Add the chile and cook for 1 minute longer. Add the onion mixture and oregano to the beans.

5. Gradually stir the cheese into the beans, reserving 2 tablespoons for garnish. If the beans are getting too thick, add more of the reserved liquid.

6. Ladle the beans into a bowl, garnish with the reserved cheese, and serve.

Five-Cheese Chile Cheesecake

This appetizer is attractive to both the eye and the taste buds. Note that it is a savory cheesecake, not a sweet one. The flavored butter adds a nice complexity. It's very easy to make compound butters at home, so you should do some experimenting.

Refrigerate any leftover cheesecake for up to five days; it doesn't freeze well.

NOTE: This recipe requires advance preparation.

1½ tablespoons compound butter, such as ButterBeautiful Champagne Tarragon (or 1½ tablespoons of softened butter mixed with ½ teaspoon finely minced fresh tarragon)

1½ ounces sharp cheddar cheese, finely grated (⅓ cup)

¼ cup fine breadcrumbs, lightly toasted

1 teaspoon New Mexican red chile powder

1 red bell pepper, seeded and thinly sliced

3 (8-ounce packages) low-fat cream cheese, softened

1 cup low-fat ricotta cheese

¾ chopped scallions

2 ounces part-skim mozzarella cheese, finely/coarsely grated (about ½ cup)

1 ounce chèvre

4 eggs

2 jalapeño chiles, stemmed, seeded, and finely chopped

1 garlic clove, halved

2 tablespoons low-fat milk

Heat Scale: Medium   12 SERVINGS

1. Preheat the oven to 325°F. Grease a 9-inch springform pan with the butter. Make sure to cover it completely.

2. Mix the cheddar cheese, breadcrumbs, and chile powder in a medium bowl. Sprinkle the mixture into the springform pan, turning it to coat the sides and bottom of the pan evenly. Refrigerate the crust until ready to bake.

3. Place half of the bell pepper slices in a food processor, reserving the rest. Add the cream cheese, ricotta, scallions, mozzarella, chèvre, eggs, jalapeños, garlic, and milk, and process until smooth.

4. Pour half of the filling into the chilled springform pan. Place the reserved bell pepper slices on top of the filling with no two touching, then pour the remaining filling on top. Set the springform pan on a baking sheet and bake for 90 minutes, or until a toothpick inserted in it comes out clean. When the cheesecake is done, turn off the oven, and cool the cheesecake in the oven with the door ajar for about 1 hour.

5. Transfer the cheesecake to a wire rack, remove the sides of the pan, and cool to room temperature before serving.

Chile, Cheese, and Grits Casserole

This recipe is a classic case of a southern staple moving to the Southwest. It is a rich dish and is best served with something simple, like roasted or grilled meats. Grits refers to any coarsely ground grain such as corn, oats, or rice, but it is important that you use corn grits in this recipe because it was tested with them. This recipe freezes well, but you should thaw it before reheating.

1½ cups corn grits

2 teaspoons salt

4 ounces Jarlsberg cheese, finely/coarsely grated (1 cup)

2 ounces chèvre, crumbled

6 tablespoons (¾ stick) butter, cut into pieces

3 eggs, or 1 egg plus egg substitute

1 tablespoon pure red ground chile, such as Chimayó

1 teaspoon sweet paprika

Heat Scale: Mild   6 SERVINGS

1. Preheat the oven to 325°F.

2. Bring 6 cups water to a boil in a large saucepan. Pour the grits into the boiling water, add 1 teaspoon of the salt, reduce the heat to low, and simmer for 30 minutes uncovered, stirring occasionally. (If you're using instant grits, follow the manufacturer's instructions.)

3. Remove the grits from the heat, add the Jarlsberg cheese, chèvre, and butter, and stir until the butter melts.

4. Beat the eggs, remaining 1 teaspoon salt, ground chile, and paprika in a bowl. Add to the grits and mix well.

5. Spread the mixture in a lightly oiled 1-quart casserole dish and bake, uncovered, for 1 hour, or until golden brown and set. If the top starts to brown too quickly, cover the dish with aluminum foil. Serve hot.

Two-Chile Chèvre Quesadilla Ecstasy

Trust me, these are not the bland, boring quesadillas you may have been subjected to in the past. When my wife, Mary Jane, taught high school in Albuquerque, the cafeteria served basic quesadillas filled with American cheese and green chiles for breakfast. According to her, they were satisfyingly good and gooey but lacked the pizzazz we've given to these quesadillas. With the addition of the sliced jalapeños, this is quite a spicy dish. Serve the quesadillas in small wedges as an appetizer or cut them into larger slices and serve as a main course with a big salad and a luscious dessert.

1–2 tablespoons butter

10–15 button mushrooms, or other mushroom variety, thinly sliced

3 (10-inch) flour tortillas

5 New Mexican green chiles, roasted, peeled, and seeds and stems removed, chopped

2 ounces chèvre, crumbled

6 ounces sharp cheddar cheese, shredded (1½ cups)

¾ cup sun-dried tomatoes, thinly sliced

¼ cup chopped fresh cilantro

2 jalapeño or serrano chiles (fresh if possible), seeds and stems removed, thinly sliced

1 teaspoon bottled hot sauce (preferably one without a lot of vinegar)

Fresh cilantro sprigs, for garnish

Heat Scale: Hot   6 TO 8 APPETIZER SERVINGS

1. Preheat the oven to 400°F.

2. Heat a tablespoon or two of butter in a small skillet over medium-low heat, then sauté the mushrooms until they soften and begin to give up their juice.

3. Place one of the tortillas on a small cookie sheet and spread half of the green chiles over the top. Sprinkle half of the chèvre and half of the cheddar over the chiles. Add half of the sun-dried tomatoes, half of the chopped cilantro, half of the mushrooms, half of the jalapeños, and half of the hot sauce. Place the second tortilla over the first one and repeat the process. Cover with the third tortilla.

4. Bake for 7 to 9 minutes, or until the quesadilla is heated through and the cheese has melted. Slice the quesadilla into triangles with a very sharp serrated knife or pizza cutter. Serve garnished with cilantro sprigs.

4 Exceptional Meats

IMAGINE A CUISINE without beef, lamb, pork, or chicken (not to mention cilantro, cumin, limes, onions, wheat bread, rice, beer, and wine). That's where New World cooking would be without the Old World, and it is particularly true of New Mexico. "Wherever Spaniards went, they took their livestock with them," writes John C. Super, author of *Food, Conquest, and Colonization in Sixteenth-Century Spanish America*. "Pigs, sheep, and cattle were as much a part of the conquest as Toledo steel and fighting mastiffs."

The Spaniards who first settled Santa Fe brought with them the necessary livestock to raise herds of cattle, sheep, and horses, as well as seeds for the crops they needed. The introduction of livestock was so successful that the animals thrived even when they escaped into the wild. Within a century after the arrival of Columbus, the estimated New World population of cattle was 800,000 and sheep numbered an astonishing 4.6 million. With all that additional meat available, no wonder the cuisines of the Americas changed radically.

With abundant pastureland in the state, New Mexico still supports large herds of both cattle and sheep, with quite a variety of breeds, such as the Churro, renowned for its ability to endure harsh climates and its delicious meat. This was the original breed brought from Spain to New Spain and introduced into northern New Mexico in the 1600s.

Meat Celebrations

Cabrito roast: Goat meat is most tender and flavorful when the *cabritos* (little goats) are between four and eight weeks old, so a spring *cabrito* roast (or grill or stew) is a popular festivity. *Cabrito al pastor*, or shepherd-style goat, is a traditional dish in New Mexico, as it is in northern Mexico, and originally involved roasting the *cabrito* on a spit over a wood fire. More likely than not, a barbecue grill with a rotisserie is used today rather than a spit. Another modern cooking method involves seasoning the carcass, wrapping it in wet burlap, and placing it on the coals of a mesquite wood or charcoal fire. When done, portions are covered with fresh salsa and served with ranch-style pinto beans.

Matanza: *La matanza* means "the killing" and refers to the ceremonial slaughter of a fattened pig in the late fall. Its roots go back two thousand years in Spain and later it was a symbol of Spanish political and religious resistance to the ruling Moors, who, of course, did not eat pork. *Matanzas* are still held in Mexico and now New Mexico, with the men doing the slaughtering and the women rendering the lard, roasting the cut-up pig, and preparing the side dishes for a family celebration or a neighborhood party. But these days, *matanzas* are held not only in the fall, but whenever anyone feels like eating pork. El Pinto Restaurant (see page 139) has a monthly *matanza* with a whole hog roasted in an outdoor oven called an *horno*. The world's largest *matanza* is held in Belén in January, attracting more than 15,000 people as a fundraiser for students.

Short Rib Chili

This recipe is from my wife, Mary Jane, and it's one of my favorite versions of chili. It's easy to make and combines the best elements of both red and green chiles. Serve it with cornbread and a big green salad. It freezes well.

2 tablespoons vegetable oil

4 pounds beef short ribs, trimmed of excess fat

1 yellow onion, chopped

1 green bell pepper, seeded and chopped

2 garlic cloves, minced

2 cups beef stock, preferably homemade

1 cup chopped roasted and peeled New Mexican green chiles

1 (12-ounce) can crushed tomatoes

2 tablespoons New Mexican red chile powder

3½ cups cooked kidney beans, pinto beans, or black beans, drained

2 cups cooked fresh corn kernels

Heat Scale: Medium   8 SERVINGS

1. Heat the oil in a large skillet over medium heat and brown the ribs for about 3 minutes a side. Increase the heat to high, add the onion, bell pepper, and garlic, and sauté for 1 minute, stirring constantly.

2. Transfer the ribs and vegetables to a slow cooker and add the stock. Add the chiles, tomatoes, and chile powder, and cover. Cook on the high setting for 6 to 7 hours, until the meat separates from the bones.

3. Just before serving, add the beans and corn and cook until heated through, about 20 minutes. For convenience, remove the meat from the cooker, cut the meat off the bones, and return the meat to the cooker and serve.

Steak à la Dave

I have been working on this recipe for 15 years, and I'm not done yet. New and different hot sauces are always adding another dimension to a dish that I originally spiced with chunks of green chile. Serve this steak dinner with a spinach salad.

NOTE: This recipe requires advance preparation.

1 tablespoon plus 1 teaspoon lemon juice

1 tablespoon bottled hot sauce

2 large 2-inch-thick steaks, sirloin preferred

2 teaspoons freshly ground black pepper

2 teaspoons minced garlic

4 ounces cheddar cheese, grated (1 cup)

Heat Scale: Medium   4 SERVINGS

1. Combine the lemon juice and hot sauce in a small bowl, then use a brush to coat both sides of the steaks with it. Sprinkle the black pepper and garlic on both sides and pound them gently into the meat. Let the steaks sit at room temperature for at least 1 hour.

2. Prepare the grill for direct grilling over high heat. Grill the steaks over a fire of mesquite wood, or a charcoal or gas fire with mesquite chips. About 4 or 5 minutes before the steaks are done — cut into the steaks to check or use a thermometer to check for a temperature of 140°F for rare — spread an equal amount of cheese over each steak. Serve just when the cheese has melted.

Recipe from ERNESTO DURAN, FORQUE

Forque's Unique "Taco Bar"

Ernesto Duran, chef de cuisine at Forque, the decidedly noncorporate restaurant at Albuquerque's Hyatt Regency, has come up with a nice spin on the classic Italian dish known as osso buco by substituting beef short ribs for veal shanks. This upscale version of a taco bar uses the braised short ribs for making designer tacos at your table. Duran combines the "osso buco" with a very quick version of a black bean stew and a number of other taco fixings. To make a "taco bar" for four, simply double the ingredients.

"OSSO BUCO"

- ¼ pound pancetta, cut in ¼-inch cubes (do not substitute bacon)
- 1 pound beef short ribs, trimmed of excess fat
- Salt and freshly ground black pepper
- All-purpose flour, for dredging
- 1 medium yellow onion, diced
- ½ cup diced peeled carrot
- ½ cup diced celery
- 1 tablespoon minced garlic
- 3–4 fresh thyme sprigs
- 1 cup dry white table wine
- 1–2 cups beef stock
- ¼ cup commercial demi-glace

BLACK BEAN STEW

- 6 Roma tomatoes, quartered
- 1 cup cooked or canned black beans
- ½ cup minced cooked bacon
- ½ roasted poblano chile, coarsely chopped
- 1 teaspoon minced garlic
- 1 teaspoon minced shallot
- 2 teaspoons ButterBeautiful habanero Dragon Breath butter or unsalted butter
- ½ cup chicken stock

TACOS

- ½ cup prepared salsa
- 10 warm corn tortillas
- 1 cup shaved red cabbage
- 1 tablespoon finely chopped fresh cilantro
- 1 lime, quartered
- ½ avocado, peeled, pitted, and minced

Heat Scale: Mild   2 SERVINGS

1. Make the "osso buco": Preheat the oven to 265°F.

2. Heat a Dutch oven on the stove over medium heat for about 5 minutes. Add the pancetta and cook, stirring occasionally, until it is crispy and most of the fat has been rendered, about 5 minutes. Transfer the pancetta to a plate and set aside.

3. Season the short ribs with salt and pepper, then dredge them in the flour and shake off any excess. Add the ribs to the hot fat in the Dutch oven. Increase the heat to medium-high and cook the ribs until well browned on each side, about 5 minutes per side. Transfer the ribs to a plate and set aside.

4. Add the onion, carrot, and celery to the Dutch oven. Cook the onion mixture over medium heat, stirring frequently, until the onion is soft, 5 to 10 minutes. Add the garlic and thyme sprigs and continue cooking, stirring frequently, until the vegetables are just beginning to brown, about 10 minutes.

5. Return the pancetta and ribs to the Dutch oven, pour in the wine, then add enough beef stock to come a little more than halfway up the sides of the ribs. Bring to a simmer. Cover the Dutch oven and put it in the oven to cook until the meat is tender, about 6 hours. When finished, sprinkle the demi-glace over the ribs.

6. Make the stew: Combine the tomatoes, black beans, bacon, chile, garlic, and shallot in a medium saucepan and sauté over medium heat, stirring occasionally, until the shallot is soft, 5 to 10 minutes. Add the butter and chicken stock and stir for 1 minute longer.

7. Make the tacos: To serve, place the short ribs on two large plates. Place a ramekin of salsa and five tortillas on each plate. Fill two small bowls with the black bean stew and place them next to the plates. Fill bowls with the cabbage, cilantro, lime wedges, and avocado, and place them on the table. Diners can then eat the stew and fashion their own tacos from the ribs and fixings.

FORQUE

WE TEND TO STEREOTYPE restaurants that are associated with major hotel chains, expecting bland, corporate, uninspired dishes. But the first time I ate at Forque, the fine-dining restaurant at Albuquerque's downtown Hyatt Regency, I was astonished when I tasted the Cajun-style Shrimp and Grits — it was remarkably delicious and decidedly noncorporate. So I got right to the point when I interviewed Ernesto Duran, Forque's chef de cuisine.

"What's going on here?" I asked him.

"We had to follow a few corporate mandates when I first arrived eight years ago," he told me. "But my predecessor and mentor, Jeremy Peterson, insisted that we try to source as much food as possible within 100 miles of this hotel. And since most of the restaurant personnel are local, trained by the Culinary Arts program at Central New Mexico Community College, that advice was easy to follow."

Forque serves cage-free eggs from nearby farms, and the chefs make their own mozzarella cheese from curds supplied by Old Windmill Dairy (see page 101). Flying Star Bakery custom-makes their bread (including a green chile–cheddar one) and Golden Crown Panaderia makes biscochitos and empanaditas for them daily. The restaurant also serves locally made beers and wines.

The menu is definitely creative: Smoked Gouda Fondue; Roasted Chicken Tortilla Soup with Pico de Gallo; Barramundi (a delicious Australian fish) with Red Bean Hummus and Calabacitas; Confit Pork Belly Salad; Organic Mushroom and Parmesan Risotto; and Osso Buco "Taco Bar" (recipe on facing page). "Besides our training and creativity," Duran told me, "we have something that many restaurants lack: Energy. Drive. The will to succeed."

He left out friendliness. While I interviewed him, at least five other staff members came over to introduce themselves. It's a very relaxing environment with great food. And not corporate at all.

Chimayó Chile Steaks with Chipotle Potatoes

From the little village of Chimayó, New Mexico, comes what many chileheads consider to be the finest tasting red chile. I use it in my enchilada sauces and for making steak rubs such as this one. The smoky taste of the chipotle potatoes is a nice complement to the grilled steak. Serve the steak and potatoes with mixed green and yellow snap beans and jalapeño cornbread (see Blue Corn–Chile Cornbread, page 50).

CHIPOTLE POTATOES

- 2 large baking potatoes
- 1 tablespoon chopped chipotle chiles in adobo sauce
- ½ teaspoon garlic powder
- 2–3 tablespoons milk
- Salt and freshly ground black pepper
- Finely chopped fresh chives, for garnish

CHIMAYÓ CHILE STEAKS

- 2 tablespoons ground New Mexican red chiles, preferably Chimayó chiles
- 1 tablespoon ground cinnamon
- 1 tablespoon sugar
- 2 teaspoons ground coriander
- 1 teaspoon salt
- ½ teaspoon ground cumin
- ¼ teaspoon dried thyme
- Olive oil
- 4 New York strip steaks

Heat Scale: Mild   **4 SERVINGS**

1. Make the potatoes: Bake the potatoes at 350°F until just done, 30 to 40 minutes. Cut the potatoes in half lengthwise and scoop out the flesh, reserving the skins. Using a hand mixer, whip the potatoes with the chipotles, garlic powder, and just enough milk to hold them together. Salt and pepper to taste.

2. Scoop the potatoes back into the skins and hold in a low oven while you prepare the steaks.

3. Make the steaks: Prepare the grill for direct grilling. Combine the chiles, cinnamon, sugar, coriander, salt, cumin, and thyme in a small bowl to create a dry rub.

4. When the grill is hot, brush the steaks with olive oil and liberally coat with the dry rub. Grill the steaks, turning often, for 12 to 16 minutes for rare (internal temperature 140°F, or 15 to 20 minutes for medium-rare, 150°F). Or slice open to check for doneness.

5. Serve the steaks with the potatoes, garnished with chives.

Recipe from SAM ETHERIDGE, FORMERLY OF AMBROZIA

Red Wine and Chile Stew

Here's another great dish by chef Sam Etheridge (see also Roasted Tomato Bisque, page 93, and Prickly Pear BBQ Sauce, page 160). He notes, "This is not your traditional red chile beef stew but instead incorporates great New Mexican flavors with the traditional French dish, beef bourguignon." This stew freezes well.

¾ pound sliced bacon

3 pounds lean stewing beef, cut into 2-inch cubes

3 tablespoons all-purpose flour

Salt and freshly ground black pepper

1 tablespoon olive oil

1 carrot, peeled and diced

1 yellow onion, diced

2 garlic cloves, crushed

½ teaspoon dried thyme

1 tablespoon tomato paste

3 cups beef stock

3 cups dry red wine, such as Milagro Winery's Corrales Red

2 potatoes, peeled and diced

1 cup chopped button mushrooms,

¼–½ cup red chile paste (see step 4)

Heat Scale: Medium   6 SERVINGS

1. Preheat the oven to 325°F.

2. Place the bacon in a large ovenproof pot over medium heat and sauté until cooked, then transfer to a bowl with a slotted spoon. Dredge the beef in the flour and add it to the pot. Cook, stirring occasionally, until brown on all sides, about 5 minutes. Salt and pepper to taste. Transfer the beef to the bowl with the bacon.

3. Add the olive oil, carrot, and onion to the pot and salt and pepper to taste. Sauté, stirring occasionally, until the vegetables are soft, 5 to 10 minutes, then add the beef, bacon, garlic, thyme, tomato paste, stock, and wine. Bring to a high simmer on the stove top, stirring often, then cover and place in the oven. Cook for 2 hours, stirring occasionally.

4. While the meat cooks, put 3 to 6 tablespoons of red chile powder, depending on how spicy you want the chile, in a small saucepan and stir in enough water to make a thick paste. Heat over low heat, stirring occasionally, until the mixture thickens.

5. Remove the pot from the oven and add the potatoes, mushrooms, and chile paste. Stir well, then return to the oven, and cook for 1 to 2 hours longer, or until the potatoes are cooked through and the meat is tender and can be pierced easily with a fork, adding water or more stock if the stew becomes too thick.

Braised Goat and Beef with Ancho Chiles

In Mexico, goat, usually tender, succulent kid meat (*cabrito*), is often saved for celebrations such as baptisms or weddings (see Meat Celebrations, page 125). This recipe, which is originally from the Mexican state of Nayarít, includes beef and is flavored with ancho chiles. This recipe serves a lot of people, so make a batch and throw a party! It freezes well.

2 pounds tomatoes, chopped

5 ancho chiles, toasted, stems and seeds removed

5 garlic cloves

8 black peppercorns

2 cloves

½ teaspoon ground cumin

Ground ginger

½ cup red wine vinegar

2 bay leaves

½ cup dry red wine

2 pounds beef, cut into 1-inch cubes

2 pounds goat, cut into 1-inch cubes

Tortillas, for serving

Salsa, for garnish

Heat Scale: Medium   8 TO 10 SERVINGS

1. Preheat the oven to 250°F. Combine the tomatoes, chiles, garlic, peppercorns, cloves, cumin, a pinch of ginger, and vinegar in a food processor or blender and purée in batches.

2. Transfer the purée to a large bowl and add the bay leaves and wine. Place the beef and goat in a large baking dish, and pour the tomato-chile mixture over it.

3. Cover the baking dish with aluminum foil and bake for 2 hours, or until the meat is done and falling apart.

4. Serve in bowls with tortillas and salsa on the side.

Texas Beef Brisket New Mexico–style

Okay, okay, I borrowed a Texas technique and changed the rub to reflect my chilehead tastes. For years, I have been perfecting brisket recipes using a smoker known as an Oklahoma Joe's. It is a horizontal, cylindrical smoker about 3½ feet long and about 14 inches in diameter. The attached, dropped firebox allows smoking with fairly cool smoke because the fire is separated a bit from the smoking area. Because smoking is so time-consuming, it makes sense to smoke several things at once. In addition to brisket, I also smoke a turkey breast.

Some cooks use the basting sauce as a mop during the smoking process and eliminate the long marinade at the end of smoking. Leftovers, if there are any, make the best barbecue sandwiches when served on a crusty hard roll with your favorite barbecue sauce. Smoked brisket will keep for a week in the refrigerator (it's already partially preserved) and it freezes well.

NOTE: This recipe requires advance preparation.

TEXAS BEEF BRISKET

- 1 (9- to 10-pound) beef brisket, "packer trimmed" preferred
- ½ cup lemon juice
- 2 cups mild New Mexican red chile powder
- ¼ cup garlic powder
- 2 tablespoons freshly ground black pepper
- 1 tablespoon cayenne pepper

BRISKET BASTING SAUCE

- 1 pound ButterBeautiful Barbecue butter (2½ tubs) or unsalted butter
- 2 yellow onions, finely chopped
- 5 garlic cloves, minced
- 1½ cups New Mexican beer, such as Marble IPA
- 4 lemons, quartered
- 2 bay leaves
- 1 bunch fresh Italian parsley, stems removed, minced
- 2 tablespoons chili powder
- ½ teaspoon cayenne pepper
- 2 cups vegetable oil
- ¼ cup Worcestershire sauce

Heat Scale: Medium   10 TO 20 SERVINGS

1. **Make the brisket:** Thoroughly coat all surfaces of the brisket with the lemon juice, rubbing it in well. Combine the chile powder, garlic powder, black pepper, and cayenne in a bowl, and sprinkle generously over the brisket, rubbing it in well. Make sure that the brisket is entirely covered in the rub. Allow to stand for 1 hour at room temperature before smoking.

2. To smoke the brisket, build a hardwood fire in the firebox using pecan, oak, or any fruitwood. When the fire is smoking nicely, place the brisket on the rack, fat side up, to let gravity and nature do the basting. Close the smoker and leave the brisket alone. The smoking will take approximately 10 hours at 200°F smoke temperature. This means a lot of beer will be consumed while you tend the fire.

3. **Make the sauce:** Melt the butter in a large pot over medium heat, add the onions and garlic, and sauté, stirring occasionally, until softened, 5 to 10 minutes. Add the beer, squeeze in the lemon juice, and add the lemon rinds to the pot. When the foam subsides, add the bay leaves, parsley, chili powder, cayenne, oil, and Worcestershire, and bring the mixture to a boil. Reduce the heat to medium-low and simmer for 20 minutes. Remove the bay leaves before using.

4. After the brisket has finished smoking, remove it from the smoker, slather it generously with the brisket basting sauce, wrap it tightly in aluminum foil, and return it to the smoker. Close off all of the air supplies to the fire, and allow the meat to "set" in the pit for about 2 hours.

5. To serve, slice the brisket very thinly across the grain of the meat.

MAYNARD CATTLE COMPANY

JIM AND KATE MAYNARD were doing fairly well raising and selling calves from their small cow herd in Las Cruces and had not really thought of wholesaling or retailing their animals directly to the consumer. But the arrival of their son in 2001 changed that.

"We had been raising these animals and simply selling them through an auction or to a buyer to put on winter pasture. When Asa was born we began to pay more attention to what we were feeding him and the ingredients in the foods. We had been running some calves with a neighbor in the Mesilla Valley and several were too small to ship with the others, so we fed them on a small pasture adjacent to our home in the North Valley, mostly with the idea that we would put one in our own freezer and have some animals for friends to purchase. We soon began to receive inquiries from people wanting beef that had not been grain fed and everything has grown from that point."

Today, Maynard Cattle Company buys calves from ranches scattered over much of southern New Mexico from the Sacramento Mountains to the Arizona state line and as far north as Mountainair to supplement their own calves raised on leased pastures in Torrance County, south of Mountainair. Family ranches receive premium prices for raising calves according to Maynard Cattle Company protocols. Calves are raised strictly on grass, either native range or irrigated pasture, without use of antibiotics or hormone supplements. The cattle are handled humanely at all times and are expected to be gentle around people.

Maynard Cattle Company currently sells meat across southern New Mexico. I asked Kate what they found to be their most popular cut of beef, and she replied, "All of them! Our customers buy every cut we put on the market." And that is something any New Mexico food producer would be proud to say.

Hot Chipotle BBQ Sauce

The smoked red jalapeño, known as the chipotle chile, has gained such popularity that there are even a couple of cookbooks devoted to it! It works particularly well in barbecuing and grilling applications, both of which have considerable smoke associated with them. This sauce, which uses the chipotle, will keep in the refrigerator for up to five days and it freezes well.

3 dried chipotle chiles

1½ tablespoons vegetable oil

3 medium yellow onions, one finely chopped and two thickly sliced

2 garlic cloves, minced

3 tomatoes, halved

2 red bell peppers, quartered and seeded

¼ cup firmly packed brown sugar

2 cups ketchup

¼ cup red wine vinegar

¼ cup Worcestershire sauce

Heat Scale: Medium

ABOUT 4 CUPS

1. Cover the chipotle chiles with very hot water in a small bowl and soak for 20 minutes to soften. Drain the chiles and finely chop.

2. Heat the oil over medium heat in a medium skillet. Add the chopped onion and sauté, stirring occasionally, until translucent, 5 to 10 minutes. Add the garlic and continue to sauté, stirring occasionally, until the garlic is soft, about 2 minutes.

3. Prepare the grill for direct grilling. Add the tomatoes, peppers, and sliced onions, and grill over medium heat, turning once until they are soft and slightly blackened. Remove, peel, and chop the vegetables.

4. Combine the chipotle chiles, onion-garlic mixture, roasted tomatoes, peppers, and onions, sugar, ketchup, vinegar, and Worcestershire in a large saucepan and bring the mixture to a low boil over medium heat. Reduce the heat and simmer for 20 minutes. Let the mixture cool and purée in a blender or food processor until smooth. You can thin the mixture with water if you so desire.

Buffalo–Green Chile Egg Rolls

W. C. Longacre, now retired, was the incredibly inventive chef and owner of the Mountain Road Cafe in Albuquerque. He was also one of the first chefs to use salsas as cooking and serving ingredients, insisting that they offered flavor dimensions far beyond their ordinary use for dipping and snacking. My wife, Mary Jane, and I dined at the café uncountable times, enjoying brunch there nearly every Sunday for years. W. C. prefers to use a bison roast in this recipe, but rare roast beef also works well. I have suggested some other dipping sauces for these egg rolls. To serve refrigerated leftovers, fry the egg rolls in oil briefly to crisp them up. They don't freeze well.

1 small bison rump roast, about 1½ pounds

1 cup shredded red cabbage

¼ cup mung bean sprouts

2 tablespoons shredded peeled carrot

3 teaspoons five-spice powder

2 teaspoons finely grated fresh ginger

1 teaspoon minced garlic

¼ teaspoon salt (optional)

1 egg

1 large package fresh egg roll wrappers

½ cup green chile strips

Oil, for frying

Habanero salsa, Sriracha sauce, or your favorite mild hot sauce, for dipping

Heat Scale: Mild   ABOUT 2 DOZEN EGG ROLLS

1. Preheat the oven to 350°F. Place the roast in a baking dish and cook it until the internal temperature is 150°F, about 1 hour. Remove the roast from the oven, place on a cutting board, and slice it into strips ½ inch by 1 inch.

2. While the roast cooks, combine the cabbage, sprouts, carrot, five-spice powder, ginger, garlic, and salt, if desired, in a bowl and mix well.

3. Combine the egg and 1 tablespoon of water in a cup and mix well.

4. Place a tablespoon of the vegetable filling in the middle of an egg roll wrapper that has a corner facing you. Add a strip of the roast and 1 or 2 chile strips. Fold the bottom third of the wrapper over the filling. Fold in the sides of the wrapper and roll up. Paint the egg mixture on the top edge using a pastry brush to seal the egg roll completely. Repeat until all of the filling, roast, and chiles have been used. If there are any left-over ingredients, wrap them and refrigerate them.

5. Heat oil to hot but not smoking. Working in batches, deep-fry the egg rolls in the oil until golden brown. The frying time will vary according to how many egg rolls you are cooking at one time. Serve with several dipping sauces.

El Pinto: The Largest Farm-to-Table Restaurant in the United States?

MOST FARM-TO-TABLE restaurants are relatively small and have an ever-changing seasonal menu, so it's not too difficult to supply the kitchen with produce from a small garden. But when your restaurant can seat a thousand customers at a time and has a mostly permanent menu of New Mexican cuisine, how do you transform it into a farm-sustainable operation? That was the challenge facing twin brothers John and Jim Thomas, who decided to give the farm-to-table concept a try after they purchased El Pinto from their parents in 1989.

Of course, they couldn't change everything overnight at the largest restaurant in New Mexico, which sits on 13 acres in Albuquerque's North Valley beneath towering cottonwood trees. So, they began with simple things.

They bought local honey and free-range eggs. They used sea salt, which has no iodine added, and replaced all cooking oils with sunflower oil. They recommended fresh salsa as a salad dressing and a replacement for butter on baked potatoes, and made their margaritas and tequila sunrises with freshly squeezed citrus. They bought organically raised beef and pork. They also planted a large garden and contracted with the Agri-Cultural Network, a collective of organic farmers, because they needed more lettuce than they could buy from their food service sources.

But their biggest challenge was sourcing the two hundred tons of red and green chile peppers they use annually. And the chile had to be grown organically — a rarity in New Mexico. So they contracted with like-minded farmers in southern New Mexico and northern Mexico to grow the chiles. Refrigerated trucks haul the pods to Albuquerque, where restaurant employees hand-roast and peel them. They either freeze the green chiles for future meals or use them in the two million jars and a half million individual portion cups of El Pinto salsa they produce each year.

John and Jim don't claim to be 100 percent farm to table yet — sourcing fresh, organic tomatoes in the quantity they need in the winter, for example, is extremely difficult. So they are considering devoting some of their land to winter greenhouses to grow tomatoes year-round and take advantage of New Mexico's three hundred days of sunshine.

El Pinto Beef Empanadas

Empanadas have a long history, going back to Indian meat-filled samosas, the concept of which appeared later in Spain and Portugal during the Moorish invasion. The "empadas," as they were first called, were a portable and hardy meal for working-class people. Now, they are common in Latin countries around the world, and sometimes known by other names, like *pastel* in Brazil. The chefs at El Pinto Restaurant in Albuquerque's North Valley have given them a decidedly New Mexican flavor, and they are a popular treat at the state's largest restaurant.

NOTE: This recipe requires advance preparation.

THE FILLING

½ teaspoon minced garlic

⅛ teaspoon freshly ground black pepper

⅛ teaspoon ground cumin

⅛ teaspoon dried oregano

¼ cup bottled French dressing

¼ cup red chile purée

2 pounds rib-eye or New York strip steak, cut into ¼-inch dice

1–2 tablespoons oil

1 red onion, cut into ¼-inch dice

1 cup ¼-inch-dice cooked red potatos

THE DOUGH

2 cups flour

1 teaspoon baking powder

⅛ teaspoon salt

¾ cup shortening

½ cup evaporated milk

½ cup whole milk

Vegetable oil, for deep-frying

Red or green chile sauce, for serving

Heat Scale: Depends on the sauce   **6 TO 8 EMPANADAS**

1. Make the filling: Combine the garlic, pepper, cumin, oregano, French dressing, and chile purée in a bowl, and add the steak. Mix well, cover, and refrigerate overnight.

2. The next day, heat the oil over medium heat in a medium skillet. Add the onion and sauté, stirring occasionally, for 3 minutes. Add the steak and cook until it begins to lose its redness, about 5 minutes, stirring occasionally. Add the potatoes and cook, stirring occasionally, for 2 minutes longer. Remove the mixture from the heat and chill until it reaches 38°F.

3. Make the dough: Sift the flour, baking powder, and salt into a bowl. Add the shortening, evaporated milk, and whole milk, and mix by hand or use a small mixer with a dough hook to mix for 5 minutes, or until smooth.

4. Make the empanadas: Roll the dough out on a flat surface to ⅛-inch thickness. Use a coffee can or other cutter to cut the dough into 6-inch circles. Add about ¼ cup of the steak mixture, fold the circle in half, and pinch the edges to seal it. Repeat with the remaining steak. Place the empanadas on a baking sheet and cover them with plastic wrap. Refrigerate for 1 hour.

5. Heat the vegetable oil to 325°F, add each empanada, and cook for 5 minutes, until lightly browned or until the internal temperature is 165°F. If your fryer is too small for all the empanadas, fry them in batches and keep them warm in the oven. Serve topped with red or green chile sauce.

RANCHLINE ALL NATURAL LAMB

I MET LAMB GROWER TODD TAYLOR at the Albuquerque Downtown Growers' Market in Robinson Park. He had driven all the way from Roswell that morning to promote and sell his lamb cuts, and I bought a small boneless leg to roast or smoke. We struck up a conversation and I was cheered by what he had to say, hopeful that more meat producers would follow Taylor's lead in raising livestock naturally.

Ranchline's lamb products are 100 percent natural, meaning the animals aren't exposed to growth hormones or stimulants. Plus, they are all grass fed. As a result, Taylor told me, his lamb meat has great flavor and is one of the most tender meats available in New Mexico. Of course, that was a sales pitch I would have to test out with the leg of lamb I had just put in my sack. As it turned out, the lamb, which I smoked, was terrific.

As Taylor claims on his website, "Just living in the western part of the United States generates a value system like no other place around the world. Ranchline All Natural is a local, New Mexico company and our lambs are raised north of Roswell, New Mexico, at Felix River Ranch in a natural environment that consists of open ranges with natural grasses and humane husbandry practices. We are simple people with a simple goal of providing each customer a product that was raised with love and care from the very beginning to the time it arrives on your dinner table."

I asked Taylor what he says to people who say they don't like lamb. "I tell them they probably had lamb that had aged on the hoof, and that was called mutton. Our lamb is young and is not gamy, and it can be used in almost any recipe that calls for beef. So I advise them to find their favorite beef recipe and substitute lamb for a change."

Since your neighborhood supermarket probably has a very limited supply of the different cuts of lamb, Ranchline All Natural has convenient online ordering and a wide selection of cuts from shanks to chops to roasts. They even sell lamb jerky. The frozen cuts are shipped to customers all over the United States.

World's Best Lamb Chili

The title of the recipe is accurate, brags Todd Taylor of Ranchline All Natural Lamb just outside of Roswell. He says it's a "delicious, classic chili with beans, herbs, and spices." He forgot to mention that it's simple to make and, if you like, can be prepared in a slow cooker set on high by combining all the ingredients after you have browned the meat. It freezes well.

2 pounds ground lamb, preferably Ranchline All Natural

2 cups canned red beans, drained

1½ cups diced yellow onion

½ cup diced celery stalks

¼ cup diced green bell pepper

¼ cup chili powder

2 teaspoons ground cumin

1½ teaspoons garlic powder

1 teaspoon salt

½ teaspoon freshly ground black pepper

½ teaspoon dried oregano, preferably Mexican

½ teaspoon sugar

⅛ teaspoon cayenne pepper

1 quart plus 2 cups tomato juice

4 cups tomato sauce

Coarsely chopped Italian parsley leaves, for garnish

Heat Scale: Medium   8 TO 10 SERVINGS

1. Cook the lamb in a large pot over medium-high heat until evenly browned, stirring occasionally, for about 5 minutes.

2. Add the beans, onion, celery, bell pepper, chili powder, cumin, garlic powder, salt, black pepper, oregano, sugar, cayenne, tomato juice, and tomato sauce to the pot. Bring the mixture to a boil, then immediately reduce the heat to low and simmer uncovered until the lamb is very tender, 1 hour to 1 hour, 30 minutes, stirring regularly. Adjust the liquid by adding some water, if needed.

3. Serve in bowls garnished with parsley.

Braised Leg of Lamb

Todd Taylor's take on cooking a leg of lamb takes a bit longer than my version (see recipe on facing page) — about a day — because of the time needed to marinate it. However, it's worth the wait, as you will see. "We serve this over risotto, but many other sides go great with this recipe," says Todd. You could try it with rice pilaf, garlic mashed potatoes, or orzo.

NOTE: This recipe requires advance preparation.

MARINADE

- 4 garlic cloves, crushed
- 2 basil leaves, finely chopped
- 1 tablespoon celery seeds
- 1 tablespoon freshly ground black pepper
- 1 teaspoon ground cumin
- 1 teaspoon salt
- ¼ cup dry sherry
- ¼ cup plus 2 tablespoons olive oil, divided
- ¼ cup red wine vinegar

LAMB

- 1 (2- to 3-pound) leg of lamb, preferably Ranchline All Natural Boneless
- 1 medium yellow onion, chopped
- 2 carrots, peeled and chopped
- 2 celery stalks, chopped
- 2 tablespoons olive oil
- 2 garlic cloves, crushed
- 2 cups dry red wine
- 3 tablespoons butter

4 SERVINGS

1. Make the marinade: Combine the garlic, basil, celery seeds, black pepper, cumin, salt, sherry, ¼ up olive oil, and vinegar in a large bowl and mix well. Place the leg of lamb in a large ziplock bag, add the marinade, and refrigerate overnight.

2. Make the lamb: The next day, heat 1 tablespoon of the olive oil over medium heat in a large skillet and sauté the onion, carrots, and celery until the carrots are slightly soft, 5 to 10 minutes. Transfer the vegetables to a slow cooker.

3. Remove the lamb from the bag and pat dry. Discard the marinade. Heat the remaining tablespoon of olive oil in the same skillet over medium heat and sear the lamb on all sides until well browned, about 10 minutes. When done, transfer the lamb to the slow cooker.

4. Sauté the garlic in the same skillet over medium heat until soft, about 3 minutes, and then deglaze the skillet with ½ cup of the wine. Pour this mixture over the lamb. Add the remaining 1½ cups wine to the slow cooker and reduce the heat to low. Cook until the lamb is just falling apart, about 8 hours. When the lamb is done cooking, remove it from the slow cooker and pull it apart.

5. Strain the slow cooker liquid into a saucepan and bring to a boil. Add the butter and stir until melted. Spoon this sauce over the lamb and serve.

Herb and Chile–infused Roasted Leg of Lamb

Navajo Churro sheep were developed by Native American tribes from Spanish breeds and for centuries were a vital part of tribal life. The rams are notable for sometimes growing four complete horns, a trait even rarer than this heritage breed, which once teetered on the verge of extinction. Largely raised for their soft, durable wool, they also produce the most flavorful lamb I have ever tasted. When I'm fortunate enough to find some — it's grown mostly in the northern part of the state — I use it with fresh herbs and chiles from the garden. After you slice it, you can freeze portions of it for later use.

4 garlic cloves, minced

3 red serrano or jalapeño chiles, seeds and stems removed, minced

¼ cup fresh rosemary leaves

¼ cup fresh oregano leaves

1 (3- to 4-pound) bone-in leg of lamb

4 large potatoes, peeled and cut into 2-inch cubes

3 tablespoons olive oil

2 tablespoons flour

Salt

Heat Scale: Medium   4 TO 6 SERVINGS

1. Preheat the oven to 325°F.

2. Crush the garlic, chiles, rosemary, and oregano in a mortar and pestle to make a coarse paste.

3. Cut slits in the leg of lamb about 1 inch deep and 2 inches apart. Work the paste into the slits using a spoon and your fingers.

4. Combine the potatoes and olive oil in a bowl and mix well until the potatoes are coated.

5. Transfer the lamb and potatoes to a large roasting pan and cook for 20 minutes per pound for medium-rare lamb, turning the potatoes every 30 minutes. The potatoes should be well browned by the time the lamb is done. Remove the lamb and potatoes from the roasting pan and keep warm while making the pan sauce.

6. Scrape the bottom of the pan with a metal spoon to loosen the drippings, add the flour, and mix well. Cook over low heat, slowly adding enough water to make a thick sauce and stirring with a whisk until smooth. Salt to taste.

7. Serve the sauce over the sliced lamb and potatoes.

Slow-roasted Breast of Lamb with Honey-Cumin Glaze

"This is a wonderful autumn or winter dish," says Chef Matt Yohalem of Il Piatto in Santa Fe. "Local lamb is plentiful and of great quality, and I usually get mine from El Rito Farms. Honey is also abundant in Santa Fe and the cumin flavor adds some familiar flavor notes from this region. I hear old-time locals talk about the dish, which they grew up with, only without the nifty honey-cumin notes, which add a great twist." It pairs nicely with egg noodles or mashed potatoes.

1 (3½- to 5-pound) bone-in breast of lamb

Salt and freshly ground black pepper

¼ cup chopped garlic cloves

Finely grated zest of 2 lemons

¼ teaspoon ground cumin

3 yellow onions, chopped

2 carrots, unpeeled and sliced

2 celery stalks, chopped

2 cups dry white wine

GLAZE

½ cup toasted ground cumin

1 cup Taos Valley Honey or other local honey

4 TO 6 SERVINGS

1. Preheat the oven to 225°F.

2. Make the lamb: Season the lamb breast with salt and pepper. Rub the garlic, half the lemon zest, and the ¼ teaspoon cumin over the lamb. Place the lamb on a roasting rack in a roasting pan and roast for 1 hour. Remove it from the oven and sprinkle the rest of the lemon zest over it. Add the onions, carrots, celery, and wine to the roasting pan, and stir to coat with the pan drippings. Wrap the lamb in aluminum foil and return to the oven with the vegetables to roast on the rack for 45 minutes longer. Remove the lamb from the oven and put it on a plate.

3. Make the glaze: Combine the pan juices and vegetables with the toasted cumin and honey in a bowl and stir. Cover and keep warm while the lamb finishes cooking.

4. Remove the roasting rack from the roasting pan. Unwrap the lamb, return it to the pan, and pour the honey-cumin mixture over it. Increase the heat to 450°F, and roast for 15 minutes. The internal temperature should be 160°F for medium. Remove from the oven. Let cool slightly and cut the ribs, which should cut easily. Serve with the pan juices.

Recipe from **AMY WHITE**, *EDIBLE SANTA FE*

Cider-braised Lamb and Turnips

"Lamb and turnips are a classic combination," says *Edible Santa Fe* contributor Amy White. "Both are available year-round in New Mexico, but we associate them especially with spring. Braising them in apple cider adds a tangy sweetness. Use a dry hard cider; you could use a nonalcoholic cider, but it makes a much sweeter dish. The cheapest, toughest cuts of lamb on the bone are great for stews like this because they are very flavorful and become perfectly tender after a long braise. Spring turnips are delicate and sweet, and can be used whole in this recipe. If you can find them with greens, use both the root and the shoot in this recipe. Find both key ingredients at early spring farmers' markets."

4 SERVINGS

1 pound lamb ribs or bone-in neck

2 tablespoons olive oil

1 medium yellow onion or 2 leeks, minced

2 garlic cloves, minced

6 cloves

1 teaspoon chopped fresh marjoram or thyme

1 teaspoon salt

¼ teaspoon freshly ground black pepper

2 cups chicken stock or water

2 cups dry hard cider

1 tablespoon cider vinegar

2 pounds turnips with greens, peeled and cut into 1-inch pieces, greens roughly chopped

½ pound carrots, peeled and cut into 1-inch pieces

Crusty bread, for serving

1. Rinse the lamb and pat it dry.

2. Heat the oil in a large skillet over medium heat, add the lamb, and brown well on all sides. Remove the lamb, then add the onion, garlic, cloves, marjoram, salt, and pepper to the skillet. Sauté over medium heat, stirring occasionally, until the onion is lightly browned, 10 to 15 minutes. Add the meat to a large saucepan and pour the stock, cider, and vinegar over it. Cover and bring the mixture to a boil, then reduce the heat to low, and simmer until the lamb is falling off the bones, 3 to 4 hours.

3. Remove the lamb from the stock, cut the meat from the bones, and chop it coarsely. Return the meat to the liquid in the pan.

4. Add the turnips, turnip greens, and carrots to the pot and simmer until tender, about 30 minutes longer. Serve with crusty bread to sop up the delicious sauce.

Grilled Piñon-crusted Lamb Chops

Here is a delicious combination of ingredients from the Southwest: piñons (pine nuts), chile, and lamb. For an authentic, smoky flavor, grill the lamb chops over mesquite wood or charcoal covered with mesquite chips soaked in water. The chops go well with rice pilaf and sautéed squash.

NOTE: This recipe requires advance preparation

3 garlic cloves

5 tablespoons roasted piñon nuts

1 tablespoon ground New Mexican red chile

¾ cup olive oil

½ cup tomato paste

¼ cup red wine vinegar

4 (1- to 1½-inch-thick) lamb chops

Heat Scale: Mild   4 SERVINGS

1. Combine the garlic, piñon nuts, chile, olive oil, tomato paste, and vinegar in a blender and purée until smooth. Paint the chops with the mixture and let them marinate, covered, at room temperature for 1 hour.

2. Prepare the grill for direct grilling. Grill the chops over medium heat, turning them occasionally, until they are medium-rare, with an internal temperature of 150°F, 7 to 10 minutes per side.

Puercos Rellenos
(Stuffed Pork Chops)

This stuffed pork chop recipe is from ButterBeautiful (see profile on page 107) and features their Savory Smoked Sage compound butter, plus New Mexican apples and pecans. Serve the pork chops with grilled endive and radicchio topped with vinaigrette dressing.

¼ cup Savory Smoked Sage butter (or softened butter puréed with a couple of smoked sage leaves), plus 2 tablespoons

½ small French baguette, cut into small cubes

3 large organic Granny Smith apples, peeled and diced into ½-inch cubes

½ cup coarsely chopped pecans

¼ cup dried cranberries

1 teaspoon brown sugar

4 (2-inch-thick) rib pork chops with pockets cut to the bone from the fat side

1. Melt the butter in a small skillet over medium heat, add the baguette cubes, and sauté until the cubes are browned. Transfer the cubes to a bowl. Add the apples, pecans, cranberries, and brown sugar to the skillet and sauté, stirring occasionally, until the apples are soft, 5 to 10 minutes. Add the apple mixture to the baguette cubes, and stir to make the stuffing.

2. Preheat the oven to 325° F.

3. Add the remaining 2 tablespoons of butter to the skillet. Cook the pork chops until lightly browned, about 5 minutes per side. Transfer the pork chops to a cutting board, let cool until you can handle them, and fill with the stuffing, using toothpicks to secure the stuffing inside the pork chops.

4. Transfer the pork chops to a glass baking dish, cover, and bake for 20 minutes. Continue baking the pork chops uncovered for 10 minutes longer, or until they are nicely browned.

Ranchero-Style Pork Chops

The addition of cumin and chiles gives these pork chops a wonderful southwestern flavor. You can grill them over charcoal, gas, or wood. Serve them with refried beans and a tomato-jicama salad.

NOTE: This recipe requires advance preparation.

6 New Mexican green chiles, roasted, peeled, stems and seeds removed, chopped

2 cloves garlic, minced

¼ cup chopped yellow onion

2 teaspoons ground cumin

1 teaspoon dried oregano, preferably Mexican

½ teaspoon ground coriander

½ teaspoon salt

¼ cup lime juice

2 tablespoons vegetable oil

4 thick-cut pork chops

Heat Scale: Medium   **4 SERVINGS**

1. Combine the chiles, garlic, onion, cumin, oregano, coriander, salt, lime juice, and vegetable oil in a shallow glass baking dish. Add the pork chops, turning to distribute the chile mixture, then cover the dish, and marinate in the refrigerator for 4 hours or overnight.

2. Prepare the grill for direct grilling. Remove the pork chops from the marinade and grill over medium heat, turning occasionally, until the lamb reaches an internal temperature of 150°F, 7 to 10 minutes a side.

Chickpea and Chorizo Stew

Here is my version of a classic Spanish stew, New Mexican–style, heated up with the addition of chorizo and red chile pods. Note that the chickpeas (garbanzo beans) require advance preparation unless you substitute canned beans. Serve this stew with a hard, crusty bread such as Spanish or Mexican bolillos. Note that the recipe calls for Spanish chorizo, which is made with a casing, not the loose Mexican chorizo.

1 pound dried chickpeas, soaked in water overnight, or 2 (15-ounce) cans

1 pound Spanish chorizo sausage, cut into 1-inch slices

1 medium yellow onion, chopped

3 tablespoons chopped garlic

1 tablespoon freshly ground black pepper

1 teaspoon salt

6 fresh Italian parsley sprigs, mostly leaves, chopped

3 bay leaves

3 New Mexican red chiles, seeds and stems removed

1 pound baby red bliss potatoes, halved

1 pound fresh spinach, coarsely chopped

Heat Scale: Medium   8 SERVINGS

1. Combine the chickpeas, chorizo, onion, garlic, pepper, salt, parsley, bay leaves, chiles, and 3 quarts water in a large pot and bring to a boil. Reduce the heat, cover, and simmer for 2 hours. If using canned chickpeas, add them only during the last hour of cooking.

2. Skim the fat from the stew, and add the potatoes and additional water if needed. Cook, stirring often, over medium heat until the potatoes are tender, about 30 minutes.

3. Add the spinach and cook for 5 minutes longer. Remove the chiles and serve.

Recipe from CALI SHAW, *LOCAL IQ*

Cali's Smoked Red Chile BBQ Ribs

Local iQ writer Cali Shaw shares her technique for smoking BBQ ribs in this recipe. "I used the 3-2-1 method: 3 hours directly on [the] grill grate, 2 hours wrapped in foil, 1 hour uncovered, mopped with your favorite BBQ sauce. (I use Santa Fe Brewery's Thick and Spicy BBQ Sauce.)"

When I made this recipe, I used chunks of apple wood for the smoking. Ribs don't freeze well, so eat all of them!

NOTE: This recipe requires advance preparation.

RUB

- ⅓ cup firmly packed brown sugar
- ⅓ cup kosher salt
- ¼ cup Chimayó red chile powder
- ¼ cup sweet paprika
- 3½ tablespoons freshly ground black pepper
- 2 tablespoons granulated garlic
- 2 tablespoons onion powder
- 1 teaspoon ground cumin

SPRAY

- ½ (12-ounce) bottle Santa Fe Pale Ale (drink the other half)
- ½ cup unsweetened apple cider
- ¼ cup olive oil

RIBS

- 1 rack pork spareribs, about 4 pounds
- Olive oil

Heat Scale: Mild

2 TO 4 SERVINGS, DEPENDING ON THE SIZE OF THE RACK

1. Make the rub: Combine the brown sugar, salt, chile powder, paprika, pepper, garlic, onion powder, and cumin in a bowl and mix well. Rub the ribs with olive oil and sprinkle the rub over them thickly. Place the ribs in a large glass baking dish, cover with plastic wrap, and refrigerate overnight.

2. Make the spray: Pour the beer, cider, and olive oil in a spray bottle and shake to combine.

3. Make the ribs: Prepare your smoker to stay at a consistent 225 to 250°F. First, smoke the ribs for 3 hours, spraying the top of them every 30 minutes. Then, wrap the ribs in aluminum foil, return them to the smoker, and cook for 2 hours. Finally, uncover the ribs and smoke them for 1 hour, spraying them twice.

4. Remove the ribs from the smoker and shut the smoker down. Cut the ribs and serve them.

FARM-TO-TABLE MEDIA SUPPORT: *LOCAL IQ*

KEVIN HOPPER, a child of the seventies, remembers the canned gray string beans of that era, and he's never going back there. Instead, as associate publisher of *Local iQ*, he makes sure that the biweekly Albuquerque magazine of arts and culture focuses on local food and fresh ingredients. "We want it all artisanal — made from scratch," he told me, "either at home or in a restaurant."

I should point out that I'm biased as I have my own monthly column in the magazine, but from what I've seen, Hopper, his wife and publishing partner, Fran, and editor Mike English are completely supportive of the farm-to-table concept. You can tell from the title that the magazine is all about local. In fact, Hopper believes that consumers should take the word convenience out of their vocabularies and shop at growers' markets and locally owned stores rather than the big chain supermarkets.

Each year they run a special issue devoted to organic farming in central New Mexico and articles throughout the growing season focus on growers' markets, restaurant openings, innovative ingredients and dishes at established restaurants, and new food products made in the state.

Hopper loves meat, so one Summer Cook-off issue featured New Mexican and worldwide-themed dishes like Smoked Red Chile BBQ Ribs, Jerk Pork Loin, Turkish Lamb Kebabs, Grilled Rib Steak with Stilton Bleu Cheese Compound Butter, and the Charcoal Companion Sausage basket. Hopper's introduction says it all: "In approaching a barbecue issue, the *iQ* staff collectively said: 'We could do this the easy way, or we could do this the fun way.' We chose fun, so that obviously meant throwing a barbecue and seeing what happened next. In doing so, we tried to appeal to all of the senses — sound, smell, taste, sight, and feel. And of course we wanted to keep things as local as possible, which meant fresh ingredients sourced from local vendors. Heck, even the beer was fresh!"

Carnita-filled Tortillas with Chile de Árbol–Tomatillo Salsa

Carnita, the diminutive for *carne*, means "a little piece of meat," usually pork, that is cooked in many different ways throughout New Mexico as well as Mexico. Fried and topped with chile sauce, carnitas make a great breakfast side dish, or as grilled here, a delicious entrée when wrapped in a warmed corn tortilla with a grilled onion and salsa. I prefer the large Mexican bulb onion, a type of spring onion here. If you can't find any, use large green onions with the green tops left on.

This recipe makes a great hands-on luncheon of soft tacos or burritos if you use flour tortillas. Serve with seasoned pinto beans.

NOTE: This recipe requires advance preparation.

CHIPOTLE-ANCHO CHILE PASTE

3 tablespoons ground ancho chile

2 tablespoons chopped fresh cilantro

1 tablespoon ground chipotle chile

1 tablespoon ground cumin

1 tablespoon garlic powder

1½ teaspoons salt

1 teaspoon freshly ground black pepper

⅓ cup vegetable oil

3 tablespoons lime juice

CARNITAS

1½ pounds boneless pork, such as shoulder, trimmed of excess fat and cut into 1-inch cubes

1 bunch large scallions, trimmed

2 tablespoons vegetable oil

2 teaspoons ground ancho chile

8 large corn tortillas

Heat Scale: Medium   4 SERVINGS

1. Make the chile paste: Combine the ancho chile, cilantro, chipotle chile, cumin, garlic powder, salt, pepper, oil, and lime juice in a bowl and mix well.

2. Make the carnitas: Rub the pork cubes with the paste until well covered. Transfer the pork to a glass baking dish, cover, and marinate in the refrigerator for 2 to 4 hours.

3. Make the salsa: Heat the oil in a medium skillet and sauté the chiles over medium heat until lightly browned, about 5 minutes. Add the garlic and onion and continue to sauté over medium heat until the onion is lightly browned, 5 to 10 minutes. Transfer the chiles, garlic, and onion to a blender or food processor, add the tomatillos and vinegar, and purée until smooth, adding a little water to thin the salsa if necessary. Set aside at room temperature while you cook the meat.

4. Thread the pork cubes on skewers. Brush the scallions with the oil and sprinkle with the ground chile. Prepare the grill for direct grilling. Grill the pork over a medium fire, turning occasionally, until well-done with an internal temperature of 175°F. They should be crisp. Cut open a test cube to see if it is done.

CHILE DE ÁRBOL–TOMATILLO SALSA

1 tablespoon vegetable oil

6–8 dried chile de árbol pods, stems removed, halved lengthwise

4 garlic cloves

2 tablespoons chopped yellow onion

1 (8-ounce) can tomatillos, drained, or about 8 medium fresh tomatillos

1 tablespoon distilled white vinegar

5. Meanwhile, place the scallions on the grill and cook, turning often, until they are browned but not burned, about 4 minutes. Wrap the tortillas in aluminum foil and warm on the grill, away from the direct flames.

6. Remove the pork, scallions, and tortillas from the grill and take the pork off the skewers. Place the pork in the tortillas, and top each one with scallions and some salsa. Wrap up the tortillas and serve.

Recipe from SAM ETHERIDGE, FORMERLY OF AMBROZIA

Chicken Braised in White Wine, Garlic, and Green Chiles

Chef Sam Etheridge loves to take traditional Italian and French recipes and "New Mexicanize" them. Here is one of his favorites, of which he notes, "This is a traditional French cooking method but utilizes the local staple of green chiles to add an extra layer to the dish while showcasing the flavor of the wine." But what about all that garlic? Sam explains, "Leaving the peel attached leaves the clove redolent of garlic, but not overly so; cooking the garlic cloves whole in their skins keeps the flavors in balance." This dish freezes well.

2 (3½-pound) whole chickens, each cut into 8 pieces

Salt and freshly ground black pepper

5 heads garlic, cloves separated (about 70), unpeeled

6 tablespoons olive oil

1 teaspoon flour

1 cup chopped roasted and peeled New Mexican green chiles

6 fresh thyme sprigs

2 cups dry white wine, such as Gruet Chardonnay

1 cup chicken stock

Heat Scale: Medium   8 SERVINGS

1. Trim the excess fat off the chicken pieces. Sprinkle the chicken with salt and pepper.

2. Lightly smash the garlic cloves to flatten slightly, leaving the peels attached and the cloves as whole as possible.

3. Heat 3 tablespoons of the oil and half of the garlic cloves in a large pot over medium-high heat. Working in two batches, add the chicken pieces and cook until brown on all sides, about 12 minutes per batch. Transfer the chicken to a plate.

4. Add the remaining 3 tablespoons oil and the remaining garlic to the pot. Cook over medium heat, stirring, until golden brown, 10 to 15 minutes. Add the flour and cook for 1 minute longer, stirring occasionally, then add the chiles, thyme, wine, and stock; bring the mixture to a boil, stirring often.

5. Return the chicken to the pot. Cover and reduce the heat to low. Simmer, moving the chicken pieces from top to bottom every 5 minutes (the sauce will not cover the chicken), until the chicken is cooked through, 20 to 30 minutes.

6. Salt and pepper to taste. Transfer the chicken to a large platter. Spoon the garlic cloves and green chiles around the chicken and drizzle the sauce over all to serve.

Prickly Pear BBQ Sauce

Chef Sam Etheridge of the late, lamented Ambrozia restaurant (see also Roasted Tomato Bisque, page 92, and Red Wine and Chile Stew, page 132) loved to barbecue, so of course he had to create a new spin on the usual barbecue sauces by using a New Mexican product that is harvested in the wild. He comments, "This is a savory use for the prickly pear that adds a nice fruitiness to a versatile barbecue sauce. [It's] great on ribs and pork."

Prickly pear pads can be purchased in Hispanic markets or online, in which case the fierce spines may be removed for you. To remove the spines, use tongs to hold the pads over an open flame to burn them off. Store the sauce in the refrigerator for up to five days or freeze it.

20 prickly pear pads, cleaned and halved

1 teaspoon vegetable oil

1 red onion, diced

2 garlic cloves, minced

2 dried New Mexico red chiles

1 tablespoon brown sugar

1 teaspoon salt

½ cup ketchup

2 tablespoons cider vinegar

1 teaspoon Liquid Smoke

1 teaspoon Worcestershire sauce

Heat Scale: Mild   ABOUT 3 CUPS

1. Place the prickly pears and 2 cups water in a medium saucepan and bring to a boil. Continue boiling the prickly pears for 3 minutes. Let the mixture cool and purée it, then strain through a fine mesh sieve.

2. Heat the oil over medium heat in a medium skillet. Add the onion and sauté, stirring occasionally, until translucent, 5 to 10 minutes. Add the garlic and cook for 1 minute longer. Add the cooled prickly pear purée to the saucepan and cook until reduced by half.

3. Put the chiles in a blender with ¼ cup water and purée. Add the purée to the saucepan along with the sugar, salt, ketchup, vinegar, Liquid Smoke, and Worcestershire. Reduce the heat to low and simmer for 30 minutes, stirring often. Let cool and purée in a blender.

Blue Corn Chicken Taquitos

A *taquito* is merely a little taco, so named because it is tightly rolled and fried before serving. These make great snacks or appetizers, especially when dipped in your favorite salsa.

CHICKEN FILLING

- 1 tablespoon olive oil
- 1 small yellow onion, thinly sliced
- 1½ teaspoons minced garlic
- 1½ pounds skinless, boneless chicken breast
- 5 Roma tomatoes, chopped
- 1 bay leaf
- 1 pasilla chile, stem removed, soaked in hot water to soften, and cut in ½-inch strips
- ½ teaspoon ground cumin
- ½ teaspoon dried oregano, preferably Mexican
- 1 cup chicken stock
- Salt and freshly ground black pepper

TAQUITOS

- ¼ cup olive oil
- 1 dozen blue corn tortillas
- Vegetable oil, for frying

Heat Scale: Mild   12 TAQUITOS

1. Make the filling: Heat the oil in a medium skillet over medium heat. Add the onion and garlic and sauté until the onion is soft, 5 to 10 minutes. Add the chicken, tomatoes, bay leaf, chile, cumin, oregano, and stock, and simmer, stirring occasionally, for 35 minutes. Strain off all the excess juices, place the chicken mixture in a bowl, and shred the chicken breasts with a fork. Add salt and pepper to taste.

2. Make the taquitos: Heat the oil in a large skillet over high heat, but don't let the oil smoke. Using tongs, dip each tortilla for 5 seconds on each side. Drain the tortillas on paper towels.

3. Heat the frying oil to high but not smoking in a heavy skillet or deep fryer. Spread about ¼ cup of the chicken filling on a tortilla. Roll the tortilla tight and deep-fry for 2 minutes. Drain the taquito on paper towels. Repeat with the rest of the tortillas, keeping the taquitos warm on a baking sheet in the oven.

BUENO FOODS

SOMETIMES ALL IT TAKES to make a successful company is a love for what you eat nearly every day. After World War II, in 1946, the Baca brothers — Joe, Ray, and August — scraped together enough money to open the Ace Food Store, which was quite successful until Piggly Wiggly and Safeway came to Albuquerque. The brothers soon realized that a small mom and pop grocery could not compete against the national supermarket chains, so they had to make a new plan.

Fortunately for the Baca family and the rest of New Mexico, they decided to specialize in New Mexican cuisine. They started with tortillas using a pie crust roller, and followed that with tamales and posole. Then the national trend of families buying home freezers steered them in another direction.

The brothers hit on the idea of roasting green chiles over an open flame as tradition dictated, then freezing them so that people could enjoy green chiles year-round. As the first in the country to flame-roast green chiles on a commercial scale, the brothers had to invent the process and build their own equipment. With a focus on frozen green chiles and a handful of related products, the brothers founded Bueno Foods in 1951. Today the company is one of the Southwest's premier producers of New Mexican and Mexican foods, and it's still owned and operated by the Baca family.

The company's vice president of marketing and communications, Ana Baca (daughter of founding brother Joe), told me that the company buys all of its green chiles, 99 percent of its dried red chiles, and some of its corn from in state. "When the ingredients are available," she says, "we source first and foremost from New Mexico." And they need a lot of those ingredients because Bueno produces more than 150 authentic, gourmet products including the original flame-roasted fresh frozen green chile, as well as red chiles, tortillas, and a line of ready-to-serve prepared products. The company also recently launched a natural and organic line.

Bueno produces all that food in a 110,000-square-foot plant next to the Barelas neighborhood in south Albuquerque, employing 220 people year-round and up to 400 during peak season in the late summer and early fall, when they process millions of tons of green chiles.

"After 62 years, we're still preserving our heritage," Baca says.

Tangy Turkey Tacos

Tacos are such an iconic southwestern food that I often feel the need to try some non-traditional ones, like these that use mashed potatoes. New Mexico doesn't have a turkey industry to speak of, but there are always plenty of them available around holiday time. You could easily substitute cooked turkey from a roast, finely chopped and barely reheated.

1 pound ground turkey

1 small yellow onion, chopped

1 medium potato, boiled and mashed

1 (8-ounce) can no-salt-added tomato sauce

½ cup Bueno New Mexico Red Chile Sauce, or any bottled red chile sauce

10 taco shells

2½ cups shredded lettuce

6 ounces cheese, like mozzarella, cheddar, or any soy cheese, grated (1 cup)

1 tomato, chopped

⅓ cup Bueno Salsa, or any bottled salsa

Heat Scale: Medium   10 TACOS

1. Brown the turkey in a skillet over medium heat, stirring occasionally. Add the onion and sauté for 2 minutes longer, stirring occasionally. Add the potato, tomato sauce, and chile sauce, and stir well. Cook, uncovered, over low heat for 15 to 20 minutes, stirring occasionally.

2. Meanwhile, preheat the oven to 350°F.

3. Place the taco shells on a large baking sheet and heat in the oven for 5 minutes.

4. Fill each shell with approximately ¼ cup of the turkey filling, top with lettuce, cheese, tomato, and salsa, and serve.

Recipe from MATT YOHALEM, IL PIATTO

Roast Duckling with Red Chile Glaze and Spiced Peaches

Chef Matt Yohalem discusses this dish: "In spite of our desert climate, peaches, apricots, cherries, and sometimes plums seem to thrive here in Santa Fe, and you can use any of these stone fruits in this recipe. Red chile is, of course, abundant and we also have a bounty of potatoes, such as Peruvian purple, fingerling, and Yukon Gold. These are so fresh that they need little or no embellishment.

"Duck hunting is also common in northern New Mexico; we have ducks of many species, plus doves, quail, and pheasant. I find this recipe works with all game birds. However, domestic duck breasts are readily available at your local gourmet grocer. Generally two breasts will serve three people, but you can do a breast per person. I always include a vegetable side."

4 Long Island duck breasts, or what type is available

Salt and freshly ground black pepper

3 tablespoons plus 1 teaspoon ground red chile

2 tablespoons berry preserves

4 peaches, peeled, pitted, and quartered, or equivalent fruit

1 tablespoon minced garlic

1 tablespoon finely chopped shallot

1 tablespoon finely chopped fresh Italian parsley

1 fresh thyme sprig

1 tablespoon olive oil

½ pound fingerling potatoes, sliced

1 cup chicken stock

2 tablespoons butter

Heat Scale: Mild   4 TO 6 SERVINGS

1. Preheat the oven to 425°F.

2. Season the duck with salt, pepper, and 1 teaspoon of the ground chile.

3. Preheat a medium ovenproof skillet over medium heat. Place the duck breasts, skin side down, in the skillet and cook until lightly browned on that side, 5 to 7 minutes. Wait until the skin begins to render fat before moving them around so they don't stick. Turn the breasts over and remove them to a plate, skin side up, and reserve, saving any juices.

4. Combine the remaining 3 tablespoons ground chile with the preserves in a small bowl. Add the peaches to the skillet and coat with the berry-chile glaze. Add the garlic, shallot, parsley, and thyme, and transfer the skillet to the oven to cook for 3 to 5 minutes, until the peaches soften. Remove from the oven, add the duck breasts and any juices back to the skillet, and reserve.

5. Meanwhile, heat the oil on high heat in a separate oven-proof skillet, and add the potatoes. Cook them for 2 minutes, stirring often. Salt and pepper to taste and place the skillet in the oven for 15 minutes. Stir the potatoes from time to time to prevent sticking.

6. Return the first skillet with the breasts and the peaches to the oven for the last 10 minutes of cooking the potatoes.

7. Remove the duck breasts and peaches from the oven and place them on a serving platter. Place the skillet over low heat and add the stock. Bring the sauce to a boil for 1 to 2 minutes, stirring with a spoon. Add the butter, and salt and pepper to taste, remove the skillet from the heat, and stir the sauce to melt the butter. Remove the potatoes from the oven, and add them to the platter.

Recipe from SOFIA ELEFTHERIOU, *EDIBLE SANTA FE*

Friday Night Skillet Breakfast

Edible Santa Fe contributor Sofia Eleftheriou observes, "Backyard chicken-keeping has become a national phenomenon, with coops popping up everywhere and an active online chicken-keeping community. There are a half dozen annual coop tours in northern New Mexico alone. Chicken keepers like me tend to have an abundance of eggs and a need for creative ways to incorporate them into meals. This delicious dish works for brunch or dinner."

THE SAUCE

2 tablespoons butter

½ cup minced oyster mushrooms

2 garlic cloves, minced

½ cup dry white wine

Salt

THE SKILLET

2 tablespoons olive oil

¼ pound sausage, casing removed

2 tablespoons chopped leeks

½ bunch braising greens, such as collards, or spinach

1 small tomato, chopped

2 tablespoons chopped fresh Italian parsley

Salt

¼ cup dry white wine

2 eggs

3 tablespoons chèvre or feta cheese, crumbled

2 SERVINGS

1. Make the sauce: Melt 1 tablespoon of the butter in a small skillet over medium heat, and sauté the mushrooms and garlic, stirring occasionally, until the mushrooms soften and release moisture, about 5 minutes. Add the wine and a pinch of salt, and continue cooking until the liquid is reduced by half. Remove the skillet from the heat and whisk in the remaining tablespoon of butter, then set aside.

2. Make the skillet: Heat the oil in a large skillet over medium heat, and sauté the sausage and leeks until the sausage is cooked through, 3 to 5 minutes. Use a spatula to break up the sausage and mix it well with the leeks.

3. Add the braising greens, tomato, parsley, salt, and wine to the skillet. Stir once to combine the ingredients but don't overmix them. Cover and cook until the greens start to soften but are still bright green, 3 to 5 minutes longer.

4. Create two small nests in the mixture and crack an egg into each one, then sprinkle the cheese on top. Cover and cook for 3 to 6 minutes, depending on how well you like your eggs cooked.

5. Scoop out each egg with as much of the green mixture as you can using a large serving spoon. Place an egg on each plate, add the remaining green mixture, and top with the mushroom sauce. Serve immediately.

THE BARBECUE COWGIRL OF SANTA FE

"IT'S EXTREMELY DIFFICULT for a restaurant our size to be completely farm to table," Barry Secular told me, "but we try." Secular, the manager of Cowgirl Restaurant Santa Fe, noted that it's easiest during the summer when there are plenty of organic tomatoes and vegetables available but much more difficult during the winter season. He depends heavily on the Santa Fe Farmers' Market to be his intermediary between the farms and his restaurant, but the produce must pass his critical quality control. "Cowgirl must be consistent in both the quality of the food we serve, and in price, and sometimes I just have to turn to my commercial suppliers."

Especially for meats, considering the restaurant's reputation for barbecue. Ironically, although they are the principal caterer for the New Mexico Cattle Growers Association, Secular finds local grass-fed beef sometimes either too lean or too tough — especially for cuts like brisket — and has to opt for Kansas-grown beef. He always uses commercial suppliers for pork, but he does buy buffalo meat from Lamont's Wild West Buffalo in Bosque Farms, New Mexico.

For a barbecue joint, Cowgirl has a surprisingly diverse menu. In addition to mesquite-smoked baby back ribs and green-chile cheeseburgers (two top choices for patrons), the restaurant offers vegetarian options like butternut squash casserole and caprese salad. New Mexican favorites include chiles rellenos, huevos rancheros, and a smoked chicken short stack (their version of enchiladas), in which the chefs combine chicken with tortillas,

black beans, Jack and cheddar cheeses, and the usual choice of red or green chiles.

To accompany these dishes, Cowgirl always has 12 microbrews on tap, of which 2 or 3 are New Mexico–brewed. They also have a full bar that specializes in tequilas — 32 of them plus 4 mescals.

A wide selection of food, the taproom, the margaritas, and live music make the Cowgirl one of the most popular restaurants in Santa Fe. It's received national attention too, including an appearance by Rachel Ray, who noted on a segment of "$40 a Day," "Not only is my lunch pick a bargain, but this restaurant is big on fun and big on down-home barbecue flavors! We have wooden floors, western decor, and tasty vittles served up by cowgirls in western wear. Talk about Girl Power!"

Recipe from KATIXA MERCIER, *LOCAL IQ*

Shrimp Tacos with Black Bean Salsa

This recipe originally appeared in *Local iQ*, the biweekly magazine of food, arts, and culture in the Albuquerque/Santa Fe area. The salsa demonstrates the versatility of black beans and works well with the shrimp.

NOTE: This recipe requires advance preparation.

BLACK BEAN SALSA

2 cups cooked black beans

1 cup cooked corn kernels

1 small bunch fresh cilantro, minced (about ¼ cup)

2 medium tomatoes, diced

1 small red onion, finely chopped

2 garlic cloves, minced

1 jalapeño chile, minced

Juice of 2 limes

Salt and freshly ground black pepper

SHRIMP TACOS

1 pound medium shrimp, peeled and deveined

2 tablespoons green chile powder

1 teaspoon ground cumin

½ teaspoon salt

⅓ cup agave nectar

¼ cup water

Vegetable oil, for frying

8 corn tortillas

Heat Scale: Medium 　　　　　　　　　　**4 SERVINGS**

1. Make the salsa: Combine the black beans, corn, cilantro, tomatoes, onion, garlic, jalapeño, and lime juice in a bowl and mix well. Salt and pepper to taste. Place the bowl in the refrigerator until an hour before the shrimp is cooked.

2. Make the tacos: Combine the shrimp, chile powder, cumin, salt, agave nectar, and water in a bowl and mix to coat the shrimp. Cover and marinate in the refrigerator for a couple hours before grilling.

3. Prepare the grill for direct grilling. Thread the shrimp onto skewers and grill over medium heat until the shrimp start to turn pink on each side.

4. In a small skillet, heat the oil until hot and fry the tortillas in the oil for 3 seconds per side and drain on paper towels. Place the shrimp on the tortillas and fold one side over. Put two tacos on each plate. Put about a half cup of salsa on each plate beside the tacos so each diner can add the salsa to the shrimp tacos at will.

5 Using Local Specialty Products

THE NATIONAL FIERY FOODS and Barbecue Show, founded in 1988, is one of two events that my wife, Mary Jane, my niece Emily, and I produce that involve the manufacturers and distributors of local foods. It is the largest show of its kind in the world, attracting some 20,000 foodies to sample and buy more than 1,000 fiery foods and barbecue products offered by the 200 vendors. The second event, the Scovie Awards Competition, established by my company, Sunbelt Shows, in 1996, typically draws more than 800 entries from about 130 food-product companies that are judged in a blind tasting judged by food professionals. New Mexico companies have won the Grand Prize six times; Lusty Monk Mustards claimed it in 2013 and repeated the win with a different product in 2014. Both of these events offer New Mexico companies (and others from around the world) much needed exposure and promotion.

Before reaching the stage of competing for acclaim, many New Mexico companies get their start at the Mixing Bowl Product Incubator, located in the center of the South Valley, a culturally rich agricultural community in southwest Albuquerque where food entrepreneurs can cook up their traditional family recipes and then some. This commercial kitchen incubator is part of the South Valley Economic Development Center. The not-for-profit business helps creative cooks test recipes and begin the process of offering their products to consumers. Many New Mexico food companies have grown up in the Mixing Bowl kitchen, learning how to successfully start their business, demo their products, and create food products that are ready for local grocery stores to carry.

This is the heart of the local food business movement in New Mexico — where micro-entrepreneurs turn raspberries into delicious chile-spiked jams, craft chocolate truffles by hand, and bake savory pies. It's a place where business owners have convened since 2006 to try each other's tasty recipes and create a community among themselves to support each other in all stages of their company's development.

Through best practice sharing and entrepreneur trainings, the Mixing Bowl is helping local foodies go beyond their dream to the reality of ownership. They help businesses navigate the hurdles of regulation, labeling, and testing.

Another program, Delicious New Mexico, in partnership with the Mixing Bowl and other commercial kitchens around the state, helps local businesses grow into even larger markets. The program holds educational seminars on manufacturing, distributing, promotions, and advertising for food producers and connects them with retailers and distributors. Consumers can join Delicious Tastebuds, a food club that offers tours of local food hotspots, gourmet farm-to-table dinners, and coupons for products, markets, and restaurants. In their own words, Delicious New Mexico is "growing the local food movement, one delicious business at a time."

CHISPA SALSA

WHEN YOU ASK RUBEN PARGA why he started Chispa Salsa, an enthusiastic and heartwarming story unfolds about a craving for the foods of New Mexico — one that's understandable to any native who's spent time away from their homeland. "You never quite appreciate things until you leave a place," says Parga, who left the Southwest after college to travel the world while serving in the military and working in the corporate world.

Parga quickly realized that the chiles and salsas ingrained in his culture were not to be found outside of New Mexico. Inspired by childhood experiences in his family kitchen, he set out to create a product that was an authentic re-creation of the homemade, red chile–based salsas found on so many New Mexican dining tables.

"Salsa" literally translates from Spanish as "sauce," and for hundreds of years, authentic salsa in New Mexico has meant a soupy, non-chunky, chile-based sauce used in cooking and for marinating as much as, if not more than, it is used as a dip for tortilla chips. Parga's Chispa Brillante salsa is a reminder of the definition of the word.

The sauce starts with red chiles, sourced directly from a farm in Hatch, immediately differentiating his salsa from others. Unlike many condiment-style salsas that have a jalapeño base, Chispa sauce uses red chile flakes. Fresh garlic and onion from a non-GMO farm that uses no synthetic pesticides replaces the powdered spices found in many other salsas. Add the fact that no flour or artificial thickening agents are in the mix and you have yourself a product that is as close to a homemade New Mexican red chile–based salsa as you can get without making it yourself.

Parga's business model is "keep it simple." His only product is Chispa Brillante because he believes that once someone learns that they can use it to cook, to marinate, and to dip, they won't need another sauce. Chispa Brillante can be found in multiple grocery sections at Whole Foods, La Montañita Co-op, and John Brooks Supermart locations throughout New Mexico.

Recipe from RUBEN PARGA, CHISPA SALSA

Chispa's Frito Pie

Frito pie is a secret (or not-so-secret) comfort food for many people. There are quite a few stories about the origin of this iconic, cheesy dish. In the '50s, Nell Morris joined Frito-Lay and helped develop an official company cookbook that included the first published Frito pie recipe. Despite that evidence, another story claims that the true Frito pie originated in the '60s with Teresa Hernández, who worked at the F. W. Woolworth's lunch counter in Santa Fe, where she supposedly invented the dish. In October 2012, a team from Frito-Lay constructed the world's largest Frito pie with 635 bags of Fritos, 660 cans of chili, and 580 bags of shredded cheddar cheese. The entire pie weighed 1,325 pounds.

1 pound lean ground beef

1 (15-ounce) can pinto beans or 2 cups home-cooked

1 (16-ounce) jar Chispa Brillante salsa/cooking sauce

1 (16-ounce) bag Fritos Original Corn Chips

½ large yellow onion, finely chopped

10 ounces sharp cheddar cheese, coarsely grated (about 2½ cups)

Heat Scale: Medium   6 TO 8 SERVINGS

1. Cook the beef in a large skillet over medium heat, stirring occasionally, until browned, about 10 minutes. Drain off any accumulated fat.

2. Add the beans and salsa to the skillet and simmer on low for 10 minutes, stirring occasionally.

3. Place the chips in the bottom of a large bowl and pour the beef mixture over them. Top with the onion and then the cheese and serve.

Lusty Mustard–Lavender Vinaigrette

Los Poblanos, located in Albuquerque's North Valley, is a farm-to-table operation that has both farms and tables because they have an on-site restaurant. One of their crops is lavender and they are cosponsors of an annual lavender festival. This great vinaigrette features their culinary lavender and the mildest of the Lusty Monk Mustards. It is a delightful topping for ripe garden tomatoes. Since fresh mustard quickly loses its potency, storing this vinaigrette is not recommended.

1 tablespoon culinary lavender

1 garlic clove, crushed

2 tablespoons Lusty Monk Altar Boy Honey Mustard or other mild, fresh mustard

1 tablespoon balsamic vinegar

1 tablespoon rice wine vinegar

6 tablespoons olive oil

Salt and freshly ground black pepper

ABOUT ½ CUP

1. Gently grind the lavender with a mortar and pestle.

2. Combine the lavender, garlic, mustard, balsamic vinegar, and rice wine vinegar in a small bowl. Slowly whisk in the olive oil. Salt and pepper to taste.

APPLE CANYON GOURMET

ANNA SHAWVER'S great-great-grandfather, Alexander Grzelachowski, owned the general store in Puerta de Luna, a little town on the Pecos River just south of Santa Rosa. On Christmas Day 1880, Sheriff Pat Garrett, a friend of Grzelachowski's, showed up at his house with Billy the Kid, who was shackled to fellow gang member Dave Rudabaugh. They were all hungry, so Grzelachowski fed them Christmas dinner, the last one The Kid ever ate. Some months later, after being convicted of murder and sentenced to hang, The Kid escaped from his cell at the Lincoln County Courthouse. Sheriff Garrett tracked him down and killed him in a shootout.

Shawver seems to have inherited some of her forebear's entrepreneurial skills. She learned how to can foods while living in the northwest, then worked for a longshoremen's company, and finally returned to New Mexico to learn about the specialty food business by working as a food broker for various small businesses. She dreamed of starting her own food company, but realizing that the world just doesn't need another salsa, she began acquiring small businesses that were faltering because of their inadequate production capacity and inability to form expansion plans.

Her first acquisition was Holy Chipotle!, which had a single product, and then Santa Fe Seasons, launched by chef Mark Miller, founder of the Coyote Cafe. After that came a dried-soup company, Comida Loca, and a beverage company called Santa Fe Mixes. Today, she lists 60 food products on her website, including soups, cookies, dips, salsas and hot sauces, jams and jellies, and spices and rubs — quite possibly the most diversified product line of any New Mexico specialty food company.

She sources her ingredients locally as much as possible. Her most interesting sourcing story comes from her Prickly Pear Margarita Mix. To make it, the fruits of the prickly pear cactus, called tunas, are harvested — with a federal license — from wild plants on B. L. M. land. The tunas are picked by hand — or rather, by hands holding tongs because they are covered with sharp spines. It's doubtful that her great-great-grandfather served margaritas to The Kid on that Christmas Day so long ago, but Shawver likes to think that they might have had a nip of whiskey from Grzelachowski's general store.

Santa Fe Seasons Quick Green Chile Stew

In this very fast recipe, Apple Canyon Gourmet's Anna Shawver uses chicken breasts and black beans in a spinoff on the traditional pork stew. Anna's use of the salsa as a recipe ingredient is a perfect example of the versatility of salsas. Serve the stew with warm corn or flour tortillas. This stew freezes well.

1 tablespoon butter

2 boneless, skinless chicken breasts, cut into bite-size pieces

1 (15-ounce) can black beans

1 (16-ounce) jar Santa Fe Seasons Fire Roasted Green Chile Salsa, or any bottled green chile salsa

Heat Scale: Medium   4 SERVINGS

1. Melt the butter in a Dutch oven over high heat and sear the chicken, turning once, for about 2 minutes per side.

2. Add the beans and salsa to the Dutch oven, stir, cover, and simmer over low heat for 20 minutes.

3. Remove the lid and cook about 10 minutes or longer if a thicker consistency is desired. Serve with warm tortillas.

Recipe from KINNA PEREZ, KINNA'S LAOS CHILE PASTE

Southwest Meets Southeast Asia Burgers

The ever-evolving traditions of New Mexico cuisine must take into consideration the state's growing Asian community, many of whom adore hot and spicy food in their own way. Green Chile Cheeseburgers are the number one seller at the Cowgirl Restaurant in Santa Fe (see page 167), but if you make this version with Kinna's Laos Chile Paste rather than green chiles, you'll add an entirely new dimension to the cheeseburger concept. Serve these delectable burgers with a fresh garden salad and dill pickles. Serve with the usual burger condiments, such as ketchup, mustard, and sliced onions.

1 pound flank steak, ground

4 ounces Old Windmill Dairy Chili & Hot Chèvre, or 1 teaspoon red chile powder and 4 ounces chèvre, combined

3 tablespoons Kinna's Laos Chile Paste, or other Asian chile paste

4 homemade or store-bought burger buns

¼ cup ButterBeautiful habanero Dragon Breath butter, or softened butter mixed with ⅛–¼ teaspoon commercial habanero sauce

Heat Scale: Medium   **4 SERVINGS**

1. Mix the ground meat, chèvre, and chile paste together in a bowl. Knead the meat thoroughly with your hands to blend. Shape the meat into four patties.

2. Prepare the grill for direct grilling over medium heat. Grill the burgers, flipping them several times, until they achieve the desired doneness (medium-rare is 150°F internal temperature).

3. While the meat is grilling, toast both sides of each bun and slather each bun with about 1 tablespoon of the habanero butter. Place the burgers on the buns and serve with the condiments.

KINNA'S LAOS CHILE PASTE

MANUEL AND KINNA PEREZ met in Albuquerque after coming from very separate parts of the world — Manuel from Chihuahua, Mexico, and Kinna from Laos in Southeast Asia. From the time they started dating, Manuel became quite accustomed to the ever-present bowl of homemade traditional chile paste on Kinna's family dining table. But when he suggested bringing his wife's family recipe to the public's table, he was met with staunch resistance.

"Are you crazy?" Kinna asked him, not out of a desire to keep the recipe secret but because the recipe, passed down through four generations, was so laborious to make that it seemed impossible to pull off on a large scale. Manuel took this as a challenge and made a bet with his wife. If he could make the chile paste by himself without Kinna looking over his shoulder *and* make it taste just like hers, they could at least continue the conversation.

The ensuing experiment made the kitchen look like it had exploded, but after a taste test by the master herself, Kinna agreed Manuel's chile paste tasted good. But her question remained: "Do you see how long it takes to make?" Manuel answered with confidence: "Now that I know how to make it, we can save time."

Kinna's Laos Chile Paste is made with fresh ingredients and health in mind. The sweetness in the otherwise spicy condiment comes from organic evaporated cane juice sourced from La Montañita Co-op. The addition of a vegan option, which has removed the traditional Asian fish sauce, means that nearly anyone can enjoy this versatile paste.

From traditional Laos dishes such as sticky rice and dried beef to mixing with mayonnaise for a delicious, slightly fiery sandwich, Kinna's Laos Chile Paste is a go-to condiment. An award from the National Fiery Foods and Barbecue Show and a place on store shelves ranging from Whole Foods to New Mexico's world cuisine grocer Talin Market are a testament to Kinna and Manuel's hard work.

Recipe from ANNA SHAWVER, APPLE CANYON GOURMET

Holy Chipotle! Flamin' Posole

Posole, a thick pork stew, is a beloved Christmas holiday dish in New Mexico, but it can be served any time of the year. The corn called for in the recipe is limed corn, also called hominy, in dried or frozen form. This slow cooker recipe takes a lot of time to make, but the flavor is worth the wait. The dish freezes well.

NOTE: This recipe requires advance preparation.

1 (2½-pound) pork tenderloin

½ (12-ounce) can Coca-Cola

6 tablespoons Holy Chipotle! Flamin' Chipotle Hot Sauce, or other bottled chipotle salsa

1 medium yellow onion, chopped

1 teaspoon garlic powder

8 ounces frozen posole corn, or dried posole corn soaked in water overnight, about 2 cups

Finely chopped fresh cilantro, for garnish

Lime wedges, for garnish

Heat Scale: Medium   8 SERVINGS

1. Place the pork in a large bowl and pierce it on all sides with a sharp fork. Combine the Coca-Cola and 4 tablespoons of the sauce in a separate bowl, then pour it over the pork. Cover with plastic wrap and refrigerate overnight.

2. Transfer the pork and marinade to a slow cooker. Add the onion and garlic powder. Set the temperature to low, cover, and cook the pork until it easily falls apart, about 7 hours. Check the liquid level in the slow cooker occasionally, adding water as needed.

3. Remove the pork to a cutting board and shred it. Transfer the pork and the liquid to a large bowl, cover, and place it in the refrigerator.

4. Add the posole corn and 6 cups water to the slow cooker, set it to hot, cover, and cook until the corn is soft, about 2 hours.

5. Drain the corn and return it to the slow cooker. Return the pork and liquid to the slow cooker, mix it with the posole corn, and add the remaining 2 tablespoons sauce. Cook for 15 minutes on high and then serve in bowls garnished with cilantro and lime wedges.

Salad Greens
with Honey Chipotle-Lime–Mustard Dressing

This salad calls for strongly flavored lettuce greens such as arugula, mustard greens, radicchio, curly endive, and spinach to balance the sweet heat and mustard bite of the assertive dressing. As an alternative to chèvre, try Mexican cotija or anejo, Parmesan, or pecorino to complement this salad.

NOTE: This recipe requires advance preparation.

DRESSING

1 chipotle chile in adobo sauce, finely chopped

1 tablespoon finely chopped fresh cilantro

1 tablespoon minced shallot

¼ teaspoon minced garlic

¼ cup Taos Valley Honey or other local honey

3 tablespoons Chipotle-Lime Mustard (recipe on facing page)

3 tablespoons extra-virgin olive oil

2 tablespoons cider vinegar

Salt and freshly ground black pepper

SALAD

4–6 cups chopped mixed salad greens, such as radicchio, curly endive, romaine, or spinach

½ red onion, thinly sliced and separated into rings

Crumbled chèvre, for garnish

Heat Scale: Mild to medium   4 SERVINGS

1. Combine the chipotle chile, cilantro, shallot, garlic, honey, Chipotle-Lime Mustard, oil, and vinegar in a small bowl and whisk to combine. Salt and pepper to taste. Allow the dressing to sit for 1 hour at room temperature to blend the flavors.

2. Combine the salad greens and onion in a salad bowl and toss to mix. Pour the dressing over the salad and gently toss to coat. Garnish the salad with chèvre and serve.

Lusty Chipotle-Lime Mustard

This Southwest-inspired mustard has a definite taste of cumin. It's spicy and tastes great with just about anything. Try it as a marinade for poultry, pork, or beef, mix it with sour cream or mayonnaise for a tasty dip, or use as a topping for vegetables. Since fresh mustard quickly loses its potency, use it up quickly.

NOTE: This recipe requires advance preparation.

2 chipotle chiles in adobo sauce

¼ cup chopped yellow onion

2 teaspoons minced garlic

2 teaspoons cumin seeds

1 teaspoon salt

1 cup Lusty Monk Burn in Hell Chipotle Mustard, or other very spicy fresh mustard

⅓ cup cider vinegar

2 tablespoons lime juice

Heat Scale: Medium ABOUT 1½ CUPS

1. Combine the chipotle chiles, onion, garlic, cumin, salt, mustard, vinegar, and lime juice in a blender or food processor and process until smooth.

2. Transfer the mixture to a small saucepan and bring to a boil over medium-high heat. Lower the heat and simmer, stirring occasionally, until the mixture thickens slightly, about 5 minutes, adding 2 to 4 tablespoons of water to thin the mustard, if necessary. (The mustard will thicken as it cools, so don't cook it too long.)

3. Spoon the mustard into a sterilized jar and refrigerate overnight before using.

Lusty Mustard–slathered Chicken Breasts

Don't let the fact that parchment paper is involved discourage you from trying this recipe — it's just another kitchen tool. In this recipe, provided by a friend of Lusty Monk Mustard cofounder Kelly Davis, it keeps the chicken and the flavorings together throughout the cooking process. Garlic-and-herb mashed fingerling potatoes would be a nice accompaniment for this classy chicken, as would some steamed broccoli tossed with your favorite infused butter from ButterBeautiful.

4 boneless, skinless chicken breast halves

Salt and freshly ground black pepper

4 tablespoons Lusty Monk Original Sin Mustard or other spicy mustard

2 medium carrots, peeled and thinly sliced

2 leeks, thinly sliced

2 teaspoons finely chopped fresh thyme, plus more for garnish

1. Preheat the oven to 400°F. Place a baking sheet on the middle rack.

2. Season the chicken with salt and pepper and rub 1 tablespoon of the mustard on each breast.

3. Toss the carrots, leeks, and thyme together in a medium bowl. Salt and pepper the mixture to taste.

4. Tear off a sheet of parchment paper about 20 inches long. Trace a circle on it with a dinner plate. Cut out the circle with scissors. Fold it in half (like you're closing a book) then open it back up. Put one-quarter of the vegetable mixture in the middle of the center fold. Put 1 chicken breast half on top of the vegetables.

5. Fold the paper over so that the two ends meet (like you are closing a book again). Beginning at either end of the center fold, make overlapping diagonal folds so that you make a tight pocket around the food. The end result will be a crescent-shape packet that looks sort of like half of a fried pie. Repeat the steps to wrap the remaining breasts.

6. Place each packet on the warm baking sheet and bake for 30 to 35 minutes, depending on the thickness of the chicken. As the chicken cooks, the packet will inflate and become aromatic. (Check the temperature early and often by inserting an instant-read thermometer through the parchment paper. The cooked chicken should be at 170°F.)

7. Place each packet on a plate and cut the flat end open with scissors or a sharp knife. Slide the paper out from under the ingredients (like you're pulling a table cloth out from underneath a set table). Garnish with additional thyme, if desired, and salt and pepper to taste before serving.

TRADITIONAL ACETO BALSAMICO OF MONTICELLO

A SINGLE 4.5-OUNCE BOTTLE of traditional, cask-aged, balsamic vinegar from Traditional Aceto Balsamico of Monticello, New Mexico, requires enough organic grape juice to make 50 bottles of wine. When you include the fact that it's aged for a minimum of 12 years and that only 1,000 bottles are released each year, you have discovered an incredibly rare treat.

Founded in 1998 by former advertising mogul Steve Darland, Traditional Aceto Balsamico of Monticello is located more than a mile above sea level, making it among the highest vineyards in the world. Grown without pesticides in this stressful environment of high heat and high altitude, the Trebbiano and Occhio di Gatto vines yield a small but powerful harvest of intensely flavorful fruit. The juice of just-harvested white grapes is concentrated and then slowly aged in handmade casks of various fragrant woods in Darland's vinegar loft. After much patience and attention to age-old crafting methods, the resulting balsamic is a luscious, viscous delicacy — with quality matching that of classics made in Modena, Italy.

With the entire process operating out of a historic New Mexico adobe village with a population fewer than 25 people, Traditional Aceto Balsamico of Monticello seems to have all the makings of a dreamy fairy tale. After tasting one drop of this liquid gold, one is reminded that this fairy tale is very true.

Steve and Jane Darland

Filet Mignon with Balsamic-Mustard Sauce

Incredibly easy and very elegant, this is the perfect dish to serve for company or for a special family celebration. Balsamic vinegar is strongly flavored and can vary greatly in quality, so I recommend splurging on good quality balsamic vinegar for a richly flavored sauce. This recipe also makes a tasty gravy for roast beef. To finish this meal, just prepare a crisp garden salad and pop some potatoes in the oven.

1 tablespoon butter, preferably unsalted

4 (8-ounce) filet mignon steaks

Salt and freshly ground black pepper

2 shallots, minced

¼ teaspoon finely chopped fresh thyme, plus more for garnish

1 cup beef stock

¼ cup balsamic vinegar

¼ cup Lusty Monk Altar Boy Honey Mustard, or other mild fresh mustard

Heat Scale: Mild

4 SERVINGS

1. Preheat the oven to 450°F.

2. Heat a large ovenproof skillet over medium-high heat and add the butter.

3. Season the filets with salt and pepper, and brown the steaks in the skillet over medium heat for about 1 minute per side. Place the skillet in the oven and bake for 5 minutes for rare meat, 7 minutes for medium-rare, or until the meat is done to your liking.

4. Transfer the steaks to a warmed platter and cover loosely with aluminum foil to keep warm.

5. Return the skillet to the top of the stove and add the shallots. Sauté over medium heat, stirring occasionally, until soft, about 5 minutes. Add the thyme, stock, vinegar, and mustard, and increase the heat to medium-high. Bring the mixture to a boil, stirring constantly and scraping the skillet until the browned bits and pieces from the skillet dissolve and the mixture reduces slightly, about 5 minutes.

6. To serve, drizzle a small amount of the sauce on individual plates, top with a steak, and garnish with thyme. Serve the steaks with additional sauce on the side.

Recipe from MARNIE BOREN, ALBUQUERQUE

Apple Canyon Orange-Sesame Chicken Coleslaw

This quick and easy coleslaw features Apple Canyon Gourmet's Orange Sesame Sauce, a Scovie Award–winning multipurpose sauce. A substantial dish, it can be served with cornbread as an entrée. It will keep in the refrigerator for up to five days. It was provided by a friend of Anna Shawver's of Apple Canyon Gourmet (see page 175).

6 TO 8 SERVINGS

1 large head green cabbage, chopped

1 red bell pepper, seeded and chopped

1 boneless, skinless chicken breast, poached and chopped

2 tablespoons mayonnaise

Apple Canyon Orange Sesame Sauce

Finely chopped fresh Italian parsley, for garnish

1. Combine the cabbage, bell pepper, chicken, and mayonnaise in a large bowl and mix well.

2. Slowly drizzle the Orange Sesame Sauce into the slaw to taste while stirring until the desired consistency is reached.

3. Sprinkle Italian parsley over the coleslaw before serving.

TAOS VALLEY HONEY

WHEN ASKED HOW HE ENDED UP in Taos, Colorado-born Jason Goodhue jokingly says, "The wind took me here." This isn't far from the truth; when he was in his early twenties, his car broke down near Taos and he never left. He started doing various jobs to pay the bills and then came across an opportunity at Questa Honey Farms. Goodhue knew about beekeeping through his uncles, an experience that gave him just enough knowledge to land the job. He started out in the warehouse, but before long he was out in the fields learning how to be a full-fledged beekeeper. It was clear that he had a natural affinity for beekeeping, one that ultimately led him to start Taos Valley Honey.

It took a couple of years before the bees produced enough honey to sell in reasonable quantities, and most of his initial business was at the Taos Farmers' Market and other local events. Now Goodhue also sells his product at Cid's, Taos Herb, and other stores in and around Taos. And the Honey Cottage in Colorado Springs ships his honey around the country.

Taos Valley Honey is unusual in that no antibiotics are used in the hives and it is cold processed with all the enzymes intact, resulting in raw honey that is not heat-processed. Most honey that is sold as raw cannot make that claim. Taos Valley Honey is known as a polyfloral honey, which offers a distinctive flavor because the bees gather the nectar from local wildflowers. The taste and aroma of wildflower honey differ from year to year depending on what is blooming.

Most commercially produced honey is blended to achieve a consistent flavor.

One of the most fascinating elements of Taos Valley Honey is where the company produces its honey. Goodhue has cultivated relationships with landowners who let him put his hives on their land, connections he enjoys, as it presents him with an opportunity to educate them about the benefits of bees and helping increase biodiversity in the region. Goodhue is also working on partnerships with other businesses and is looking to sell honeybees to people looking to get into beekeeping. His passion for teaching has led him to offer a summer camp for young people with the Field Institute of Taos, where he can continue the tradition of inspiring kids to become interested in bees.

Jason Goodhue

Pasilla Scones with Red Chile Honey

These tender flaky scones are best served warm from the oven. The pasilla chile adds a little bit of heat and a really nice raisiny taste. Serve the scones for breakfast with the red chile honey. Cut out the scones with a heart- or chile-shaped cookie cutter, and you've got the beginnings of a great day.

PASILLA SCONES

- 2 cups all-purpose flour
- 1 tablespoon baking powder
- 1 teaspoon salt
- ⅓ cup finely chopped seeded pasilla chiles
- 1 teaspoon ground cinnamon
- 1 cup plus 2 tablespoons heavy cream

RED CHILE HONEY

- 1 tablespoon New Mexican red chile powder
- 1 (8-ounce) jar Taos Valley Honey or other local honey

Heat Scale: Medium   16 SCONES

1. Make the scones: Preheat the oven to 425°F.

2. Mix together the flour, baking powder, and salt in a large bowl. Add the chiles, cinnamon, and 1 cup of the cream, and stir until a soft dough forms. Place the dough on a floured work surface and knead 10 times, or until the dough forms a ball.

3. Divide the dough into two pieces. Working with one ball of dough at a time, roll out the dough on a floured surface until it is about ½ inch thick, then cut out the scones with a cookie cutter, and place them on a baking sheet. Repeat with the remaining ball of dough.

4. Brush the top of each scone with the remaining 2 tablespoons cream. Bake for 15 minutes, or until golden brown.

5. Make the honey: While the scones are baking, mix the chile powder thoroughly into the honey.

6. Drizzle the honey over the scones and serve. Leftover honey can be stored at room temperature.

LUSTY MONK MUSTARD

"LUSTY MONK has nothing to do with sex," company owner Steve Monteith told me. "The word 'lust' means a passionate hunger or craving for a number of things, like certain foods." In medieval Europe, where the belief that mustard was an aphrodisiac was widespread, many monks were forbidden to eat it for fear that it would give them carnal desires. So Kelly Davis, Monteith's sister-in-law, created the character of a monk with a lust for mustard when she invented the brand. Naturally, the mustard varieties are called Altar Boy for a milder mustard, Original Sin for a medium one, and Burn in Hell for the one with chipotle peppers in it.

This clever branding has been the secret of their success, along with the fact that the company makes refrigerated mustards, which hold heat and flavor better. Unlike capsaicin — the active ingredient in chile peppers that's impervious to cooking or freezing — isothiocyanate, the active or spicy principle in mustard, horseradish, and black pepper, very quickly breaks down by cooking, oxidation, or even if you look at it wrong. That's why good recipes that have mustard as an ingredient call for fresh (not shelf-stable) refrigerated mustards.

So what do you do after you've ordered two tons of mustard seed from Minnesota? For starters, you grind some of it into mustard flour so when you make the finished mustard, it's not too grainy. Without revealing the Monk's secrets of mustard-making, the basic process for making fresh mustard is to soak the yellow, brown, or black mustard seeds in vinegar for at least eight hours before adding any other flavorings like beer, horseradish, or herbs. The mixture is processed to leave a few whole seeds in it, then covered and refrigerated.

Based in Corrales, Steve and Kris Monteith run the western branch of Lusty Monk, while Kelly runs the eastern branch in Asheville, North Carolina. Both branches create the same mustards with the same recipes.

For the owners of Lusty Monk, their challenges are their successes. Even though they are limited by their small-scale production and having to be displayed in the refrigerated section, their mustards are carried by Whole Foods, La Montañita Co-op, La Cumbre Brewery, and soon-to-be Sprouts. Those deficits and that Lusty Monk himself give them a cachet of a true specialty food, one that refuses to be relegated to a shelf.

Lusty Mustard Broccoli Soup

Do you ever wonder what to do with all those broccoli stems you wind up with when you buy a fresh bunch? Well, they can be made into a base for this great-tasting soup, which is quick and easy to prepare. The mustard gives the soup a creamy texture without the addition of any cream, so this "cream" soup is low in fat! For a vegetarian version, just substitute vegetable stock for the chicken stock. This soup freezes well.

1 pound fresh broccoli, stems roughly chopped and florets reserved

1 medium yellow onion, coarsely chopped

2 chicken bouillon cubes

4 chiltepín or piquín chiles

2 teaspoons chopped fresh rosemary

1 teaspoon chopped fresh Italian parsley

½ teaspoon dried marjoram

½ teaspoon dried thyme

Salt

½–¾ teaspoon freshly ground white pepper

3–4 tablespoons Lusty Monk Altar Boy Honey Mustard, or any mild fresh mustard

Finely chopped fresh chives, for garnish

Heat Scale: Medium   4 TO 6 SERVINGS

1. Combine the broccoli stems, onion, bouillon cubes, chiltepíns, rosemary, parsley, marjoram, thyme, and 2 quarts of water in a large stockpot. Bring the mixture to a boil, reduce the heat, and simmer uncovered for 30 minutes.

2. Remove the broccoli mixture from the heat and let cool slightly.

3. Transfer the mixture to a blender or food processor and purée until smooth. Strain the soup back into the stockpot and discard any solids. Salt to taste.

4. Add the broccoli florets and white pepper to the stockpot and bring the soup to a simmer over medium-low heat. Simmer until the florets are just done, slightly crisp and still bright green, about 7 minutes.

5. Remove the soup from the heat and stir in the mustard to taste. Ladle the soup into a tureen or individual bowls, garnish with chives, and serve.

Recipe from KACIA DUNCAN, SOURWOOD INN

Pig Rollin' in Lusty Monk Cream Sauce

Kacia Duncan is the head chef of the Sourwood Inn in Asheville, North Carolina, where Lusty Monk Mustards were born (see page 192). So although this recipe is from the Southeast, the mustard is now made in Albuquerque, so it has southwestern ties as well. Serve this with a rice pilaf made with chicken stock (top it with the cream sauce, too) and grilled carrots.

1 tablespoon canola oil

1 (12-ounce) pork tenderloin, with silver skin removed

Salt and freshly ground black pepper

2 tablespoons dried Italian herb mix

1 shallot, finely chopped

1 garlic clove, minced

1 cup good dry vermouth

2 cups heavy cream

2 tablespoons Lusty Monk Original Sin Mustard or other medium-hot fresh mustard

4 TO 6 SERVINGS

1. Preheat the oven to 350°F.

2. Heat the canola oil in a medium skillet over medium heat. Season the pork tenderloin with salt and freshly ground black pepper. Brown the pork in the skillet over medium heat, turning occasionally, about 3 minutes per side.

3. Transfer the pork to a large ovenproof baking dish, reserving the skillet for the next step. Sprinkle the pork with the Italian dry herb mix and cook for approximately 12 to 15 minutes, or until an instant-read thermometer reaches 130°F. Let the pork rest before slicing.

4. While the pork is cooking, sauté the shallot and garlic in the skillet over medium heat, stirring occasionally, until translucent, 5 to 10 minutes.

5. Remove the skillet from the heat and add the vermouth. Return the skillet to the heat and cook, scraping the brown bits from the bottom of the pan, until the vermouth has reduced by half.

6. Add the cream and mustard to the skillet and stir over medium heat. (Warning: Stay with the skillet as the cream can overflow and catch on fire!) Stir and reduce the sauce until thickened, about 3 minutes. Salt and pepper to taste.

7. Serve the thinly sliced pork with the cream sauce spooned over it.

Puglia-style Pasta with Chispa Salsa

It is difficult to believe that a pasta recipe could be this quick and easy to prepare and taste so wonderful, but it's true. The pasta absorbs the water and juices, making this a one-pot pasta dish. Serve with an avocado salad and freshly baked bread slathered with one of ButterBeautiful's infused butters. My wife, Mary Jane, adapted this recipe from one we tasted in Italy. She suggests adding precooked meat, such as sausage, and just heating it through before adding the cheese. You can freeze the leftovers.

¼ pound angel hair pasta, broken in half

2 medium tomatoes, chopped

2 garlic cloves, minced

1 large shallot, finely chopped (¼ cup), or several thin slices of yellow onion

1 teaspoon chopped fresh Italian parsley, or more as desired

1 teaspoon chopped fresh basil, or more as desired

1 teaspoon chopped fresh oregano, or more as desired

1 cup Chispa Brillante Salsa, or other medium-hot salsa

2 tablespoons olive oil

Grated Parmesan or pecorino cheese

Freshly ground black pepper

Heat Scale: Medium   2 SERVINGS

1. Combine the pasta, tomatoes, garlic, shallot, parsley, basil, oregano, salsa, olive oil, and enough water to cover all the ingredients in a large saucepan. Bring to a boil, reduce the heat to low, and simmer, partially covered, for 5 to 8 minutes, adding more water if necessary.

2. When the pasta is tender, add the cheese and pepper to taste and serve.

New Mexican Baklava

Here is my take on this famous Greek dessert that is so time-consuming to prepare but so delicious to eat. Instead of the usual walnuts, I'm using New Mexico–grown pistachios and, of course, local honey. Store leftovers, covered, at room temperature for up to five days.

16 SERVINGS

BAKLAVA

- 1⅓ cups unsalted shelled New Mexican pistachios
- 1⅓ cups sliced almonds
- ⅓ cup dry, unflavored breadcrumbs
- 2 teaspoons ground cinnamon
- 1 (1-pound) box phyllo dough, thawed
- 1 cup (2 sticks) unsalted butter, melted

SYRUP

- 2 cups sugar
- 1 (3-inch) cinnamon stick
- 3 cloves
- ½ cup Taos Valley Honey or other local honey

1. Make the baklava: Place about half of the pistachios and half of the almonds in a food processor and pulse several times to chop the nuts finely, but do not pulverize them or you'll get a paste. Transfer the nuts to a bowl and repeat with the remaining pistachios and almonds. Add the breadcrumbs and cinnamon and toss until the mixture is well blended.

2. Preheat the oven to 350°F. Remove the phyllo from the package, transfer to a clean work surface, and smooth out the stack of sheets. Place one sheet of phyllo on a parchment paper–lined, rimmed baking sheet. Brush the sheet with melted butter. Repeat this procedure 9 more times, until you have 10 sheets of buttered phyllo in a stack.

3. Sprinkle about ¾ cup of the nut mixture on top of the stack of phyllo sheets. Top the nuts with 4 more sheets of buttered phyllo, then sprinkle on the remaining nut mixture. Cover that with 4 more sheets of buttered phyllo. With a very sharp knife, carefully cut the layers into thirds lengthwise. Then cut the strips diagonally into diamond shapes.

4. Bake the baklava for 1 hour, or until golden brown on top. Remove the baking sheet from the oven and put it on a rack to cool.

5. Make the syrup: While the baklava is cooling, combine the sugar, cinnamon stick, cloves, honey, and 1½ cups water in a saucepan. Bring to a boil, stirring constantly, until the sugar dissolves. Boil for 5 minutes longer. Set aside to cool until lukewarm, then pour it over the cooled baklava.

6. Cover the baklava tightly with plastic wrap and let sit for several hours or overnight before serving.

HEIDI'S RASPBERRY FARM

WHEN MY WIFE, Mary Jane, and I went to pick raspberries on Heidi Eleftheriou's farm in Corrales, the first thing I noticed wasn't the raspberries, but the flock of wild turkeys hanging around the brambles. That's me — birder first, berryman second.

"Don't they eat your berries?" I asked Eleftheriou.

"Nope," she replied, "they prefer the grasshoppers."

Eleftheriou's farm occupies 13 acres beside the Rio Grande, of which 5 are planted in raspberries, or to be botanically correct, four different varieties of Primocane, which are the ever-bearing form of raspberries. The farm is certified organic by the New Mexico Department of Agriculture's Organic Program, and a few years ago, she added more acreage in Los Lunas to supplement berry production.

To make her jams, Eleftheriou depends on the Mixing Bowl community kitchen at the South Valley Economic Development Center, and she's one of the biggest producers there. "I slowly cook the raspberries to a brief and delicate boiling phase," she says. "This method ensures that the precious vitamins and beautiful color of the natural fruit are preserved for your exquisite raspberry experience. I developed this delicious low-sugar recipe in my kitchen at home."

Her initial product was the simplest, Heidi's Organic Raspberry Jam. Then she did two variations, the first by adding Hawaiian ginger to make Heidi's Raspberry Ginger Jam, and the second combining the original jam with New Mexican red chiles to make Heidi's Raspberry Red Chile Jam. Finally, in a fit of creativity, she combined the two and came up with my favorite flavor, Heidi's Raspberry Red Chile Ginger Jam. If she adds anything more to it, the name of the product won't fit on the label!

Eleftheriou sells her jams at the Corrales Farmers' Market on Sundays and also at the growers' markets in downtown Albuquerque, Los Ranchos, and Santa Fe Market. So, is Eleftheriou planning any expansions, like adding strawberries or blackberries to her farms or planting mulberry trees for another unique fruit that could become a jam? In a word, no. She's the raspberry queen of New Mexico and plans on staying that way.

Heidi's Spicy Chocolate-Raspberry Muffins

The combination of the convenience and the flavor of New Mexico's specialty foods was never more evident than in this muffin recipe that utilizes Heidi's Raspberry Red Chile Jam (see profile on page 197). The organic berries are from Heidi's extensive brambles in Corrales, and the fresh berries are so fragile and the shelf life so short that only 10 percent of them are sold fresh. As jam, however, they are stable and easy to use in recipes.

2 cups all-purpose flour

½ cup sugar

2 teaspoons baking powder

½ teaspoon baking soda

6 ounces semisweet chocolate, finely chopped

1 egg

2 tablespoons butter, melted

½ cup buttermilk

1 cup Heidi's Raspberry Red Chile Jam, or other raspberry jam mixed with 1 teaspoon of red chile powder

Finely chopped pecans, for sprinkling

Heat Scale: Mild   12 MUFFINS

1. Preheat the oven to 375°F. Lightly grease a standard 12-cup muffin pan or use paper liners.

2. Blend the flour, sugar, baking powder, baking soda, and chocolate in a large bowl. Beat the egg, butter, and buttermilk in a separate bowl until smooth. Pour the egg mixture into the dry ingredients and blend well. Add the raspberry jam, gently folding it into the batter.

3. Spoon the batter into the muffin cups, filling them about three-quarters full. Sprinkle the muffins with the pecans and bake for 12 to 15 minutes, or until a toothpick inserted into the center comes out clean.

4. Cool the pan on a rack and serve the muffins warm.

Spatchcocked Game Hens with Heidi's Jam Glaze

When we think of jam, we automatically think of spreading it on bread or some other baked item. In this case, think out of the jar and onto the grill, where a spicy jam enhances a couple of Rock Cornish game hens. These small chickens are a hybrid of the Cornish and White Rock breeds. To spatchcock or butterfly the hens, place one breast side down on a cutting board and use kitchen shears to cut along each side of the backbone to remove it. Then use a paring knife to cut along the breastbone and remove it. Flatten out each hen and they're ready for the grill. These hens also could be roasted in the oven.

1½ cups balsamic vinegar

¾ cup Heidi's Raspberry Red Chile Ginger Jam, or other raspberry jam mixed with ½ teaspoon red chile powder and ½ teaspoon grated fresh ginger

Zest of 1 orange

2 tablespoons apple cider or orange juice

2 Rock Cornish hens, spatchcocked

4 tablespoons butter, melted

Salt and freshly ground black pepper

Heat Scale: Mild   2 TO 4 SERVINGS

1. Preheat the grill to medium.

2. While the grill is heating, cook the balsamic vinegar in a saucepan over medium heat until it is reduced by half, about 20 minutes. Add the jam, orange zest, and apple cider, stir well, and heat for 5 minutes longer to blend the flavors.

3. Place the hens on the grill and cook until nicely browned, about 20 minutes, turning a couple of times and basting alternately with the glaze and melted butter frequently. The hens are done when they have reached an internal temperature of 170°F on an instant-read thermometer.

4. Transfer the hens to a cutting board to rest for 5 minutes, then serve with some of the glaze drizzled over them.

Santa Fe Seasons Baked Stuffed Apples *en Croûte*

Apples, probably New Mexico's top fruit, shine when prepared as a spicy dessert with a delicious specialty sauce from Apple Canyon Gourmet's Santa Fe Seasons brand. You can make your own puff pastry, but perfectly acceptable versions are available in the frozen foods section of markets. Serve the apples with a scoop of homemade ice cream. These can be stored in the refrigerator for up to five days, but do not freeze them.

3 tablespoons lemon juice

4 tart apples, peeled and cored

1 (2-sheet) box of puff pastry, thawed overnight in the refrigerator

1 (9.5-ounce) jar Santa Fe Seasons Red Chile Cranberry Sauce, or other cranberry sauce mixed with 1 teaspoon of red chile powder

Egg wash (1 egg yolk whisked with ¼ cup water)

Heat Scale: Mild   4 SERVINGS

1. Preheat the oven to 350°F.

2. Combine the lemon juice and 1 cup of water in a bowl and roll the apples in it.

3. Using one pastry sheet from the box, cut the pastry sheet into 4 squares, each large enough to cover an apple.

4. Place an apple in the center of each square of puff pastry and fill the cores with the Red Chile Cranberry Sauce. Wrap the apples with the puff pastry and invert them onto a baking sheet. Brush the egg wash onto the pastry-covered apples and bake for 40 to 50 minutes, or until the puff pastry is golden brown.

Recipe from DORY WEGRZYN AND NERISSA MUUS, RED TRACTOR FARM

Red Tractor Farm Blue-Corn Pancakes

In recent years, blue corn has had a commercial renaissance. It has a sweeter, nuttier flavor than white or yellow field corn, which may explain why chefs such as Mark Miller popularized blue corn tortillas and ignited blue corn's renaissance at his Coyote Cafe in Santa Fe back in the '80s. The ladies at Red Tractor Farm in Albuquerque's South Valley grow blue corn and like to make blue corn pancakes stuffed with bacon and green chiles.

8 bacon strips

¼ pound roasted, peeled whole green chiles

1¾ cups blue corn flour

¾ cup unbleached all-purpose flour

1 tablespoon baking powder

½ tablespoon brown sugar

4 eggs, beaten

1¾ cups milk, or a 50/50 combination of milk and buttermilk

4 tablespoon butter, melted and slightly cooled

Maple or elderberry syrup, for serving

Heat Scale: Medium   8 PANCAKES

1. Cook the bacon in a skillet until crisp. Cut the slices in half and set aside. Cut the chiles to the size of the bacon strips. Set aside.

2. Combine the blue corn flour, white flour, baking powder, and brown sugar in a large bowl and set aside. Beat the eggs and milk in a separate bowl, then slowly add the butter.

3. Add the wet ingredients to the dry ingredients. Stir gently, until the lumps disappear. Let the batter stand for 5 minutes. Add more milk if you desire a thinner batter.

4. Prepare a medium-hot, greased griddle. Place two of the bacon strips in an X on the griddle. Place two chile pieces on top of the bacon. Ladle the pancake batter over the X. Cook until the batter is firm and then flip and repeat the procedure. Repeat with the remaining bacon, chile pieces, and batter. Serve the pancakes warm with heated maple or elderberry syrup.

Recipe from ANA BACA, BUENO FOODS

New Mexican Green Chile Quiche

Ana Baca, vice president of Bueno Foods, makes this quiche regularly in her own kitchen. Of course she recommends using her company's products but there's no law about it. That said, their frozen green chile has come in very handy on occasions when I've run out of my homemade supply. Bueno was the first company in the world to sell frozen green chile (see page 162).

1 (9.5-inch) homemade or prepared pie or tart shell

1 ear sweet corn

1 yellow onion

1 (13-ounce) container Bueno Frozen Autumn Roast Green Chile, or ¾ cup roasted and peeled green chiles

6 eggs

1 cup milk

2 tomatoes, chopped

1 teaspoon salt

½ teaspoon ground cumin

8 ounces cheddar cheese, shredded (about 1 cup)

Heat Scale: Medium   1 (9½-INCH) QUICHE

1. Preheat the oven to 425°F. Place the pastry shell in a 9½-inch pie dish and bake for 8 to 10 minutes, or until slightly browned.

2. Prepare your grill for direct grilling over medium heat. Shuck the corn and cut the onion in half. Place the corn and the onion halves on the grill and roast, turning occasionally, until both are slightly blackened, about 5 minutes. Remove from the heat and cut the kernels off the corn cob and coarsely chop the onion.

3. Place the frozen chile in a saucepan, cover, and cook on low heat until most of the liquid evaporates, 15 to 20 minutes. Meanwhile, whisk the egg and milk together in a bowl and set aside.

4. Combine the corn, tomatoes, onion, salt, and cumin in a separate bowl. Transfer the vegetable mixture to the prebaked pastry shell and reduce the oven temperature to 400°F.

5. Top the vegetable mixture with ½ cup of the cheese. Pour in the egg mixture and spread the chile evenly on top. Sprinkle with the remaining ½ cup cheese.

6. Wrap the edges of the crust with aluminum foil to prevent them from burning. Bake the quiche for 50 to 60 minutes, or until a toothpick inserted into the center comes out clean. Let the quiche stand for 10 to 15 minutes before serving.

6 Brilliant Beverages

THE TWO OLDEST wine-producing regions in the United States are New Mexico and El Paso, which was on the Camino Real, the road linking Mexico City to Santa Fe. A Franciscan friar, Augustín Rodríguez, is credited with bringing grape vines to southern New Mexico in 1580, about a hundred years before the friars in California planted their vineyards. By 1662, priests in the Mesilla Valley were regularly producing sacramental wine for Mass.

As winemaking gradually spread north, grapes, wine, and brandy were common subjects in the reports of explorers and travelers to New Mexico. In 1846, W. H. H. Davis, a traveler and the author of *El Gringo, or New Mexico and Her People*, commented about the wines of the Mesilla Valley and El Paso: "The most important production of the valley is grapes, from which are annually manufactured not less than two hundred thousand gallons of perhaps the richest and best wine in the world. This wine is worth two dollars per gallon, and constitutes the principal revenue of the city."

The European grapes that were established in southern New Mexico in the seventeenth century did well, and, by the 1800s, wine was being produced from the Mexican border to Bernalillo, which was the heart of wine production country. In the middle of the nineteenth century, New Mexico was producing more wine than California, bottling just under a million gallons in 1880. But a series of natural, economic, and political disasters ruined the wine industry, which took over a century to recover. Since the 1970s, however, many new vineyards have been planted, and New Mexico boasts some 46 wineries and numerous wine festivals.

The New Mexico Wine Festival in Bernalillo, held over the Labor Day weekend for the past 26 years, is the state's largest, with attendance of more than 20,000 people. In addition to the wineries represented, there are arts and crafts vendors, lots of live music, and plenty of New Mexican food. Featured wines include the most popular varietals produced in the state: Chardonnay, Cabernet Sauvignon, Merlot, Pinot Noir, and Chenin Blanc.

The state's brewmeisters have been brewing for nearly as long as the winemakers have been in business — both industries undergoing a forced hiatus during Prohibition, of course (see A Brief History of Beer in New Mexico, page 212). Today the state is home to a number of craft breweries that turn out quality ales and lagers to go with our favorite dishes, spicy and otherwise. And we have our own distilleries, too, for those all-important margaritas and other specialty cocktails.

SANTA FE SPIRITS DISTILLERY

JUST WALKING INTO the tasting room at Santa Fe Spirits is enough to give you a contact buzz. The barrel room of this micro-distillery on the city's south side is right off the tasting room, sending out intoxicating whiffs of the whiskey that has been aging for the last couple of years. In the tasting room, you can sample the clear whiskey called Silver Coyote or try a sip of locally sourced and produced vodka, gin, or apple brandy. I've come for the gin and apple brandy. I'm also interested in finding out why local booze matters in this economy.

"You don't *need* alcohol. We know that. It's a luxury item. So if you are going to buy it, why not buy a better product?" says owner Colin Keegan. He's referring to his micro-distilled products, which are infused with so much localism and love that you can smell it the moment you walk in the door. The apples in Santa Fe Spirits' Apple Brandy grow on about four acres on Keegan's own property. And he sources the ingredients for his gin from within a 30-mile radius of Santa Fe. Talk about hyper-local.

And they keep it even more local by throwing "picking parties" for the staff and family and friends of the distillery. At these fun get-togethers everyone picks, plucks, pulls, sorts, and stems ingredients for the spirit production. For the gin botanical parties, the crews head out to the Bonanza Creek property to pick cholla cactus blossoms. After a good rainstorm, when the cholla is in full bloom, crews armed with tin snippers and heavy gloves head out to pick as many blossoms as they can. Cactus blooms are in short supply and who knows when the next rain will come these days? At his orchard, Keegan hosts picking parties for the apple harvest as well, serving the picking crews everything from local elk to homemade apple pie. It's a family-like affair and everyone pitches in.

Designer Cocktails from Santa Fe Spirits

New Mexico's premier craft distillery offers these four updated classics (next page) featuring their own liquors along with two other locally sourced spirits, from Albuquerque and Taos. Choose among a mint julep sweetened with maple syrup, an apple brandy combined with grenadine and citrus, a Tom Collins made with New Mexican vodka, and a punch using local honey.

Maple Julep

2 ounces Silver Coyote Tequila

6 mint leaves, plus more for garnish

½ ounce pure maple syrup

Gently muddle the mint leaves and maple syrup in a tall glass. Fill the glass with crushed ice, pour in the tequila, and stir gently. Garnish with additional mint leaves.

Western Jack Rose

2 ounces Santa Fe Spirits Apple Brandy

½ ounce grenadine

½ ounce fresh lime juice or lemon juice

Apple slice, for garnish

Maraschino cherry, for garnish

Fill a cocktail shaker with ice. Pour in the apple brandy, grenadine, and lime juice, and shake. Strain into a short glass. Garnish with an apple slice and maraschino cherry.

Colin's Collins

3 ounces sparkling water

1½ ounces Expedition Vodka

½ ounce fresh lemon juice

½ ounce simple syrup

1 lemon wedge

Combine the sparkling water, vodka, lemon juice, and simple syrup in a cocktail shaker with ice. Stir gently and pour the mixture into a tall glass. Garnish with the lemon wedge.

Wheeler Peak Punch
(pictured)

½ ounce Taos Valley Honey or other local honey

1½ ounces Wheeler's Gin

½ ounce fresh lemon juice

2 ounces tonic water

Seasonal berries, for garnish

Combine the honey and 1¼ teaspoons of water in a cocktail shaker and stir. Add the gin and lemon juice and fill the shaker with ice. Shake well and strain into a tall ice-filled glass. Add the tonic water and garnish with berries.

Craft Stout Michelada

The michelada is a popular cocktail south of the border that has only recently traveled north. Essentially it's a cocktail prepared with beer and served over ice, and is very refreshing on a sweltering day. It has been touted as a surefire cure for the "tequila flu."

1 lime, preferably a Key lime

Coarse salt or margarita salt

2 dashes Worcestershire sauce

Dash soy sauce

Dash habanero hot sauce

Freshly ground black pepper

1 (12-ounce) bottle New Mexican stout or dark beer such as Marble Oatmeal Stout, Santa Fe Porter, or Java Stout

Heat Scale: Medium to hot   1 COCKTAIL

1. Cut the lime in half and rub one half around the rim of a large pint glass. Reserve the other half.

2. Pour the salt onto a plate and dip the rim of the glass in the salt to coat.

3. Fill the glass with ice and squeeze the juice from the reserved lime half into the glass. Add the Worcestershire, soy sauce, habanero hot sauce, and a few grindings of pepper to taste. Pour in the beer, stir, and serve.

A BRIEF HISTORY OF BEER IN NEW MEXICO

When George Schneider opened the Pacific Brewery in Santa Fe in 1864, he was among the first to attempt to produce beer in the state. Ten years later, breweries were operating in Elizabethtown (now a ghost town), Fort Union, Golondrinas, Lincoln, Santa Fe, and Silver City. Given that long history, New Mexico even has its own beer museum, the Hammel Museum in Socorro, which features the history of the Illinois Brewing Company.

Jacob Hammel settled in St. Louis with his friend Eberhard Anheuser, who wanted him to go into partnership in a brewery. Hammel decided to start his own brewery, the Illinois Brewing Company, instead. (Anheuser then joined forces with a guy named Busch, so things turned out pretty well for him after all.) Hammel's sons brought the family business to Socorro in the 1880s. Two of their beers were Export Beer and Magdalena Beer. A newspaper, the *Chieftain*, reported on May 29, 1884, that "Hammel's beer garden will be quite a resort in the near future. Many trees have been planted and the place promises to be a perfect little park, where one may go, and in the delicious shade, quietly enjoy a cooling glass of the foaming beverage brewed but a few yards away."

But disaster struck when Congress and the states amended the Constitution to prohibit the production, distribution, and consumption of alcoholic beverages. The Illinois Brewery was shut down and his son William Hammel died a year later, bankrupt. The beer garden building lasted long enough to become the Hammel Museum.

A few years after the Illinois Brewery came to the state, Don and Harry Rankin founded the Southwestern Brewery in Albuquerque; it was later taken over by Jacob and Henry Loebs, who were brewmasters from Germany. The five-story brewery or barrel house was one of several buildings, including a stable, built on the site in 1899. The company's mainstay beer, Glorieta, sold for a nickel

in a tall mug at local saloons with names like the White Elephant, Free & Easy, and Bucket of Blood.

By the start of the twentieth century, Southwestern Brewery was one of Albuquerque's largest employers and its flagship product, Glorieta Beer, was distributed throughout the Southwest. The enactment of Prohibition forced the company out of the brewing business, but its ice-making operations remained profitable. The facility changed hands several times, but continued to produce ice for most of the twentieth century. It finally closed in 1997.

The repeal of Prohibition in 1933 opened the way to brewing companies again. When Paul von Gontard relocated to Albuquerque from the Midwest in 1937, he raised money to purchase a struggling start-up called New Mexico Brewery. With the help of brewmaster Max Leischner, von Gontard opened the plant as the Rio Grande Brewing Company. Alas, the company went bankrupt in 1939, the beginning of a gap of nearly 50 thirsty years for fans of local brew, only relieved when the first microbrewery in New Mexico opened in 1988 (see Santa Fe Brewing Company, page 226.)

Gurlz Green Bean Bloody Mary

I love creative Bloody Mary garnishes like a long, thin section of jicama, a raw asparagus spear, or a thin section of a New Mexican chile. Picklers and Bloody Mary drinkers Maria Gamboa and Angie Rodriguez of Valley Gurlz Goodz (see profile on page 64) prefer the pickled green beans used here.

¾ cup tomato juice

¼ cup vodka

1 tablespoon Valley Gurlz Goodz Pickled Green Beans brine

2 teaspoons Worcestershire sauce

½ teaspoon bottled hot sauce

Dash of freshly ground black pepper

Dash of horseradish (optional)

2 lime wedges

2 Valley Gurlz Goods Pickled Green Beans, for garnish

Heat Scale: As hot as you like   1 COCKTAIL

1. Fill a 16-ounce glass with ice.

2. Add the tomato juice, vodka, brine, Worcestershire, hot sauce, pepper, and horseradish, if desired.

3. Squeeze the lime wedges into the glass. Stir, garnish with pickled beans, and serve.

MARBLE BREWERY

THE OPENING OF MARBLE BREWERY in 2008 was a boon to the reemergence of downtown Albuquerque. It was the first brewery to open in the city since the Rio Grande Brewery closed in 1929. Visit the company's headquarters on any day of the week and you are likely to see a wide range of people from business professionals to college students enjoying events like weekend concerts, mini beer festivals, and food-truck extravaganzas.

Of course this success would not have happened were it not for the excellent beer! Marble Brewery offers a consistent lineup of six beers, including standouts like the very hoppy IPA, the delicious Red Ale, and the mellower Wildflower Wheat, which utilizes local wildflower honey. In addition, they usually have at least a couple of specialty beers in rotation including the tasty Double White, a Belgian-inspired wheat ale that is quite refreshing on a hot summer's day.

Marble Brewery is quite the innovator. It was one of the first New Mexico breweries to use locally grown hops, which they still source from farmer Mike de Smet. The brewery recently launched a beer in honor of the popular television series *Breaking Bad*, which was filmed in Albuquerque and occasionally featured Marble Brewery. The beer, an India Black Ale, is called "Heisenberg's Dark" after one of the main characters, Jesse Heisenberg. Head brewer Ted Rice has also compiled a handy beer pairing guide so you know exactly how to complement your favorite style of beer!

In addition to its downtown location, Marble Brewery has a taproom in Santa Fe at the Plaza and a newly opened location on Albuquerque's Westside. All their taprooms have delightful patios, which are well suited to the enjoyable climate of New Mexico.

If you are not able to make it to the taproom locations, you are likely to see Marble beers on tap at fine restaurants throughout the state. Two such restaurants, the Grove Cafe and Market and Zinc, have dishes specifically designed to be paired with Marble's beers.

Cucumber Margarita

Local iQ writer Ben Williams says, "Of all the current mixology trends, there are two that I embrace emphatically: the use of fresh ingredients and emphasizing premium spirits. Sure, you could make a margarita with Cuervo Gold and Mrs. T's Sweet and Sour — just don't expect it to taste anything like the Patron Silver Coin you had at the hip new bar down the street where the bartender squeezed the limes right in front of your eyes. Fresh ingredients paired with a little creativity make for a doubly refreshing and rewarding beverage. Case in point: this Cucumber Margarita."

1 (1-inch) slice of cucumber, peeled, seeded, and roughly chopped

⅓ ounce agave nectar

Juice of 1 large lime

2 ounces premium silver tequila, like Herradura

⅛ ounce mescal

Cucumber wheel, for garnish

1 COCKTAIL

1. Fill a metal cocktail shaker with ice. Add the cucumber to the shaker with the agave nectar. Muddle until the ice is crushed and the cucumber is reduced to a pulp.

2. Add the lime juice and tequila. Shake well and strain into an old-fashioned glass filled with ice.

3. Top the cocktail by gently pouring the mescal on top so that it floats. Do not mix. Garnish with a cucumber wheel.

Fiery Frozen Margarita

This drink has enough basic flavors to please anyone, being sweet, spicy, salty, and sour at the same time — not to mention icy! I prefer to use the small, spherical Key limes, if possible.

8 fresh limes
Salt
1½ cups *Tequila Enchilada* (see recipe facing page)
⅓ cup Cointreau or Triple Sec
Crushed ice
4 lime slices

Heat Scale: Medium

4 COCKTAILS

1. Juice the limes. (You should have ½ cup juice.) Rub the rims of four margarita glasses (or long-stemmed goblets) with a piece of the rind. Dip the rims in the salt and then place the goblets in the freezer for at least 30 minutes.

2. Place the lime juice, tequila, and Cointreau in a blender. Add enough crushed ice to fill the blender halfway and blend.

3. Taste the result and adjust the flavors by adding more Cointreau to make it sweeter, more lime juice to make it more tart, more tequila to increase the heat level, or more ice to decrease the heat level. Pour the margarita into the frosted goblets and garnish with the lime slices.

Variation: For a milder margarita with the flavor of green chiles, substitute any New Mexican green chile wine for the fiery tequila. Several wineries in New Mexico add green chiles to their finished wines.

Tequila Enchilada
(Chilied Tequila)

This recipe is a variation on spiced vodkas but made with Mexican spices. It can be used in any drink recipe requiring tequila, or downed straight. It will keep indefinitely in your liquor cabinet and becomes stronger the longer it sits without being strained.

NOTE: This recipe requires advance preparation.

1 (750 ml) bottle white tequila
10 chiltepíns or chile piquíns
10 coriander seeds
10 black peppercorns
2 fresh cilantro sprigs
2 (2-inch) sections of lime peel
2 tablespoons salt
1 teaspoon chile piquín powder
   Lime wedges, for serving

Heat Scale: Medium   750 ML

1. Open the bottle of tequila and add the chiltepíns, coriander seeds, peppercorns, cilantro, and lime peels. Close the bottle and refrigerate for at least 4 hours. Taste for heat and spice level, then strain the added ingredients out if you're happy with it. The longer you leave the flavoring agents in, the stronger and stronger the infusion will become.

2. Combine the salt and chile powder in a shallow bowl and mix.

3. To serve, pass the lime wedges over the rims of shot glasses, dip the glasses in the salt mixture, and pour in the chilled and chilied tequila.

Prickly Pear Margarita

Les Baker, a writer for *Local iQ*, developed this recipe and I made a couple of substitutions, one of which is using Anna's Prickly Pear Margarita Mix from Santa Fe Mixes (see profile on page 175) to feature a locally made product. Baker noted, "I chose El Tesoro Reposado tequila because it is mellow and rich, with subtle wood tones and a hint of sweetness that does not overpower the agave flavor."

2 ounces Anna's Prickly Pear Margarita Mix

1½ ounces El Tesoro Reposado tequila

1 ounce fresh lime juice

½ ounce Cointreau

¼ ounce agave nectar

¼ ounce St-Germain liqueur

Lime wedge, for garnish

1 COCKTAIL

1. Fill a cocktail shaker with ice. Add the margarita mix, tequila, lime juice, Cointreau, and agave nectar.

2. Shake *very* vigorously. Salt the rim of a rocks glass by running a lime wedge around the rim and then dipping it in salt. Fill it with crushed ice and pour in the drink. Use a bar spoon to mix.

3. Gently pour the St-Germain on top so that it floats. Do not stir. Garnish with a lime wedge and serve.

Zingtopia Sparkler

The folks at Villa Myriam (see profile on facing page) make their Zingtopia juices in a number of different flavors, most of them exotic and unique. This refreshing, nonalcoholic summer cooler makes great use of any of them. Multiply the ingredients to make a full pitcher to serve by the pool.

8 ounces sparkling water
1 ounce Zingtopia juice
¼ lemon

1 SERVING

Fill a tall glass with 1½ cups of crushed ice. Add the sparkling water, juice, and a squeeze of lemon juice. Mix well and serve.

VILLA MYRIAM

WHEN MOST PEOPLE SAY coffee runs in their blood, they usually mean they really enjoy coffee, but in the case of Villa Myriam owners David and Juan Certain, they actually mean it! The brothers are originally from Colombia, where their grandfather owned a coffee-producing hacienda in the lush green hills of Piendamo. Colombia has a rich tradition of coffee production, and coffee from the Piendamo area is among the most exceptional in the world, with a very balanced acidic profile and smooth taste. The Certains' grandfather built the coffee hacienda in the 1960s in honor of his daughter Myriam. It is still family owned and the owners maintain the same high quality control standards.

The Certains spent their childhood learning about coffee, including how to spot the perfect bean and understand the highly technical roasting process. In addition, they gained an appreciation for the work that goes into harvesting great coffee beans by hand, as it still is today. This childhood experience served the brothers well when they launched Villa Myriam in 2011 shortly after their move to Albuquerque. At first, it was a small, single-source roaster. But before long, they opened their own café and began supplying coffee to a number of popular establishments such as the Range Cafe, the Standard Diner, and the Hotel Parq Central.

The consistency, quality, and freshness of Villa Myriam coffee is undeniable. Their three main coffees are Juan's Roast (medium-dark), David's Roast (medium), and Ron's Roast (espresso). Villa Myriam also produces seasonal roasts and special roasts for many of its restaurant clients.

Besides the delicious coffee, the other thing that sets Villa Myriam apart is that their coffee is both Rainforest Alliance Certified and UTZ Certified (*utz kapeh* is Mayan for "good coffee"), meaning that they use sustainable farming practices and are committed to maintaining the biodiversity of the area as well as the economic livelihood of the farmers so you can enjoy their coffee and feel good about it!

The Certains have also developed a product line called Zingtopia, a unique and flavorful line of exotic fruit juices from Colombia in easy-to-use packaging. Just as with their coffee, Juan and David ensure that the juices are all-natural. The juice flavors include Bana, Lulo, Maca, Paya, Uvvo, and Verde.

My personal favorite is Bana, which comes from the tropical fruit *gunabana* (soursop) and has a delicious citrus flavor but at the same time is creamy like coconut or banana. The Zingtopia Sparkler (facing page) is a simple, yet great, addition to any summer drink lineup, and with all the different flavors mentioned above, it is unlikely you'll become bored drinking them anytime soon. Zingtopia is extremely versatile; it tastes great poured over ice cream or yogurt and makes a splash in fruity cocktails.

Café Diablo

At last, here's a use for that chafing dish you couldn't give away at your last yard sale! Use it to make this flaming coffee known in some circles as *café brûlot*. However, it is doubtful that the French would spice it up quite as much as we do in New Mexico. This recipe is adapted from one by John Philips Cranwell in *The Hellfire Cookbook* (1975).

1 (½-inch by 2-inch) piece and 4 small twists of lemon peel

1 (½-inch by 2-inch) piece of orange peel

5 small sugar cubes

1 teaspoon finely ground ancho or pasilla chile

¼ teaspoon ground cloves

¼ teaspoon ground cinnamon

1½ cups cognac

¼ teaspoon vanilla extract

3 cups hot strong brewed coffee

Heat Scale: Mild

4 COCKTAILS

1. Combine the larger piece of lemon peel, the orange peel, 4 of the sugar cubes, the chile, cloves, cinnamon, cognac, and vanilla in the bottom pan of a chafing dish and bring to a simmer over low heat.

2. Put a large metal ladle into the mixture and heat until the ladle is hot, a matter of a few seconds. Fill the ladle almost full with the mixture and add the remaining sugar cube. Ignite the mixture in the ladle. When it is burning well, carefully pour the contents of the ladle into the chafing dish. This will set the mixture on fire.

3. Add the coffee to the chafing dish and mix well. When the flame has subsided, place a twist of lemon peel into each of 4 small cups and pour the coffee mixture over the top. Serve immediately.

Recipe from BEN WILLIAMS, *LOCAL IQ*

Biscochito in a Glass

Developed by Ben Williams and first published in the biweekly *Local iQ*, this drink was inspired by the official New Mexico State Cookie. Ben writes, "Much like its confectionary counterpart, there are many variations of the biscochito cocktail that have been unselfishly shared by past generations of local barkeeps. The warm cocktail is designed to emulate the semisweet, anise-laced pastry dunked in a hot cup of coffee, which is my favorite way to enjoy it."

1 ounce Tia Maria liqueur

1 ounce White Sambuca

2 ounces half-and-half, steamed or warmed

Ground cinnamon, for garnish

1 COCKTAIL

Combine the Tia Maria and White Sambuca in a warm snifter. Top with the half-and-half and dust with cinnamon before serving.

Royal Chocolate with Chile

Although this drink was once served to royalty in the large Mayan cities, the discovery of chile peppers in conjunction with cacao at the Cerén archaeological site indicates that even commoners knew how to make this concoction. Simple to prepare, this spicy drink is more bitter than most hot chocolate but will warm you much quicker than mundane hot chocolate with marshmallows.

¼ cup unsweetened cocoa powder

¼ teaspoon hot chile powder, such as piquín

1 tablespoon local honey

1 vanilla bean pod

Heat Scale: Medium

1 SERVING

Bring 1½ cups water to a boil in a small saucepan. Add the cocoa, chile powder, and honey, and stir to mix. Pour into a mug, garnish with the vanilla bean, and serve immediately.

Java Stout Bundt Cake

A stout dessert? This surprising recipe produces a rich, moist cake full of complex flavor. A porter or dark ale would work just as well. Adding a scoop of ice cream would make this a truly decadent end to any meal.

1 cup (2 sticks) unsalted butter, plus more for greasing the pan

Unsweetened cocoa powder

2½ cups all-purpose flour

¾ teaspoon baking soda

½ teaspoon kosher salt

¾ cup coffee stout, preferably Santa Fe Brewing Imperial Java Stout, or another dark beer

12 ounces semisweet chocolate, roughly chopped

1 cup firmly packed dark brown sugar

1 cup granulated sugar

3 eggs

½ cup sour cream

½ cup heavy cream

8 SERVINGS

1. Preheat the oven to 350°F.

2. Butter a 12-cup Bundt pan and dust it with cocoa powder, tapping out the excess.

3. Whisk together the flour, baking soda, and salt in a medium bowl and set aside.

4. Combine the butter and stout in a small saucepan. Cook over medium heat, stirring, until the butter melts. Remove the saucepan from the heat, add 8 ounces of the chocolate, and whisk until smooth.

5. Beat the 1 cup brown sugar, granulated sugar, and eggs with an electric mixer on medium-high until fluffy. Beat in the chocolate mixture and sour cream. Reduce the speed to low and gradually add the flour mixture until just combined. Do not overmix.

6. Pour the batter into the prepared pan and bake for 45 to 55 minutes, or until a toothpick inserted into the center comes out with just a few moist crumbs attached. Let the cake cool for 30 minutes in the pan, then invert it onto a rack to cool completely.

7. When the cake is completely cool, bring the heavy cream just to a boil in a small saucepan over high heat. Remove the saucepan from the heat, add the remaining 4 ounces chocolate, and let sit for 5 minutes. Whisk until smooth.

8. Set the cooling rack with the cake over a large baking sheet. Drizzle the cake with the glaze and let set before serving.

SANTA FE BREWING COMPANY

SANTA FE BREWING is a groundbreaker on the New Mexico beer scene. When they opened in 1988, they were the first microbrewery in New Mexico. Currently the state's largest brewery, they distribute beer throughout the Southwest. In 2010, they became the first brewery in New Mexico to start canning most of their beers, starting with the Freestyle Pilsner in the bright green can and the very popular Happy Camper IPA, which looks like the New Mexico state flag on a beer can and makes local beer drinkers proud to hoist a few.

Many breweries might settle for being the oldest and biggest brewery in the state, but Santa Fe Brewing is constantly seeking to push the envelope with their beers. Since taking over in 2003, owner Brian Locke has pushed the company to new levels from its humble roots in Galisteo. This included moving their main Santa Fe location to a bigger building in 2005, where facilities include a large tasting room and an excellent outdoor stage for hosting concerts, celebrations, and events. They also still have a smaller tasting room in town.

Santa Fe Brewing produces more than 20,000 barrels of beer annually and is always aiming to increase that amount. In addition to the sheer quantity of microbrew they produce, Santa Fe Brewing releases a robust lineup of seasonal beers. These include the age-old favorite Chicken Killer Barleywine (one of the few beers they don't can), the Black IPA, the Oktoberfest, and the Imperial Java Stout, which uses locally roasted coffee from Ohori's Coffee House.

Most recently, Santa Fe Brewing released their Saison 88 to celebrate their 25th anniversary. Saison 88 (*saison* being French for season) is a balanced summer beer with citrus notes as well as a slight spice that creates a very refreshing beverage. The Saison, in its distinctive can, is easy to spot in Santa Fe on the north side of town.

Recipe from SANTA FE BREWING COMPANY

Brewmaster Brats

We're not speaking about the unruly kids of brewers here, but rather my favorite sausage, the bratwurst. Brats and beer are an unbeatable combination for dinner, but what would happen if you marinated the brats overnight in a craft beer? If you can't resist finding out, try this recipe from Santa Fe Brewing Company. With this method, the beer flavor really comes through because the sausage is not overly cooked.

NOTE: This recipe requires advance preparation.

10 bratwursts

3 white onions, chopped

2 green bell peppers, seeded and chopped

2 (12-ounce) bottles Santa Fe Pale Ale, chilled

10 hot dog/bratwurst buns

Spicy mustard, for serving

5 TO 10 SERVINGS

1. Prepare the grill for direct grilling. Take the brats and do a very quick sear on the grill over high heat for 3 minutes just to brown the outside — they are not cooked at all, just browned.

2. Place the brats, onions, and peppers in a stainless steel pot and pour the beer on top. Cover and refrigerate overnight.

3. About 30 minutes before you want to eat, put the pot on the stove over low heat and bring to a simmer. Simmer until the brats are cooked through and the onions and peppers are barely softened, about 20 minutes.

4. Drain the brats, onions, and peppers. Serve the brats on the buns topped with the cooked onions and peppers, and a slather of spicy mustard.

Turkey and Porter Chili

This is the Santa Fe Brewing Company's beery take on one of New Mexico's favorite dishes. Now, what do you suppose should be your beverage of choice while gobbling down this bowl o' red? This chili freezes nicely for up to three months.

5 pounds ground turkey

2 tablespoons canola oil

2½ pounds yellow onions, chopped

1½ pounds red bell peppers, seeded and chopped

1½ pounds yellow bell peppers, seeded and chopped

2 jalapeño chiles with seeds, finely chopped

7 tablespoons chili powder

2 teaspoons chipotle chiles in adobo sauce, minced

2 (28-ounce) cans crushed tomatoes

2 (15-ounce) cans kidney beans, drained

1 (12-ounce) bottle porter, preferably State Pen Porter

Salt and freshly ground black pepper

Sour cream, for garnish

Shredded cheddar cheese, for garnish

Chopped scallions, for garnish

Heat Scale: Medium   12 OR MORE SERVINGS

1. Sauté the ground turkey in a large pot over medium-high heat, stirring occasionally and breaking it up with a spoon, until cooked through, 10 to 15 minutes.

2. Heat the canola oil in a medium pot or skillet over medium heat, and sauté the onions, bell peppers, and jalapeños , stirring occasionally, until softened, about 10 minutes.

3. Transfer the vegetables to the pot with the cooked ground turkey. Mix in the chili powder and chipotle chiles. Cook over medium heat, stirring frequently, for 5 minutes.

4. Add the tomatoes, beans, and porter to the pot. Bring to a boil, stirring occasionally. Reduce the heat to low and simmer, uncovered, for about 20 minutes, stirring often. Salt and pepper to taste.

5. Serve in bowls garnished with sour cream, cheddar cheese, and scallions.

Recipe from VIVÁC WINERY

Dolcetto Wine Pizza Sauce

The Vivác Winery (see facing page) makes a rather unique pizza sauce by incorporating their Dolcetto red wine into the recipe. After spreading it over the pizza dough, Jesse and Chris Padberg sprinkle on a generous layer of grated mozzarella, then top the pizza with mushrooms, crumbled chorizo sausage, and onions. Want to bet that they serve it with Vivác Dolcetto?

This sauce can also be served over cooked pasta. Store it in the refrigerator for up to five days. It freezes well.

1 (28-ounce) can whole peeled tomatoes

1 (6-ounce) can tomato paste

¼ cup olive oil

4 garlic cloves, minced

¼ cup chopped fresh Italian parsley

1½ teaspoons salt

½ cup dry red wine, preferably Vivác Dolcetto

ABOUT 1 QUART

1. Mix the tomatoes and paste together in a medium bowl; set aside.

2. Warm the olive oil over medium-low heat in a large saucepan, then add the garlic and cook for a few minutes, stirring occasionally, but do not let it brown.

3. Pour the tomato mixture into the saucepan and stir; cook over medium heat for 10 minutes.

4. Add the parsley, salt, and wine to the saucepan. Reduce the heat to low and simmer, stirring occasionally, until the sauce thickens, about 15 minutes. Remove from the heat and use in your favorite pizza recipe.

VIVÁC WINERY

THE BEAUTIFUL TOWN OF DIXON is nestled in the lush Embudo Valley near the Rio Grande between Taos and Santa Fe. This idyllic location is the backdrop for Vivác Winery, whose name in Spanish means "high-altitude refuge." Inspired by traditional winemaking culture in Italy and France, brothers Jesse and Chris Padberg and their wives, Michele and Liliana, started Vivác in 2003.

The property includes a tasting room and gallery at the intersection of Highways 75 and 68 where visitors can taste delicious wines and browse for accessories such as corkscrews, wine racks, and glasses. Plus, there is a lot of literature available for true connoisseurs. The organically farmed vineyard next door produces some of the grapes used in Vivác's wines. Most of their grapes come from southern New Mexico's Mimbres Valley, currently the state's only American Viticultural Area (AVA), due to its distinctive growing conditions and features. Vivác hopes at some point to make Embudo Valley an AVA as well, which will allow them to get more of their grapes from their own backyard.

Jesse and Michele are certified executive sommeliers. For the best wines to use in both cooking and drinking, their first recommendation is a dry Rosé of Dolcetto, made in a traditional way with short exposure to skins and free run juice. Dry rosés are very food friendly and Vivác is currently the only winery in the state making one in this style.

Their next recommendation is the Refosco, the name of the wine and the grape, which is very rare to see as a varietal release. It has incredible aging ability, which transforms the young, fruity, lush wine into one with a dense dried-fruit flavor profile. The Refosco is also amazing paired with strong cheeses like blue or cheddar and smoked meats like bacon, making it one of the only bold reds to knock your socks off with a savory salad!

Finally, the couple recommends the Divino red wine blend. This wine is part of their Heaven and Hell artist series, in which they release two wines as a pair. The Divino, the lighter wine in its set, has a spectacular versatility with food. Primarily a Nebbiolo base, this wine has the depth to pair with exotic foods while not compromising more ordinary fare.

Recipe from SANTA FE SPIRITS

Apple Brandy Crepes

This delicious recipe for a slightly sweetened crepe is fantastic for dessert, breakfast, or brunch. Serve with either crème fraîche or vanilla ice cream to take this dish to the next level! Those marinated apples are pretty great on their own, too!

4 small apples, peeled, cored, and thinly sliced

½ cup plus 4 tablespoons Santa Fe Spirits Apple Brandy

1 tablespoon plus 1 teaspoon all-purpose flour

1 tablespoon plus 1 teaspoon sugar

Kosher salt

4 eggs, at room temperature

⅓ cup heavy cream

½ teaspoon vanilla extract

3 tablespoons plus 1 teaspoon unsalted butter, softened

Confectioners' sugar, for garnish

Caramel sauce, for garnish

4 SERVINGS

1. Put the apple slices in a small bowl and pour ½ cup of the brandy over them. Marinate at room temperature for 30 minutes.

2. Whisk the flour, sugar, a pinch of salt, the eggs, heavy cream, and vanilla in a medium bowl until blended.

3. Heat ½ tablespoon of the butter in an 8-inch nonstick skillet over medium-high heat. Add ⅓ cup of the batter and cook until the bottom is golden brown, about 2 minutes.

4. Flip the crepe, remove the skillet from the heat, and add 1 tablespoon of the brandy to the skillet around the edges of the crepe. Return the skillet to the heat and cook until the brandy thickens slightly, about 20 seconds. Repeat to make 3 more crepes. Keep the crepes warm in the oven as you make the rest.

5. Slide each crepe onto a plate, then spread with butter and dust with confectioners' sugar. Drizzle caramel sauce over the warm crepe. Serve with the sliced apples.

7 Nuts, Fruits, and Extraordinary Desserts

EVEN DESSERTS are influenced by New Mexico's ubiquitous "state vegetable": Of the 23 dessert recipes in this chapter, 8 of them have green or red chiles as an ingredient. But one of the main reasons green chiles appear in the nationally famous New Mexican Green Chile–Apple Pie is that fruits go well with other fruits, and we've learned in this book that the chile is a fruit, not a vegetable. But why red chile in pecan pie? That's just because New Mexicans are nuts about desserts — literally. Our two main nut crops, pistachios and pecans, are used mostly in desserts and candies.

For instance, Marianne Schweers, owner of Heart of the Desert Pistachios in Alamogordo, sells 12 different pistachio candies and 2 pecan candies, and she has 16 pistachio dessert recipes on her website. Her main competitor, McGinn's Pistachio Tree Ranch, sells the Atomic Hot Chile Pistachio Brittle that beat out more than five hundred other products to win the grand prize two years running in my annual food contest, the Scovie Awards Competition.

And then there is the inspiring story of how the New Mexico State Cookie — which really is a cookie — became famous and inspired a cookie business launch. In a state that takes its cookies as seriously as chiles and nuts, biscochitos — anise-flavored sugar cookies — were named the New Mexico State Cookie in 1989, making them the only official state cookie in the country.

Celina Aldaz-Grife, an Albuquerque real estate agent, enjoyed giving her clients small packages of these traditional delicacies at Christmas. They were made from her Grandma Maggie's authentic family recipe that had been passed down through generations (the secret is using lard, not butter or shortening).

As word spread about Aldaz-Grife's special biscochitos, the delectable treats became so popular that perfect strangers would stop her to ask if they could buy some. With an established customer base, an exceptional traditional recipe, and a struggling housing market, Aldaz-Grife took the hint. She left her real estate job, recruited her husband, David, and officially started Celina's Biscochitos in 2010. Current varieties include traditional, lemon, and a newly released red chile version — see what I mean? Special orders are fulfilled for celebrations such as weddings, baptisms, baby showers, and more. Celina's Biscochitos are sold at local farmers' markets, candy shops, and online.

So might I suggest a dessert that combines biscochitos with a cup of Royal Chocolate with Chile from the beverages chapter?

NUTS ABOUT NEW MEXICO

Though chile peppers are the state's iconic crop, the pecan industry is actually more valuable, as evidenced by the huge pecan groves that stretch north and south of Las Cruces. Pecan trees were introduced to New Mexico from Texas and northern Mexico and planted at the Fabian Garcia Agricultural Science Center in Mesilla in 1915 and 1916. The original planting was just four acres, and many of those trees are still producing. The main problem with the trees is their water consumption. A single, mature tree uses as much water during the growing season as an acre of chile plants!

The first recorded commercial pecan production in New Mexico was in 1920, when a mere 626 pounds were harvested. By the '60s, orchards totaled 6,000 acres. It takes a lot of room to grow pecans, and with the nut's increasing popularity, the state now has more than 25,000 acres planted with 1.3 million trees, an average of about 52 trees per acre. In 2006, 46 million pounds of pecans were produced, and growers in New Mexico rejoiced at earning the title of America's number one pecan producer.

By contrast, Texas has more than 70 million pecan trees, but most of them are wild. The saying that "Texans will buy anything with pecans in it," bodes well for the New Mexico crop.

Pistachios

Also in the shell game of nut growing in New Mexico are pistachios, though on a much smaller scale. They thrive in the Tularosa Basin because the climate and altitude are quite similar to those of Iran and Turkey, noted pistachio-growing regions. Pistachio trees are smaller than pecans, growing only about 30 feet tall, so many more trees can be planted per acre, about 120. They are hardy and tolerant of drought and alkaline soils and can live to be hundreds of years old.

The primary pistachio grower in New Mexico is Eagle Ranch Pistachio Groves in Alamogordo, which markets the tasty nuts under the name "Heart of the Desert." Eagle Ranch is owned by Marianne and George Schweers, who started their groves in 1974 with 200 two-year-old trees. They now have more than 3,000 trees and can harvest as much as 1,800 pounds of pistachios an acre.

The Alamogordian pistachios are marketed in small designer burlap bags and sold by mail order and in gift shops. These "health nuts" are cholesterol-free, high in fiber, and low in saturated fats. They are a popular snack; a wonderful ingredient in pâtés, sausages, and ice cream; and a good substitute for other nuts in cooking. They make an excellent pesto if piñon nuts cannot be found.

Piñon Nuts

New Mexico's State Tree, the tough piñon tree (*Pinus edulis*), was nearly as important to Native Americans of the Southwest as the bison was to the tribes of the Great Plains. The Ramah Navajo, for example, utilized all parts of the tree in their daily lives and gave credit in legend to the squirrel for planting the first piñon tree.

The only problem with the nuts of the piñon is that there aren't enough of them to go around. The cones containing the nuts mature during the second year after flowering, and this fact combined with weather variations results in a good crop of nuts in the same region only every four or five years. The crop depends on the amount of moisture received each year, and insufficient rainfall in the years preceding flowering means a scant supply of nuts from a given tree.

And once ripe, the tasty nuts are devoured in great quantities by deer, turkeys, javelinas, bears, birds, squirrels, and other rodents. But probably the most voracious consumer of piñons is mankind, cracking some three to five million pounds of the nuts that are collected each year in the Southwest and Mexico.

Pecan grove

Recipe from JIM HEYWOOD, FORMERLY OF THE CULINARY INSTITUTE OF AMERICA

Red Pepper–spiced Pecans and Dried Cranberries

The recipe for this great cocktail snack was provided by my late friend Chef Jim Heywood, a former associate professor at the Culinary Institute of America in Hyde Park, New York. The nuts are both salty and mildly spicy, so when you bite into a cranberry, the sweetness is a pleasant, tasty surprise. Jim liked to use Spanish paprika rather than the Hungarian type (which is darker) and table salt rather than sea salt, as it sticks to the nuts better. This snack will keep for a couple of weeks in a sealed container at room temperature.

1 pound raw pecan halves
½ pound dried cranberries
1 tablespoon light brown sugar
1 tablespoon Spanish paprika
1 teaspoon cayenne pepper
2 teaspoons salt
4 tablespoons butter

Heat Scale: Medium   1½ POUNDS

1. Toss the pecans and cranberries together in a large bowl.

2. Combine the sugar, paprika, cayenne, and salt in a small bowl and stir to mix.

3. Heat a skillet over medium heat and add the butter. Cook the butter until it gets foamy and has a nutty aroma, about 5 minutes, stirring occasionally and being careful that it doesn't burn.

4. Pour the brown butter over the nuts and cranberries, and toss well to coat. Add the sugar mixture to the nuts and cran-berries, and toss well to coat. Allow to cool to room tempera-ture and serve.

Green Chile–Piñon Pesto

This southwestern adaptation of the Italian specialty uses green chiles, spinach, and parsley in place of the traditional basil in the pesto. It has a very concentrated flavor, as do all pestos, so a little bit goes a long way. Toss this pesto with hot pasta instead of using a traditional sauce. It's also good on grilled meats or fish, burgers, and sandwiches. Store the pesto in the refrigerator for up to five days or freeze it.

1½ cups fresh spinach

½ cup fresh cilantro or parsley

1 tablespoon chopped fresh basil

6 New Mexican green chiles, roasted, peeled, and stems and seeds removed

3 garlic cloves

2 tablespoons piñon nuts

1 tablespoon lime juice

¼–½ cup vegetable oil

Salt and freshly ground black pepper

Heat Scale: Mild   1½ CUPS

1. Combine the spinach, cilantro, and basil in a food processor or blender and pulse to finely chop.

2. Add the chiles, garlic, nuts, and lime juice, and continue to pulse until a coarse paste forms.

3. With the machine running, slowly add just enough of the oil to make a smooth paste. (You may not need all of the oil.) Salt and pepper to taste.

Margarita Pie

My live-in pastry chef, Mary Jane, also known as my wife, developed this refreshing, alcoholic dessert with a crunchy crust. As she says, "What more can you ask for? It's just like a margarita, except you eat it with a fork." The recipe comes together quickly, and can be made ahead of time and chilled.

NOTE: If you do not want to use raw egg whites, you can substitute ⅓ cup heavy cream. Whip the cream and slowly add the remaining ½ cup of sugar and fold into the chilled, cooked mixture.

CRUST

- 1 cup coarsely crushed salted pretzels
- ⅓ cup plus 3 tablespoons butter, melted

FILLING

- ¼ cup lemon juice
- ¼ cup lime juice
- 1 (¼-ounce) envelope plain gelatin
- 4 eggs, separated
- 1 cup sugar
- ¼ teaspoon salt
- ½ teaspoon finely grated lemon zest
- ½ teaspoon finely grated lime zest
- ⅓ cup white tequila
- 3 tablespoons Triple Sec or other orange liqueur

1. Make the crust: Combine the pretzels and butter in a small bowl and mix. Press the mixture into the bottom and sides of a 9-inch pie pan and chill for 1 hour.

2. Make the filling: Pour the lemon juice and lime juice into a small bowl and sprinkle the gelatin over the top. Let stand until the gelatin is soft.

3. Place the egg yolks in the top of a double boiler. While heating slowly, beat in ½ cup of the sugar, the salt, lemon zest, and lime zest. Add the gelatin mixture and cook over gently boiling water, stirring constantly, until the mixture is slightly thickened, about 5 minutes.

4. Transfer the egg yolk mixture to a medium bowl and blend in the tequila and Triple Sec. Chill the filling for 1 hour, uncovered.

5. Beat the egg whites in a separate bowl until foamy. While beating, gradually add the remaining ½ cup sugar. Continue beating the egg whites until they form stiff peaks. Gently fold the egg whites into the chilled egg yolk mixture.

6. Pour the filling into the crust and chill for 1 hour, or until firm.

New Mexican Green Chile–Apple Pie

I think New Mexicans will put chile in anything. I remember a visit by John T. Edge of the Southern Foodways Alliance, who was in Albuquerque researching green chile pies for his food history book and cookbook, *Apple Pie: An American Story*. He was researching the origin and popularity of the only spicy apple pie he had ever come across, and he featured it in the book. His recipe is very similar to this one from chef Shawn Weed.

APPLE FILLING

- 4 large Granny Smith apples, peeled, cored, and cut into ½-inch slices
- 1 cup sugar
- ½ cup chopped Bueno Frozen Autumn Roast Green Chiles, or 3 green chiles, roasted, peeled, and chopped
- 3 tablespoons flour
- 3 teaspoons ground cinnamon
- ¾ teaspoon ground nutmeg
- 1 tablespoon lemon juice

DOUGH

- 1½ cups flour
- 1 teaspoon ground cinnamon
- 1 teaspoon salt
- ¼ teaspoon baking powder
- 4 tablespoons cold, salted butter
- ¼ cup shortening
- 1 egg
- 1 teaspoon distilled white vinegar

Heat Scale: Mild   1 (9-INCH) PIE

1. Preheat the oven to 425°F. Spray a 9-inch pie pan with cooking spray and set aside.

2. Make the filling: Combine the apples, sugar, chiles, flour, cinnamon, nutmeg, and lemon juice in a large bowl. Mix well and set aside to blend flavors while preparing the crust.

3. Make the dough: Combine the flour, cinnamon, salt, and baking powder in a large bowl, then cut in the butter and shortening.

4. Whisk the egg, vinegar, and ½ cup ice water together in a separate bowl. Add the egg mixture to the flour mixture and blend with your hands until the dry ingredients are moistened. If the mixture is still dry after adding all the egg mixture, slowly add more ice water 1 tablespoonful at a time.

5. Divide the dough into two sections. Roll out one section on a lightly floured work surface to fit a 9-inch pie pan. Place the crust into the pan. Spoon the apple-chile mixture into the pan, forming a mound in the center of the crust. Roll out the second section of dough and place that crust over the pan. Press the edges together and flute, then cut three small vent holes into the center of the top crust.

6. Bake the pie for 15 minutes, then reduce the temperature to 400°F and bake for 1 hour longer. The pie is done when the juices bubbles up around the edges and the crust is golden brown.

Easy New Mexico–style Apple Pie á la Mode

Believe it or not, New Mexicans often add green chiles to fruit pies, with winning results, so feel free to add a ½ cup of chopped chiles while cooking the apples if you wish. Using New Mexico–grown apples and pecans makes this liberal interpretation of traditional apple pie even more of a southwestern favorite.

¼ cup sugar

1 tablespoon cornstarch

½ teaspoon ground cinnamon

2½ tablespoons butter

¼ cup brandy

2 medium baking apples, peeled, cored, and thinly sliced

½ cup roughly chopped pecans

16 Celina's Biscochitos, or substitute other sugar cookies

Vanilla ice cream, for serving

4 SERVINGS

1. Mix together the sugar, cornstarch, and cinnamon in a medium bowl.

2. Heat a skillet over medium-high heat. Add the butter and, once it melts, add the brandy. Whisk the cinnamon-sugar mixture into the skillet and cook for 2 minutes, stirring well.

3. Add the apples and pecans to the skillet. Stir until all the apples and nuts are coated with the sauce. Continue to cook the apples, stirring occasionally, until they are soft and tender, 10 to 15 minutes. Remove the mixture from the heat and let cool slightly before assembling the dessert.

4. To assemble, place 4 biscochitos on a dessert plate. Add a scoop of vanilla ice cream. Top with one quarter of the caramelized apple mixture and crumbled biscochitos. Repeat with the remaining cookies, ice cream, and caramelized apple mixture.

Recipe from ANDREA SCHULTE, NEW MEXICO PIE COMPANY

Pie Shake

This recipe was invented by Andrea Schulte of New Mexico Pie Company, and she's prejudiced, of course, advising that this shake is especially wonderful made with a slice of the company's Caramel Apple Green Chile Pie, but any of your favorite pies will do nicely. If using pecan pie or any variety with whole nuts or large pieces of fruit, cut it into small chunks before blending. You'll need a spoon to finish this delicious treat — a straw just won't do the trick.

1 large slice pie, about ¼ of a 9-inch pie

2 large scoops vanilla ice cream

2 tablespoons milk

2 SERVINGS

Combine the pie, ice cream, and milk in a blender and pulse until the ice cream and milk are blended, but some chunks of pie still remain. Divide the milk shake between 2 tall glasses and start slurping!

NEW MEXICO PIE COMPANY

"PIE IS COMING BACK," owner Andrea Schulte says, explaining the growing trend for replacing the traditional cake with pie at events like weddings. New Mexico Pie Company is the culmination of more than a decade of Shulte's professional pastry and culinary arts experience. Numerous awards, including the New Mexico Chocolate Fantasy and National Bacardi Classic, have put New Mexico Pie Company in the spotlight. With a mission of offering handmade sweet and savory pies using simple, pure flavors and natural local ingredients, Schulte satisfies every taste.

Pies range from classic — pecan, pumpkin, and seasonal fruit — to several with a modern New Mexico twist — caramel apple green chile, chocolate pecan red chile, and a savory turkey green chile cheddar handpie. Seasonal quiches, cookies, and traditional biscochitos round out the delicious offerings, and Schulte makes each product with unadulterated ingredients such as unbleached flour, cage-free eggs, and pure butter and cream cheese instead of shortening.

For the future, in addition to catering, Schulte plans to open a retail bakery to expand her operation and allow the company to grow.

Andrea Shulte

Double Pepper–infused Strawberries

According to the California Strawberry Advisory Board, 90 percent of Americans eat strawberries, consuming more than five pounds of fresh or frozen berries per person annually. Here's a slightly shocking way to use up some of your annual amount: a dish in which the sharp flavors of the pepper tequila and black pepper strangely complement the sweetness of the strawberries. You can enjoy them by the bowlful, perhaps with a few crisp sugar cookies or some buttery shortbread on the side. Or serve them over a scoop of vanilla or dark chocolate ice cream. (A truly daring chilehead might choose a chile-infused ice cream.)

¼ cup tequila

2 piquín chiles, crushed

4 pints of strawberries, hulled and halved (about 6 cups)

2 teaspoons freshly ground black pepper

½ cup orange juice

2 teaspoons balsamic vinegar

Fresh mint sprigs, for garnish

Heat Scale: Mild
6 SERVINGS

1. Pour the tequila over the chiles in a small bowl. Soak for 1 to 4 hours before straining. The longer you leave the chiles, the stronger the flavor will be.

2. Combine the strawberries, pepper, orange juice, vinegar, and infused tequila in a bowl and toss well. Cover and chill for at least 3 hours, stirring occasionally.

3. Spoon the mixture into 6 small glass bowls and garnish with mint sprigs before serving.

Red Chile–Piñon Ganache

This ganache is wonderful spread on biscochitos or shortbread cookies. To turn the ganache into a chocolate sauce, increase the cream to 1½ cups. For a firmer ganache to use for making truffles, reduce the cream to 1 cup. Always use the best ingredients available. This ganache will keep for up to two weeks in a sealed container in the refrigerator, but it's unlikely to last that long once your family and friends get a taste.

1 pound semisweet dark chocolate (55 percent), roughly chopped

1¼ cups heavy cream

2 tablespoons medium-hot red chile powder

2 tablespoons agave nectar

2 tablespoons unsalted butter, softened

2½ ounces (½ cup) piñon nuts, toasted and finely chopped

1 tablespoon ground cinnamon

Heat Scale: Mild ABOUT 3½ CUPS

1. Place the chocolate in a large metal bowl and set aside.

2. Heat the cream in a saucepan over medium heat. Once it is warm but before it reaches a boil, add the chile powder and stir to mix completely. Add the agave nectar and stir to mix completely.

3. Bring the cream just to a boil, then pour it over the chocolate. Let the cream and chocolate mixture sit for 1 minute to melt the chocolate.

4. Stir the chocolate-cream mixture, starting with small circles in the center of the bowl. Gradually expand the stirring to incorporate all of the chocolate. The mixture will become shiny with a puddinglike consistency. This mixture is now a ganache.

5. If all the chocolate has not melted, reheat the bowl over a pan of hot water. Heat just until the chocolate has melted to avoid overcooking. Keep in mind that the chocolate and the bowl will retain heat after you remove it from the hot water.

6. Add the butter and stir to incorporate completely. Stir in the piñon nuts and cinnamon. Let the ganache sit for 5 minutes to set, then stir again to encourage the ganache to complete setting. If making a soft ganache, it is now ready to spread or pour.

7. To make truffles, let the ganache set until firm in the refrigerator (overnight is fine), then scoop it into balls with a melon baller. The ganache centers can then be dipped in tempered chocolate, rolled in cocoa powder, or finished to your liking.

WHAT THE FUDGE!

APPLES HAVE ALWAYS BEEN part of Valerie Clark's life. As a child growing up north of Santa Fe, she helped in the family orchard by picking up apples off the ground that didn't quite make the cut for market. Decades later, she moved to Albuquerque, married a man who owned a candy company, and started to experiment with combinations of apples, caramel, chocolate, and other sweets. Today, Clark makes delectable, gourmet caramel apples that are primarily available through a heartfelt, community-based program.

Her company, What the Fudge!, arose from a need that Clark noticed in the community for a delicious, easy, and, above all, local fundraising option for schools and nonprofit organizations. For so many years, the choices had always been cheap, mass-produced, corporate products that lacked real quality and were often made outside of the United States. Clark wanted to change this, and a flood of support from parents and leaders of community organizations who shared her concern made her vision possible.

What the Fudge! provides its wonderful creations to sports leagues, churches, hospitals, and fundraising events to benefit the United Way. Clark even works with a local orthodontist to reward patients who just got their braces removed with a treat they may have waited years to enjoy.

Clark starts with crisp, tart Granny Smith apples, coating each one by hand with made-from-scratch caramel. The apple is then drizzled

with dark chocolate and sprinkled with peanuts or other mouthwatering toppings. Each treat is made to order, and orders totaled more than 65,000 apples in 2013. As the demand for What the Fudge! caramel apples has grown, so has Clark's vision to expand. After so many people asked where they can buy her apples, she is planning to eventually open a retail store. For now, What the Fudge! can be found at Albuquerque's Downtown Growers' Market and online.

El Pinto Biscochito Squares

In 1989, the New Mexico State Legislature named the biscochito the New Mexico State Cookie, but with the spelling "bizcochito" as it is spelled in Mexico. It is also called "biscocho" in the southern part of the state. But no matter how it's spelled in the New World, it originated in Spain as the *montecado*, or "crumble cake," a Christmas cookie. Indeed, most biscochitos are made and sold during the holidays — except at El Pinto, where they are available every day in two forms: a round cookie or, as this recipe specifies, as a square ingredient for an incredibly rich dessert called levante (see page 250). You can order the round cookies from the restaurant but the squares are only used to make levante.

If your oven is large enough to hold three baking sheets, you can make these all at once. If not, make them in batches.

COOKIES

- 1 pound lard
- 2 cups sugar
- 2 eggs
- 8 cups all-purpose flour
- 1 tablespoon baking powder
- ¼ teaspoon anise powder
- ½ cup Patron XO Cafe Tequila

TOPPING

- 2 cups sugar
- ¼ cup ground cinnamon

ABOUT 6 DOZEN COOKIES OR 5 DOZEN LEVANTE SQUARES

1. Make the cookies: Combine the lard and sugar in a stand mixer fitted with the paddle attachment and mix on medium speed for 3 minutes. Add the eggs and mix on low speed for 2 minutes. Add the flour, baking powder, and anise, and mix on low speed for 3 minutes. Add the tequila and mix on low speed for 3 minutes longer.

2. Preheat the oven to 325°F. Line 3 large baking sheets with parchment paper and set aside.

3. Sprinkle some flour over a clean work surface and roll the dough out to a thickness of ⅛ inch. Cut the dough into 3-inch squares to make levante or use a round 2½-inch cookie cutter to make cookies. Place the bars or cookies on the prepared baking sheets and bake for 10 to 12 minutes, or until the cookies are light brown on top.

4. Make the topping: Meanwhile, combine the sugar and cinnamon in a bowl and mix well.

5. Take the cookies out of the oven and sprinkle a good amount of the topping over them. Allow them to cool on the baking sheets. Repeat the process with any remaining dough.

MOMO & COMPANY

LESLIE THOMPSON fancies herself a bit of an alchemist when it comes to the delicious creations she makes at Momo & Company, her gluten-free and mostly vegan café in Santa Fe. Creating savory and sweet waffles, dairy-free ice-cream sandwiches, gorgeous cupcakes, and gluten-free muffins poses interesting challenges in mile-high Santa Fe. "Gluten-free and vegan baking is hard at high altitudes," Thompson says, describing the countless recipe modifications necessary for that bursting-with-flavor, melt-in-your-mouth experience. Her persistent, artistic food experimentation has met rave reviews from the beginning, having won an Eat Local Week community baking competition at the local farmers' market before she even opened Momo's doors.

Leslie Thompson

A Bronx native, Thompson came to New Mexico in 2005 to pursue art therapy. Instead, inspired by her immersion in Santa Fe's health conscious culture and having experienced the healing effects of going dairy-free herself, Thompson followed a calling to the art and therapy of allergen-free baking.

The real story for locals and tourists who love Momo & Company is that Thompson creates favorites with a flair for fun. Her menu is full of treats with names like the Mint Chocolate Fudge Fat Pants cupcake and features an entire line of Belgian waffles named after New York–inspired hip-hop culture, such as Wu Tang and Fly Girl. The savory green chile and cheese Big Pun waffle, topped with maple syrup, is quickly becoming a local favorite, with its nod to allergy-free living combined with the ubiquitous New Mexican chile crop. It's hard not to have a little fun while noshing at Momo & Company.

Levante

Levante is a New Mexican–style tiramisu made with tequila rather than espresso and with biscochitos substituting for lady fingers. It's so rich I don't even want to estimate the number of calories in it — if you have to ask, don't make it. It is one of the favorite desserts at El Pinto Restaurant, the largest in the state, located under the cottonwoods next to the Rio Grande in Albuquerque's North Valley (see profile, page 139).

NOTE: This recipe requires advance preparation.

LEVANTE LIQUOR

1 (750-ml) bottle Patron XO Cafe
   Tequila, or your favorite tequila

LEVANTE CUSTARD

¾ cup sugar

4 egg yolks

2 tablespoons levante liquor

1 (16-ounce) package mascarpone
   cheese

2 cups whipped cream

1 batch biscochito squares (see
   recipe page 248)

2 cups whipped cream

   Grated chocolate, for garnish, if
   desired

8 TO 10 SERVINGS

1. Make the liquor: Pour the tequila into a 2-quart stainless steel pot, bring to a boil, then reduce the heat to low and simmer until the volume is reduced by half, about 10 minutes. Remove the saucepan from the heat and pour the liquor into a bowl to cool.

2. Make the custard: Combine the sugar, egg yolks, and liquor in the top of a double boiler over boiling water and whisk vigorously until the egg yolks thicken considerably, 7 to 10 minutes. Remove the double boiler from the heat and set aside.

3. Whip the mascarpone on medium speed with a hand mixer in a mixing bowl. Add the warm yolk mixture and continue mixing well. Add the whipped cream and whip on low speed until completely blended, about 1 minute. Scrape off the hand mixer and reserve the custard.

4. Assemble the levante: Place 18 biscochito squares evenly in a 15- by 10- by 2-inch glass baking dish. Fill a squeeze bottle with the reserved liquor and squeeze it carefully over the biscochito squares, taking care not to soak them too much. Spread a ½-inch-thick layer of the custard over the top, using about one-third of the total. Add a second layer of biscochito squares and repeat the procedure. Add a third layer of biscochitos and soak this layer with the liquor a little more than the previous two. Add the final layer of custard and spread the whipped cream over the top. If you have any liquor left, it will keep indefinitely in the refrigerator until you make the next batch of levante.

5. Cover and refrigerate for 24 hours before serving.

Red Chile–Amaretto Truffles

If you've ever wondered if there's a connection between this delectable confection and the famous French fungus, it's that early truffles were rather free-form in appearance and, after being dusted with cocoa, they somewhat resembled that other sought-after treat. Traditional flavors tend toward the fruity or alcoholic, so when chocolatiers first starting combining chiles and chocolates, people thought they'd lost their senses.

These treats are well worth the extra effort it takes to make them. The chile takes a back seat — it's mild but in the background. Store them in containers in the pantry for up to two weeks.

NOTE: This recipe requires advance preparation.

---

1 pound semisweet chocolate, preferably Lindt or Valrhona

2 tablespoons unsalted butter

1 tablespoon light cornstarch

½ cup heavy cream

2–3 teaspoons Chimayó or other New Mexican chile powder

2 tablespoons amaretto liqueur

Heat Scale: Mild   ABOUT 2 DOZEN TRUFFLES

1. Roughly chop or break 9 ounces of the chocolate into small pieces and combine it with the butter and cornstarch in a heat-resistant bowl.

2. Pour the cream into a heavy saucepan and bring it to a rolling boil over medium-high heat. Pour the warm cream over the chocolate mixture and stir until all the chocolate has melted. Allow the mixture to cool, then add the chile powder and amaretto and mix well. Cover the bowl and refrigerate overnight to set. The filling should be firm like frosting.

3. Line a baking sheet with wax paper. Drop tablespoons of the filling onto the baking sheet and roll to form balls. (This is easier if your hands are cold. If the filling is becoming sticky, put it back in the refrigerator to chill and wash your hands with cold water before continuing.) When you have rolled all the balls, put the baking sheet in the refrigerator until the candies are firm.

4. Meanwhile, place the remaining 7 ounces chocolate in the top of a double boiler set over simmering water. Stir the chocolate continuously until melted, being careful that absolutely no water gets into the chocolate. Dip the chilled truffles in the melted chocolate to cover and return them to the baking sheet. Place the baking sheet back in the refrigerator to set the coating.

Mulberry Country Cake

Any kind of fruit or berries works beautifully in this tasty, easy dessert. Out of season, I use frozen mulberries instead of fresh mulberries and the flavor and texture are identical. You can serve this cake warm or at room temperature, and a scoop of ice cream or a dollop of whipped cream wouldn't go amiss. (Leftovers go nicely with a cup of coffee the next morning, too.)

2 cups fresh or frozen mulberries

⅓ cup granulated sugar, plus ¼–½ cup for the berries

6 tablespoons butter

¾ cup flour

2 teaspoons baking powder

½ teaspoon salt

⅓ cup firmly packed brown sugar

½ teaspoon finely grated lemon zest

¾ cup milk

6 TO 8 SERVINGS

1. Preheat the oven to 350°F.

2. Combine the mulberries and ¼ to ½ cup of the granulated sugar (depending on how sweet the berries are) in a bowl and set aside.

3. Melt the butter in an 8-inch square glass baking dish and set aside.

4. Sift the flour, ⅓ cup granulated sugar, baking powder, and salt into a medium bowl, and stir in the brown sugar; add the lemon zest and milk and mix until just combined.

5. Pour the batter over the melted butter in the baking dish. Do not mix. Sprinkle the mulberries over the batter and bake for 40 to 50 minutes, or until the mulberries are set.

FORAGING FOR MULBERRIES

When speaking of mulberries in New Mexico, the farm-to-table concept becomes forage-to-table. During the late spring and early summer, I take long walks in the South Valley of Albuquerque with specific destinations in mind: the spots with fruiting mulberry trees. I bring along a plastic bag and spend some quality time harvesting the ripe berries and staining my hands reddish purple. But the stains are worth it — they wash off easily and the berries are used in surprisingly varied recipes, including both spicy ones and cool-down desserts.

There are two principal methods of picking the berries: one by one by hand, or spread a large cloth like an old, clean sheet underneath the tree and vigorously shake the branches. I don't advise climbing into the tree to pick them, although I did that as a kid. Rather, use a sturdy ladder to pick fruit from the higher branches. Pick only the darkest and ripest berries as the lighter-colored ones are very sour and not nearly as flavorful. Because birds will have been feeding in the trees, avoid picking berries with white spots!

Clean the berries by soaking them in water for an hour or so, then rinse well. The berries will keep for several days in the refrigerator in a covered bowl, and they freeze well. You can use mulberries in any recipe calling for blackberries or raspberries and they blend well with other fruits, especially apples and pears.

Ginger Crème Anglaise over Fresh Peach Shortcake

Crème anglaise, or English custard, is made from the same recipe that you would use for making crème brûlée, but it is cooked on top of the stove and stirred so that it doesn't form into a custard. The trick to making this sauce is to heat it slowly and stir it constantly to prevent curdling. This very rich sauce transforms a simple dessert into an elegant ending to a special meal; to simplify menu prep, it can be made up to two days in advance and refrigerated until ready to serve. I like to serve it over fruit shortcake in place of the usual whipped cream, with a touch of freshly grated ginger to the sauce to complement the fruit.

CRÈME ANGLAISE

- 1 tablespoon finely grated peeled fresh ginger
- 1 cup milk
- ½ cup heavy cream
- ⅓ cup sugar
- 5 egg yolks
- 1 teaspoon vanilla extract

PEACH SHORTCAKES

- 3 cups sliced fresh peaches
- ¼ cup sugar
- 4 shortcakes or biscuits
- Fresh mint leaves, for garnish

4 SERVINGS

1. Make the crème anglaise: Combine the ginger, milk, and cream in a heavy saucepan and slowly heat over medium heat, stirring well, until hot. Remove the saucepan from the heat and let the mixture steep for 15 minutes. Return the saucepan to the stove and reheat over medium heat until small bubbles form around the edges of the liquid.

2. Combine the sugar and egg yolks in a medium bowl and whisk until slightly thickened. Slowly strain the hot milk into the eggs while whisking. It's important to do this slowly so that the eggs temper, rather than cook. Discard the solids from the sieve.

3. Transfer the mixture to a small saucepan and cook over medium-low heat, stirring constantly, until the sauce thickens and coats the back of a spoon or reaches a temperature of 170°F, about 5 minutes. Do not let the mixture boil.

4. Pour the sauce into a bowl, stir in the vanilla, and cover the surface with plastic wrap to prevent a "skin" from forming. Cool and chill for an hour.

5. Make the shortcakes: Place the peaches in a bowl, sprinkle with the sugar, and set aside.

6. To serve, place each shortcake on an individual plate and top with the peaches. Ladle the crème anglaise over the peaches, garnish with mint leaves, and serve.

Green Chile–Piñon Ice Cream

Don't let its mild appearance fool you — this is not an innocent ice cream, though you can control the heat level by the chile you use. A 'Big Jim' pepper will give you a mild ice cream and a 'Sandia' or 'Barker', a much spicier one. With its combination of heat and coldness, this is a wonderful dessert to finish a summer barbecue.

⅔ cup sugar

¼ teaspoon salt

2 cups heavy cream

1 cup milk

3 egg yolks

1 cup mashed avocado

¼ cup Galliano (optional)

1 tablespoon lemon juice

⅓ cup chopped El Pinto Roasted Green Chile, or 2 New Mexican chiles, roasted, peeled, and chopped

3 tablespoons piñon nuts

Heat Scale: Mild to medium   ABOUT 1 QUART

1. Combine the sugar, salt, cream, and milk in the top of a double boiler set over boiling water, and mix well. Bring the mixture to a boil while stirring constantly. Remove from the heat.

2. Whisk the egg yolks in a medium bowl. Continue whisking while slowly adding one-third of the hot cream mixture to the bowl. Transfer to a medium saucepan and add the remaining two-thirds cream. Cook the mixture over medium heat, stirring constantly, until moderately thickened, about 5 minutes. Remove and chill in the refrigerator for an hour.

3. Combine the avocado, Galliano, and lemon juice in a blender or a food processor fitted with the steel blade attachment and process until smooth. Slowly add the avocado mixture to the chilled cream mixture, and stir to mix. Add the chiles and piñon nuts and mix. Chill the mixture for 1 hour.

4. Freeze the ice cream in a commercial ice cream freezer according to the manufacturer's directions.

Recipe from AMY WHITE, *EDIBLE SANTA FE*

Red Chile–Pecan Pie

"Pecan pie is a classic, and it's truly spectacular with a little red chile in it," says Amy White, one of *Edible Santa Fe*'s excellent food writers. "Did you know the pecan is a species of hickory, native to the southern United States and Mexico? New Mexico pecans are in season in late winter and early spring, and many orchards sell them online. At some winter farmers' markets you can find small-batch pecans from local growers, but most come from large commercial orchards in the southern part of the state."

DOUGH

- 1¼ cups flour
- 1 teaspoon salt
- 1 teaspoon sugar
- ½ cup (1 stick) unsalted butter, cut into ½-inch cubes and chilled

FILLING

- 2 eggs
- 1 cup firmly packed light brown sugar
- ¼ cup granulated sugar
- 2 tablespoons red chile powder
- 1 tablespoon flour
- ¼ cup butter, melted
- 2 cups finely chopped pecans
- 1 tablespoon milk
- 1 teaspoon bourbon or vanilla extract

Heat Scale: Mild   1 (9-INCH) PIE

1. **Make the dough:** Combine the flour, salt, and sugar in a food processor fitted with the steel blade attachment. Add the butter and pulse until the mixture resembles very coarse cornmeal. Add about 2 tablespoons ice water and pulse for 10 seconds at a time, until the dough begins to ball up around the blade of the food processor.

2. Transfer the dough to a lightly floured work surface, form it into a flat disk about 1 inch thick, and wrap it in plastic wrap. Refrigerate the dough for at least 1 hour or up to 2 hours.

3. Preheat the oven to 400°F.

4. Allow the dough to sit at room temperature for 5 to 10 minutes before rolling it out on a well-floured work surface to fit a 9-inch pie plate. Transfer the dough to the pie plate. If you roll your dough out before the filling is ready, put the pie plate back in the fridge until you're ready to bake the pie.

5. **Make the filling:** Beat the eggs in a large bowl until foamy. Stir in the brown sugar, granulated sugar, chile powder, flour, and melted butter. Mix thoroughly, then gently stir in the pecans, milk, and bourbon.

6. Pour the filling into the unbaked pie shell. Cover the edges with aluminum foil, and bake for 10 minutes.

7. Remove the foil, reduce the temperature to 350°F, and bake 20 to 30 minutes longer, until the center is just set. The whole pie should jiggle as one mass when gently shaken. Let the pie cool before serving, and serve à la mode.

Chilled *Natillas* (Little Pudding) with Shaved Chocolate

This custardy pudding, which also goes by the name "Spanish cream," is one of the ways New Mexicans tame the flames of the chiles. Though it's commonly served plain, I like to add some chocolate shavings for a boost of flavor. To shave chocolate, chill a bar until almost frozen and use a vegetable peeler to peel long thin curls off the bar. *Natillas* is an easy dessert to prepare, and the cook has the enjoyable task of eating the rest of the chocolate bar after shaving off enough for the garnish.

3 eggs, separated
¾ cup sugar
2 tablespoons all-purpose flour
2 cups milk
¼ teaspoon ground cinnamon
⅛ teaspoon ground nutmeg
Shaved semisweet chocolate curls, for garnish

6 TO 8 SERVINGS

1. Beat the egg whites in a bowl, and gradually add 1 tablespoon of the sugar. Beat until they are stiff but not dry and set aside.

2. Combine the egg yolks, flour, and 1 cup of the milk in another bowl and beat to form a smooth paste.

3. Combine the remaining sugar and remaining 1 cup milk in a saucepan over medium heat, and cook until the milk is just below the boiling point, or scalded. Add the egg mixture and continue to cook over medium heat until it reaches a soft custardlike consistency.

4. Remove the hot custard mixture from the heat and stir in the cinnamon and nutmeg. Gently fold the reserved egg whites into the mixture. Divide the mixture among individual shallow bowls and chill until ready to serve.

5. Serve the pudding either chilled or warmed to room temperature and garnished with shaved chocolate curls.

Recipe from MATT THOMAS, MATT'S GLUTEN-FREE GOODNESS

Rhubarb and Strawberry Polenta Cake

"This has become my go-to cake in spring and early summer for sharing with friends or bringing along to potlucks when rhubarb and strawberries are in season," says Matt Thomas of this delicious dessert. "It really should be called an almond cake, as it has more almonds than polenta, but you can't help but notice the texture the polenta adds to the cake. The combination of orange and rhubarb with bright red strawberries makes this a cake that even nongluten gluttons will want seconds of. In a pinch, I have topped this with strawberry jam or orange marmalade."

NOTE: Orange blossom water is available online from Amazon.com and other sources.

POLENTA CAKE

- ½ cup plus 6 tablespoons (1¾ sticks) butter, softened, plus more for greasing the pan
- 1 cup sugar
- 3 eggs
- Finely grated zest of 2 oranges or 1 lemon
- 2 teaspoons orange blossom water
- 2 cups almond meal
- ⅔ cup polenta
- ½ cup Matt's Bakery Gluten-Free Flour Mix or other gluten-free flour
- ¾ teaspoon baking powder
- ½ teaspoon sea salt

RHUBARB JAM

- 2½ pounds rhubarb, chopped
- 2 cups sugar
- 3 teaspoons finely grated orange zest
- ⅓ cup orange juice

- 1 pint strawberries, hulled and thinly sliced

8 TO 10 SERVINGS

1. Make the cake: Preheat the oven to 350°F. Butter an 11-inch round tart pan. (You can use a 9-inch round cake pan, buttered and lined with parchment paper; add 10 minutes to the baking time.)

2. Beat the butter and sugar in a medium bowl until well blended. Add the eggs, orange zest, and orange blossom water and mix well.

3. Whisk together the almond meal, polenta, flour, baking powder, and salt. Add the flour mixture to the egg mixture and mix until well combined. Spread the batter in the prepared tart pan and bake 35 to 45 minutes (depending on the pan used), or until the top is golden brown.

4. Make the jam: While the cake is baking, combine the rhubarb, sugar, orange zest, and orange juice in a large saucepan and bring to boil over high heat. Reduce the heat to low and cook, stirring occasionally as the jam thickens, for 45 minutes. Remove the jam from the heat and place in a bowl. The jam will thicken further as it cools.

5. Remove the cake from the oven and allow to cool for 1 hour at room temperature. Once the cake has cooled completely, transfer carefully onto a plate. Lightly glaze the cake with the rhubarb jam. Spread the strawberries flat on top of the glaze. Follow with a final glaze of rhubarb jam. You will not need all of the jam, so store the rest in a jar in the refrigerator, where it will keep for several weeks.

MATT'S GLUTEN-FREE GOODNESS

WHEN MATT THOMAS DISCOVERED he had celiac disease after more than a decade of experiencing constant allergies, pain, and fatigue, it was both a time of celebration and concern. A celebration in that adopting a new lifelong gluten-free diet would be the answer to feeling better and a concern in that he would have to give up many great-tasting foods. "How am I ever going to survive?" Thomas remembers thinking, wondering how to go about replacing the tasty gluten-heavy goods he used to enjoy with equally tasty gluten-free options.

Curiosity turned to action and, as his kitchen experiments yielded increasingly positive feedback from friends, family, and even local press, Thomas decided to bring his creations to the public by starting Matt's Gluten-Free Goodness out of the Mixing Bowl, the South Valley commercial kitchen incubator.

Thomas proves the notion that "gluten-free doesn't taste good" is just plain wrong. His very popular chocolate cupcake with butter cream is said to convert noncupcake eaters into big-time fans. Made with wholesome, fair-trade, organic ingredients like cocoa, organic milk, and eggs, offerings include a melt-in-your-mouth lemon pound cake, a double chocolate cookie with walnuts, and a deliciously unique quinoa cookie, to name a few.

Matt's Gluten-Free Goodness acts as part of a local support system for young people with gluten sensitivities and continues to expand their product line to provide healthy, wholesome food to celiacs and nonceliacs alike. Matt's Gluten-Free Goodness products are found throughout New Mexico in bakeries, coffee shops, markets, co-ops, and online.

NIN'S NUTZ

AS A CLINICAL NURSE specialist with a motherly pet name inspired by her grandchildren, it's no surprise that Helen Poling (Nin) sprang into action when a dear friend's autistic child needed a snack that fit his special dietary needs. Thus began the quest to cook up a delicious, all-natural snack that was gluten- and preservative-free and made with as few ingredients as possible. The result was a mouthwatering sweet-and-salty granola nugget that became such a hit with kids and adults that Nin's Nutz was born in 2009.

Since then, the original Nin's Nutz treat has seen the addition of tasty dried fruits and has expanded into tempting specialty products with rich chocolate and caramel. She uses local ingredients in her treats ranging from raw honey from the Rio Grande Valley to specialty caramels from Sheila's Sweets and What the Fudge! (see profile on page 247). These versatile treats can be sprinkled on yogurt for breakfast, mixed with sherbet for dessert, or just enjoyed straight out of the bag. As Nin's Nutz continues to grow, food allergies are always kept in mind. New nut-free and vegan product lines will make it possible for more people with a range of dietary needs to snack safely and deliciously.

When Nin's Nutz isn't giving back to the community through charities that benefit health-conscious organizations like the American Lung Association, they can be found at the Albuquerque Downtown Growers' Market advocating smart snacking. Nin's products can be purchased at family-owned Sheila's Sweets, local Whole Foods stores, and online.

Nin's Peach and Blueberry Crisp

From Helen Poling (known as Nin to her grandchildren and others) comes this perfect summer dessert for lunch or dinner using Blueberry Nuggets from her company (see profile on facing page). How about a nice dessert wine to accompany this from one of our New Mexican wineries? Works for me.

3 cups sliced fresh peaches

½ cup sugar

1 teaspoon ground cinnamon

⅛ teaspoon ground nutmeg

1 tablespoon lemon juice

¾ cup flour

½ cup firmly packed light brown sugar

6 tablespoons butter, cut into small chunks and chilled

¾ cup Nin's Nutz Blueberry Nuggets, crumbled, or use dried blueberries

ABOUT 6 SERVINGS

1. Preheat the oven to 350°F.

2. Combine the peaches, sugar, cinnamon, nutmeg, and lemon juice in a large bowl. Pour the peach mixture into an 8-inch square baking dish.

3. Mix together the flour, sugar, and butter using a fork until pea-size balls form. Fold in the crumbled nuggets and pour the mixture over the peaches. Bake for 40 minutes, or until browned.

4. Serve warm with ice cream or whipped cream. It's also delicious at room temperature.

SOUTHWESTERN COOKING TERMS AND INGREDIENTS

achiote. The orange-colored seeds of the annatto tree; used as a coloring agent and seasoning.

adobado or adovada. In New Mexico and El Paso, a marinade for pork made with New Mexican red chiles, garlic, and oregano; in Texas, a sour marinade paste made with herbs, chiles, and vinegar.

adobo. A thick cooking sauce comprising tomatoes, vinegar, and spices.

aguas frescas. Fresh fruit drinks.

ajo. Garlic.

albóndigas. Meatballs.

al carbon. Charcoal-grilled.

al pastor. Cooked on a spit over a fire.

Anaheim chiles. Misnomer for New Mexican chiles; now the term for a very mild New Mexican cultivar grown only in California.

ancho chiles. The dried from of poblano chiles. Substitute: pasilla chiles.

antojito. Literally, "little whim"; an appetizer.

árbol chiles. Hot dried red chiles from Mexico. Substitute dried New Mexican red chiles or piquíns.

arroz. Rice.

asada or asado. Roasted or broiled.

asadero. A type of rubbery white cheese at first made only in the Mexican states of Chihuahua and Michoacán but now produced in the United States as well. Substitute: Monterey Jack.

azafrán. Saffron.

barbacoa. In Texas, pit-barbecued meat; in Mexico, the barbecued flesh of a cow's head.

biscochitos. (Sometimes bizcochitos) in New Mexico, anise-flavored cookies.

bolillo. Mexican hard roll; similar to French bread.

borracho. Literally, "drunken"; foods containing beer or liquor.

burros (AZ) and burritos (NM and TX). Flour tortillas stuffed with meats, cheeses, beans, and chile sauces, or a combination thereof.

cabrito. Roasted kid (young goat, that is).

calabacita. Squash, usually zucchini types.

calamari. Squid.

caldillo. Literally, "little soup"; a thick stew with beef and chiles, commonly served in El Paso and Juárez.

caldo. A broth, stock, or clear soup.

canela. Cinnamon.

capriotada. A bread pudding dessert.

carne. Meat.

carnitas. Literally, "little pieces of meat"; small chunks of pork fried to a crisp texture.

cascabel chiles. Literally, "jingle bells"; small, round, hot chiles that rattle when shaken. Substitute: árbol chiles.

ceviche. Raw seafood combined with lime juice, which "cooks" the fish by combining with its protein and turning it opaque.

chalupas. Literally, "little boats"; in New Mexico, a fried corn tortilla in the shape of a boat containing shredded chicken or beans topped with salsa, guacamole, or cheese.

chicharrón. Crisp-fried pork skin.

chicos. Corn kernels that are roasted, then dried.

chilaquiles. A casserole made of tortilla wedges, salsa, and cheese.

chile. Referring to the plants or pods of the *Capsicum* genus.

chile caribe. A red chile paste made from crushed or ground red chiles of any type, garlic, and water.

New Mexican Green

New Mexican Red

Jalapeño

Yellow Hot

Serrano

Habanero

Piquín (Árbol)

Chipotle

chile con queso. A cheese and chile dip.

chile pasado. Literally, "chile of the past"; sun-dried, roasted, and peeled green chile.

chile piquín or chilipiquín. Also called "chiltepíns," or "chile tepins," these small dried red chiles are quite hot. Substitute: cayenne pepper or hot red chile powder.

chili. Chile sauce with meat; chili con carne.

chiltepíns. Small, round, wild chiles that grow in Arizona. Another variety is called "chilipiquín" in Texas.

chimichanga. A deep-fried stuffed burro topped with cheese and chile sauce.

chipotle chiles. Smoked and dried jalapeño chiles. Substitute: moritas, smoked serranos.

chorizo. A spicy sausage made with pork, garlic, and red chile powder.

cilantro. An annual herb (*Coriandrum sativum*) with seeds that are known as coriander. Substitute: Italian parsley or culantro (*Eryngium foetidum*). Commonly used in salsas and soups.

comal. Griddle.

comino or cumin. An annual herb (*Cuminum cyminum*) whose seeds have a distinctive odor; the dominant flavor in Tex-Mex dishes such as chili con carne.

desayuno. Breakfast.

empanada. A pastry turnover.

enchiladas. Rolled or stacked corn tortillas filled with meat or cheese and covered with chile sauce.

epazote. Known as "ambrosia" in English, this perennial herb (*Chenopodium ambrosioides*) is strong and bitter and used primarily to flavor beans.

escabeche. Vegetables, especially chiles, marinated or pickled in vinegar.

fajitas. Literally, "little belts"; marinated and grilled skirt steak.

flan. A baked caramel custard dessert.

flautas. Literally, "flutes"; tightly rolled, deep-fried enchiladas.

frijoles. Beans.

gorditas. Stuffed corn cakes; literally, "little fat ones."

guacamole. Literally, "mixture of vegetables"; in this case, a blend of avocados, tomatoes, garlic, and chiles.

habanero chiles. Literally, "from Havana"; small orange or red chiles from the Caribbean and Yucatán that resemble a tam or bonnet; the hottest in the world. Substitute: jalapeños or serranos.

hongos. Mushrooms.

huevos rancheros. Literally, "ranch-style eggs."

jalapeño chiles. Small, fat chiles that are pickled, stuffed, or used in fresh salsas. Substitute: serranos.

jamaica. A Mexican flower that flavors drinks and teas.

jamón. Ham.

jicama. A white tuber (*Pachyrhizus erosus*) used in salads that tastes like a cross between an apple and a potato.

lengua. Tongue.

lima. Lemon.

limón. Lime.

machaca. Meat that is stewed, roasted, or broiled and then shredded.

maíz. Corn.

manteca. Lard.

masa. Corn dough.

masa harina. Corn dough flour.

menudo. Tripe soup, often with chiles.

mescal. A liquor distilled from the agave plant.

metate. A stone for grinding corn.

migas. In Texas, eggs scrambled with chorizo, tortilla chips, onions, tomatoes, cheese, and serrano chiles.

molcajete. A mortar made out of volcanic stone.

mole. Literally, "mixture"; usually refers to a thick chile sauce made with many spices and chocolate.

nachos. Tostados topped with cheese and sliced jalapeño chiles.

natillas. Custard dessert.

New Mexican chiles. "Long green" chiles grown in New Mexico; varieties include 'Big Jim', 'No. 6-4', 'Sandia', 'Española,' 'Chimayo'. Substitute: poblanos.

nopales or nopalitos. Prickly pear cactus pads, spines removed.

olla. A round, earthenware pot.

pan. Bread. Pan dulce is sweet bread.

papas. Potatoes.

parrilla. Grill or broiler.

pasilla chiles. Literally, "little raisin"; an allusion to the aroma and dark brown color of this long, thin, Mexican chile. Substitute: ancho chiles.

pepitas. Roasted pumpkin seeds.

pescado. Fish.

picadillo. Shredded beef, spices, and other ingredients usually used as a stuffing.

picante. Hot and spicy.

pico de gallo. Literally, "beak of the rooster"; a salsa with tomatoes, onions, cilantro, and serrano chiles.

piloncillo. Brown, unrefined cane sugar.

piñons. The nuts of the piñon tree (*Pinus edulis*).

pipián. A sauce containing ground nuts or seeds and spices.

poblano chiles. Literally, "peppers of the people"; these dark green fat chiles are commonly used in Mexico and the Southwest. The dried form is called ancho, "wide."

pollo. Chicken.

posole. A thick stew made with pork, chiles, and hominy.

puerco. Pork.

quelites. Spinach and bean dish seasoned with chiles and bacon.

quesadilla. A flour tortilla turnover, which is usually stuffed with cheese, then toasted, fried, or baked.

queso. Cheese.

rajas. Strips; usually refers to strips of chiles.

refrito. Used mainly to describe beans that are mashed and fried in lard.

relleno. Stuffed.

res. Beef.

ristra. A string of red chile pods.

salpicón. A Mexican shredded meat salad.

salsa. Literally, "sauce"; usually used to describe uncooked sauces (salsa cruda).

saguaro. Tall cactus found in Arizona; its fruits are made into jams and jellies.

serrano chiles. A small, hot Mexican chile that is usually pickled or used green or red in fresh salsas. Substitute: jalapeño chiles.

sopa. Soup.

sopapilla. From sopaipa, a fritter soaked in honey; in New Mexico, a puffed, fried bread, served with honey or filled with various stuffings.

taco. A stuffed corn tortilla, either soft or a crisp, fried shell.

tamal. (Plural, tamales) any filling enclosed in masa, wrapped in a corn shuck, and steamed.

tamarindo. Tamarind.

taquito. A rolled, deep-fried taco.

tequila. A type of mescal produced near Tequila in the state of Jalisco, Mexico.

tomatillo. A small, green husk tomato (*Physalis ixocarpa*); substitute small regular tomatoes.

torta. A sandwich, often made with a bolillo.

tostados. Tortilla chips.

tunas. Prickly pear cactus fruits.

yerba buena. Mint.

NEW MEXICO FOOD AND BEVERAGE EVENTS

January

Annual Taos Winter Wine Festival
Events include Taste of Taos and reserve Tasting, grand Tasting, seminars, winery dinners, and apres ski tastings.
www.taoswinterwinefest.com

The Souper Bowl XIX (Santa Fe)
Sample amazing soups prepared by several dozen of Santa Fe's finest chefs, then cast your vote for your favorites. This annual soup competition benefits the Food Depot, northern New Mexico's food bank.
www.thefooddepot.org

March

National Fiery Foods & Barbecue Show (Albuquerque)
Taking place the first weekend in March, the most popular food show in the Southwest has been delighting chileheads for more than 25 years with more than a thousand different products to taste and buy.
www.fieryfoodsshow.com

Southwest Chocolate & Coffee Fest (Albuquerque)
Celebrate all things coffee and chocolate at the end of March.
www.chocolateandcoffeefest.com

May

Albuquerque Blues & Brews Festival
In early May, beer fans can enjoy live music with top blues bands, dozens of regional craft breweries, and homebrew demonstrations at the Isleta Amphitheater.
www.abqbluesandbrews.com

Albuquerque Wine Festival
Held in late May at Balloon Fiesta Park, this festival combines wines from around the state with food, arts and crafts, live music, and educational opportunities.
www.abqwinefestival.com

Southern New Mexico Wine Festival (Las Cruces)
More than 12,000 people mark the start of summer with this event at the Southern New Mexico Fairgrounds by tasting wines and attending hourly seminars about wine and how to pair it with food. Live music, arts and crafts, and a wide variety of agricultural products enliven the scene.
www.snmwinefestival.com

June

Savor the Flavor (Santa Fe)
Held in early June at the Museum of International Folk Art, this celebration of local food includes tastings, cooking demos, live music, and free entry into the museum. It's produced by Delicious New Mexico to help promote local food awareness.
www.deliciousnm.com

Smokin' on the Pecos (Artesia)
There's lots to do here in late June, with New Mexico State BBQ Championship, Kids' Q, and Backyard BBQ categories, as well as entertainment and crafts exhibits.
www.smokinonthepecos.us

July

Lavender in the Village Festival (Los Ranchos de Albuquerque)
A celebration of all things lavender!
www.lavenderinthevillage.com

August

Hot Chili Days, Cool Mountain Nights (Red River)
Visit Brandenburg Park in mid-August for live music and multiple chili cook-offs, including CASI "Red River Red" cook-off, the New Mexico State Green Chile Championship, and the Lone Star BBQ Society cook-off.
http://larryjoetaylor.com/red_river.htm

September

Expo New Mexico (Albuquerque)
As at all state fairs, you'll find many different styles of food. Try the smoked turkey legs.
http://exponm.com

Hatch Chile Festival
Held on Labor Day weekend, this is a celebration of the chile in a county fair atmosphere.
www.hatchchilefest.com

New Mexico Wine Festival (Bernalillo)
Taking place on Labor Day weekend, this is the largest of many wine festivals in the state.
www.newmexicowinefestival.com

Old Town Salsa Fiesta (Albuquerque)
Held in mid-September on the Plaza in Old Town, the fiesta features salsa bands and dancers on the gazebo and throughout Old Town, and a salsa dip cooking competition. Competitors make their salsa on the spot in front of everyone, and attendees get to taste and cast their votes for the winners.
www.cabq.gov/culturalservices/historic-old-town/events/salsa-fiesta

Santa Fe Wine & Chile Fiesta

Ease into fall at the Santa Fe Opera with samplings of wine and food from the city's best restaurants.
www.santafewineandchile.org

Tularosa Basin Wine & Music Festival (Alamogordo)

Held in mid-September, the festival offers wine tastings and food vendors during their hot air balloon invitational at Alameda Park.
www.tularosabasinwinefest.com

October

Albuquerque Grecian Festival

Enjoy food, music, and dancing, and a Greek marketplace in early October at St. George Greek Orthodox Church, Lead Avenue.
http://abqgreekfest.com

Albuquerque Hopfest

The largest beer festival in the state, with 50 breweries in attendance, takes place in late October at Isleta Casino.
www.albuquerquehopfest.com

Harvest Festival (El Rancho de las Golondrinas)

This festival, held in early October, spotlights native foods.
www.golondrinas.org

Local Food Festival and Field Day (Albuquerque's South Valley)

Held at historic Gutierrez-Hubbel House in early October, this festival highlights local food and agriculture.
http://mrcog-nm.gov/local-food/local-food-festival

New Mexico Brew Fest (Albuquerque)

Held in the beautiful Villa Hispana outdoor venue at Expo New Mexico during the Albuquerque International Balloon Fiesta in early October, the New Mexico Brew Fest pours local and regional microbrews in the state and region to thousands of craft beer enthusiasts. Presented by *Local iQ* magazine and set to an Oktoberfest-inspired backdrop, this burgeoning event features live music, German bratwursts, and inventive food truck fare.
www.nmbrewfest.com

New Mexico Pecan Festival and the Rootin' Tootin' Rib Cook Off (Las Cruces)

Two days of nuts, nutty fun, nutty food, and even nutty art that occur in late October at the Mesilla Valley Maze Family Fun Farm.
www.nmpecanfestival.com

Whole Enchilada Fiesta (Las Cruces)

Celebrate chiles and New Mexican food in early October; don't miss the making of the World's Largest Enchilada.
www.enchiladafiesta.com

NEW MEXICO FARMERS' MARKETS

Alamogordo
Alamogordo Alameda Park Farmers' Market
Alameda Park, 1987 White Sands Blvd.

Alamogordo Farmers' Market
Otero County Fairgrounds' Frontier Village

Albuquerque
ABQ Uptown Growers' Market
NE parking lot of ABQ Uptown Shopping Center,
Uptown Loop and Uptown Blvd.

Albuquerque Downtown Growers' Market
Robinson Park, 8th and Central

Albuquerque Northeast Farmers' and Artisans' Market
West side of Albuquerque Academy, 6400 Wyoming Blvd. NE

Armijo Village South Valley Growers' Market
SW corner of Isleta Blvd. and Arenal Rd.

Caravan Nouveau Growers' and Artisans' Market
Wilson Park, San Pedro Dr. and Anderson Ave. SE

Le Jardin Verde Urban Growers' Market
Mesa Verde Park
7900 Marquette Ave. NE

Nob Hill Growers' Market
Morningside Park, Lead and Morningside SE

South Valley Growers' Market
3907 Isleta Blvd. SW

Aztec
Aztec Farmers' Market
West Side Plaza, 1409 W. Aztec Blvd.

Bayard
Bayard Farmers' Market
Bayard Lions Club
808 Tom Foy Blvd.

Belén
Belén Growers' Market
Anna Becker Park, Reinken Ave.

Bernalillo
Bernalillo Farmers' Market
301 Camino del Pueblo

Capitan
Capitan Farmers' Market
115 Smokey Bear Blvd.

Carlsbad
Carlsbad Downtown Farmers' Market
Eddy County Courthouse
Mermod and Canal

Cedar Crest
Cedar Crest Farmers' Market
12144 N. Hwy. 14

Chaparral
Chaparral Farmers' Market
101 County Line, corner of county and state lines

Clovis
Clovis Farmers' Market
Corner of 4th and Pile

Corrales
Corrales Growers' Market
Recreation Center, 500 Jones Rd. at Corrales Rd.

Cuba
Cuba Farmers' Market
St. Francis of Assisi Park, off NM 126

Deming
Copper St. Farmers' Market
216 Copper St.

Dixon
Dixon Co-op Farmers' Market
215 Hwy. 75

Eagle Nest
Moreno Valley Farmers' Market
Golden Eagle RV Park, Hwy. 64

Edgewood
Edgewood Farmers' Market
Wildlife West Park
87 N. Frontage Rd.

Española
Española Farmers' Market
1005 N. Railroad Ave.

Farmington
Farmington Growers' Market
Farmington Museum at Gateway Park, 3041 E. Main St.

Gallup
Gallup Farmers' Market
Downtown Walkway between Coal and Aztec

Gila
Gila Farmstand
414 Hwy. 211

Glencoe
Glencoe Farmers' Market
27489 Hwy. 70

Jemez/Jemez Pueblo
Jemez Pueblo Farmers' Market
Red Rocks, north end of Pueblo

Jemez Springs Community Farmers Market
Civic center on Hwy. 4, next to credit union

Las Cruces
Las Cruces Farmers' and Crafts Market
Downtown Mall

Sunday Growers' Market
Mountain View Co-op parking lot
1300 El Paseo

Las Vegas
Las Vegas: Tri-County Farmers' Market
6th & University

Los Alamos
Los Alamos Farmers' Market
Mesa Public Library, 20th & Central

Los Lunas
Los Lunas Farmers' Market
Main St., at the river

Los Ranchos de Albuquerque
Los Ranchos Growers' Market
6718 Rio Grande Blvd. NW

Mimbres
Mimbres Valley Farmers' Market
La Tienda in San Lorenzo
2674 Hwy. 35

Mora
Mora Valley Farmers' Market
Mora Valley Ranch Supply, Hwy. 518

Mountainair
Mountainair Farmers' Market
Roosevelt St. next to post office

Ojo Caliente
Ojo Caliente Farmers' & Ranchers' Market
St. Mary's Church parking lot

Pecos
Pecos Farmers' Market
Canelas Restaurant
29 Glorieta Hwy. (Hwy. 50)

Pojoaque
Pojoaque Valley Farmers' Market
Poeh Cultural Center, 78 Cities of Gold

Portales
Portales Farmers' Market
Corner of W. 1st and Ave. B

Ramah
Ramah Farmers' Market
½ mile west of Ramah on Hwy. 53

Raton
Raton First Street Market
100 block of historic downtown on First St.

Ribera
El Valle Farmers' Market
Route 3 in Ribera

Rio Rancho
Rio Rancho Farmers' Market
24th Ave & 10th St.

Roswell
Roswell Farmers' Market
Chaves County Courthouse lawn

San Felipe Pueblo
San Felipe Pueblo Farmers' Market
I-25 exit 252, west side of casino

Santa Fe
Eldorado Farmers' Market
La Tienda parking lot, 7 Caliente Rd.

Santa Fe Farmers' Market
1607 Paseo de Peralta at Guadalupe

Shiprock
Shiprock Farmers' Market
Shiprock Chapter House, north of Hwy. 64

Silver City
Silver City Farmers' Market
7th and Bullard

Socorro
Socorro Farmers' Market
Socorro Plaza Park

Sunland Park
Ardovino's Desert Crossing Farmers' Market
Ardovino St.

Taos
Red Willow Farmers' Market, Taos Pueblo
Red Willow Center, 885 Starr Rd.

Taos Farmers' Market
Town Hall lot on Camino de Placitas

Truth or Consequence
Sierra County Farmers' Market
Ralph Edwards Park

Tucumcari
Tucumcari Farmers' Market
Wailes Park, Tucumcari Blvd. and Date St.

Tularosa
Tularosa Farmers' Market
Corner of N. Bookout and Central Ave.

RECIPE CONTRIBUTORS AND SUPPLIERS

Apple Canyon Gourmet 175
800-866-4695
www.applecanyongourmet.com

Amore Neapolitan Pizzeria 104
2929 Monte Vista Boulevard
Northeast
Albuquerque, NM 87106
505-554-1967
www.amoreabq.com

Bueno Foods 162
El Encanto, Inc.
2001 Fourth Street Southwest
Albuquerque, NM 87102
800-952-4453
www.buenofoods.com

ButterBeautiful 107
6 Dovela Place
Santa Fe, NM 87508
505-577-1978
www.butterbeautiful.com

Camino de Paz School and Farm 113
PO Box 669
Santa Cruz, NM 87567
505-747-9717
www.caminodepaz.net

Celina's Biscochitos 235
multiple locations
505-269-4997
www.celinasbiscochitos.com

The Chispa Company 172
318 Isleta Boulevard Southwest
Albuquerque, NM 87105
info@chispasalsa.com
www.chispasalsa.com

Cowgirl 167
319 South Guadalupe Street
Santa Fe, NM 87501
505-982-2565
www.cowgirlsantafe.com

El Pinto Restaurant & Salsa 139
10500 Fourth Street Northwest
Albuquerque, NM 87114
505-898-1771
www.elpinto.com

Forque Kitchen and Bar 129
Hyatt Regency Albuquerque
330 Tijeras Northwest
Albuquerque, NM 87102
505-842-1234
www.albuquerque.hyatt.com/en/ hotel/dining/ForqueKitchenandBar. html

Hartford Square 61
300 Broadway Boulevard Northeast
Albuquerque, NM 87102
505-265-4933
http://hartfordsq.com

Heidi's Raspberry Farm 197
PO Box 1329
Corrales, New Mexico
505-898-1784
www.heidisraspberryjam.com

Il Piatto 95
95 West Marcy Street
Santa Fe, NM 87501
505-984-1091
http://ilpiattosantafe.com

Kinna's Laos Chile Paste 179
Albuquerque, NM
505-228-7345
www.kinnas.net

La Montañita Co-op 98
multiple locations
www.lamontanita.coop

Lusty Monk Mustard 192
505-975-6498
www.lustymonk.com

Marble Brewery 214
111 Marble Ave. Northwest
Albuquerque, NM 87102
505-243-2739
www.marblebrewery.com

Matt's Bakery LLC 263
PO Box 1075
Taos, NM 87571
575-613-0601
www.mattsbakerytaos.com

Maynard Cattle Co. 136
260 Cactus Patch Way
Las Cruces, NM 88007
575-644-9845
kmaynard@zianet.com

Momo & Co. 249
229 Johnson Street
Santa Fe, NM 87501
505-983-8000
www.momoandcompany.com

New Mexico Pie Company 244
4003 Carlisle Blvd. Northeast
Albuquerque, NM 87107
505-884-3625
http://nmpiecompany.com

Nin's Nutz 264
505-379-6768
http://ninsnutz.com

The Old Windmill Dairy
PO Box 834
McIntosh, NM 87032
505-384-0033
http://theoldwindmilldairy.com

Old Town Farm 67
949 Montoya Street Northwest
Albuquerque, NM 87104
505-764-9116
http://oldtownfarm.com

Ranchline All Natural 142
866-402-2836
www.ranchlineallnatural.com

Red Tractor Farm
Albuquerque, NM
www.redtractorfarm.net

Santa Fe Brewing Co. 226
35 Fire Place
Santa Fe, NM 87508
505-424-3333
www.santafebrewing.com

Santa Fe Spirits 206
7505 Mallard Way, Unit 1
Santa Fe, NM 87507
505-467-8892
www.santafespirits.com

The Seasonal Palate 72
505-934-3866
http://theseasonalpalate.com

Sichler Farms 18
820 San Mateo, NE
Albuquerque, NM 87108
505-255-3338
www.sichlers.com

Taos Valley Honey 189
HCR 74 Box 24374
El Prado, NM 87529
575-770-5953
taosvalleyhoney@inbox.com

Tio Frank's Red and Green Chile Sauce 45
505-715-3046
www.tiofranks.com

Traditional Aceto Balsamic of Monticello 186
info@organicbalsamic.com
www.organicbalsamic.com

Valley Gurlz Goodz 64
valleygurlzgoodz@yahoo.com
www.valleygurlzgoodz.com

Villa Myriam Specialty Coffee 221
2420 Midtown Place Northeast #H
Albuquerque, NM 87107
800-609-0250
www.villamyriam.com

Vivác Winery 231
2075 State Highway 68
Dixon, NM 87527
505-579-4441
http://vivacwinery.com

What the Fudge! 247
505-489-1035
valerie@whatthefudge.org
www.whatthefudge.org

RECIPES BY CATEGORY

VEGETARIAN MAIN DISHES

MEAT DISHES

POULTRY DISHES

SEAFOOD DISHES

DESSERTS

INDEX